A.L.A.
Cataloging Rules for
Author and Title
Entries

ADVISORY BOARD

A.L.A. Cataloging Rules, Second Edition

RUDOLPH GJELSNESS

EVELYN M. HENSEL   MARY HAYS MARABLE
M. RUTH MACDONALD   LUCILE M. MORSCH
HARRIET D. MACPHERSON ARNOLD H. TROTIER

(ex officio) ETHEL BOND, *President*
American Library Association
Division of Cataloging and Classification

June 1949

67440

A. L. A.
Cataloging Rules for Author and Title Entries

Prepared by the Division of Cataloging and
Classification *of the* American
Library Association

SECOND EDITION

Edited by
CLARA BEETLE

American Library Association
Chicago, 1949

The Preliminary American Second Edition of *A.L.A. Catalog Rules*, on Part I of which the present volume is based, was prepared by:

AMERICAN LIBRARY ASSOCIATION

Catalog Code Revision Committee
Rudolph Gjelsness—*Chairman and Editor-in-Chief*
Nella J. Martin—*Executive Assistant and General Editor*
Charles Martel—*Consultant*

EXECUTIVE COMMITTEE

Rudolph Gjelsness, *Chairman*

T. Franklin Currier
J. C. M. Hanson

Harriet D. MacPherson
Margaret Mann

Keyes D. Metcalf

CHAIRMEN OF SUBCOMMITTEES AND EDITORS OF SECTIONS

Definitions—Anna M. Monrad and Clara Newth de Villa S.
Documents—James B. Childs
Societies and institutions—Harriet W. Pierson
Religious entries—Julia Pettee

Anonymous classics—Amelia Krieg
Periodicals—Mary W. MacNair
Capitalization—Della J. Sisler
Incunabula—T. Franklin Currier
Maps and atlases—Frances Ambuhl
Music—Eva J. O'Meara

Index—Katherine E. Schultz

EDITORIAL SUBCOMMITTEE

Margaret Mann

Harriet D. MacPherson

Arnold H. Trotier

ADVISORY COMMITTEE

Effie G. Abraham, Frances Ambuhl, Hazel Bartlett, Bertha Bassam, Ethel Bond, James B. Childs, Flora Eckert, Mrs. Anna S. Erichsen, Reverend Colman Farrell, Sophie K. Hiss, Amelia Krieg, Mary W. MacNair, Lucy W. Markley, Anna M. Monrad, Isadore G. Mudge, Theodore A. Mueller, Eva J. O'Meara, Julia Pettee, Miss Clyde Pettus, Harriet W. Pierson, Harriet B. Prescott, Mrs. Elizabeth S. Radtke, William M. Randall, Marion M. Root, Bertha M. Schneider, Katherine E. Schultz, Della J. Sisler, Arnold H. Trotier, Mrs. Clara Newth de Villa S., Ruth Wallace, Katherine Warren, Wyllis E. Wright.

(BRITISH) LIBRARY ASSOCIATION. CATALOGUING RULES COMMITTEE

James D. Stewart, Bermondsey Public Library (Chairman); Henry W. Acomb, Durham University (Honorary secretary); E. Ansell, Cambridge University Library; Herbert M. Cashmore, Birmingham Public Library; F. J. King, Bodleian Library; C. B. Oldman, British Museum; C. J. Purnell, London Library; James Ross, Bristol Public Library; F. E. Sandry, Edmonton Public Libraries; Henry A. Sharp, Croyden Public Libraries; Margaret S. Taylor, School of Librarianship, University College, London.

Preface

The cataloging rules here presented are an expansion and revision of the rules of entry and heading of the 1908 edition of CATALOG RULES, AUTHOR AND TITLE ENTRY. They go back in origin to the rules presented at the Buffalo conference of the American Library Association in 1883, which were printed in the *Library journal* of that year (v. 8: 251-54) and reprinted in Cutter's *Rules for a dictionary catalog*, 3d edition, 1891. For an earlier forerunner, with its concise statement of many of the principles underlying the rules, reference should be made to Pannizi's British Museum *Rules* of 1841, the most important codification up to that time and one which greatly influenced subsequent rules in many countries and especially in the United States. Incidentally it may be noted that these revised rules have profited from a study of the application of existing rules to specific cases as revealed in the British Museum *Catalog* and other catalogs of comparable character, especially the files of printed cards of the Library of Congress.

History.—The *Rules* of 1908 were the product of an American Library Association committee which was organized in 1901, a year notable also for the initiation by the Library of Congress of its printed card service to other libraries. The rules formulated by that committee were developed over a period of experimentation when libraries were beginning in a tentative way to incorporate these printed cards into their catalogs. The chairman of that committee was James C. M. Hanson, for many years chief of the Catalog Division of the Library of Congress. It was a fortunate circumstance that the Library of Congress was engaged in revising its own rules and its own catalogs at a time when the Association was seeking a standardization of cataloging practices in order to further cooperative or centralized cataloging. The committee which drew up the 1908 rules was in a position to reconcile to a great degree the practices of the Library of Congress with those of other scholarly libraries in the United States.

Since that time there has been steady progress in the standardization of library catalogs, furthered by the increasing use of Library of Congress printed cards. American libraries have revised their catalogs extensively, frequently at great cost, in order to incorporate easily these printed cards. It has followed that cards prepared in individual libraries for purely local use have also tended to observe Library of Congress practices with such modifications as the local situation might prescribe. In the absence of any supplementary rules from the American Library Association between 1908 and 1941, libraries had to formulate their own rules, relying for guidance chiefly on rules issued occasionally by the Library of Congress, added to such deductions relating to practice as could be made from the printed cards as examples.

In 1930, the American Library Association Committee on Cataloging and Classification, in response to an inquiry from the Association regarding needed publications in the field of cataloging, suggested among other projects a revised code of cataloging rules as being of first importance. A subcommittee, the Catalog Code Revision Committee, with Charles Martel of the Library of Congress as chairman, was appointed to begin work on a revision. This subcommittee was made an independent committee of the Association in 1932 "to make necessary revisions in the A. L. A. Catalog rules with authority to cooperate with the Library Association of Great Britain and with such other national library associations as it may think appropriate."

The work was actually inaugurated during the years 1930 to 1935. In this period, cataloging groups studied and discussed the direction the revision should take, and material pertinent to the revision was assembled. Opinions were sought from members of the profession and a considerable body of data was collected. This included suggested new rulings, additional examples to accompany old rules, and numerous questions which the old *Rules* did not answer. The Committee met at annual conferences, and some new rules were promulgated and approved.

Being dependent entirely on voluntary effort, progress was necessarily slow. This was perhaps not unfortunate as it provided a period of stock taking, allowed a preliminary investigation of the extent of the project and some experimentation in its execution. From the evidence before the Committee, it soon became apparent that dissatisfaction with the 1908 code rested not with its inclusions but rather with its omissions. The basic rules were on the whole satisfactory but did not meet the present day needs of the cataloger in the large scholarly or specialized collection. Expansion was needed rather than change. This was clearly brought out in a meeting of the New York Regional Group of Catalogers in April, 1931, under the chairmanship of Minnie E. Sears, where revision needs were discussed.[1] It was emphasized further in Mr. Hanson's address before the Catalog Section at the A. L. A. Conference of 1932.[2]

---

[1] New York Regional Group of Catalogers, "Summary of discussion of need for revision of catalog code," *Catalogers' and classifiers' yearbook* no. 3 (1932), p. 20-29.
[2] J. C. M. Hanson, "Revision of A. L. A. Catalog rules," *ibid.*, p. 7-19.

The needs were emphasized and elaborated upon by a member of the Committee, Julia Pettee, in the *Library Journal* of April 15, 1936.

Relation to cooperative cataloging.—In the meantime cooperative cataloging activities had experienced considerable growth under a committee of the American Library Association (Keyes D. Metcalf, chairman) aided by a grant from the General Education Board. As a consequence, a larger number of libraries became involved in the work of supplying copy for printing and distribution by the Library of Congress, and the amount of copy provided by libraries previously cooperating was greatly increased. This created an urgent demand from such libraries for rules which would answer the many questions arising in the preparation of this copy. Much time was lost by individual catalogers seeking precedents in the files of printed cards, and, if this source failed, engaging in complicated correspondence with cooperative cataloging headquarters at the Library of Congress. It was this demand, along with the growing realization that voluntary effort could not produce a new code within a reasonable time, which culminated in a decision to seek a subvention to hasten the revision.

Carnegie Corporation grant.—With the aid of the Executive Committee of the Catalog Code Revision Committee in December, 1935, the chairman prepared a statement outlining the plans and stating the financial needs of the Committee. This was endorsed by the members of that committee (W. W. Bishop, James C. M. Hanson, Harriet D. MacPherson, Margaret Mann, Keyes D. Metcalf), was submitted by the chairman to Carl H. Milam, Executive Secretary of the American Library Association, and by him to the Executive Board of the American Library Association, urging that a subvention be secured. The Carnegie Corporation, friend of so many worthy publishing projects in the library field, made a grant in April, 1936 to further the revision. Nella Martin from the staff of the Library of Congress was appointed executive assistant and began work in September, 1936.

Plan of work.—The revision progressed in two main directions: from the central headquarters under the direction of the executive assistant; and in the field through subcommittees appointed to prepare rules for special classes of material.

The committee met at annual conferences of the American Library Association to discuss questions which arose in the progress of the work and to make necessary decisions. The subcommittees were responsible for the inclusion of much new material not previously available in so systematic or full a form. These subcommittees and their chairmen were as follows: Definitions (Anna M. Monrad), Religious entries (Julia Pettee), Anonymous classics (Amelia Krieg), Documents (James B.

Childs), Music (Eva J. O'Meara), Incunabula (T. Franklin Currier), Societies and institutions (Harriet W. Pierson). In most cases the rules were circularized first by the subcommittees and revised by them, and were later edited by Miss Martin to bring them into conformity with the rest of the code. The rules for music were developed in collaboration with a committee of the Music Library Association.

The formulation of definitions of cataloging terms, recognized as one of the major tasks of the committee from the beginning, was investigated carefully by the subcommittee from 1935 to 1938, and a considerable number of tentative definitions were formulated. The task of carrying this on and preparing the list for printing was entrusted to Mrs. Clara Newth de Villa S. who is chiefly responsible also for the form in which it appears in the revised second edition.

The preliminary edition.—The preliminary edition, published in 1941, expanded the rules of 1908 to make more provision for special classes of material, e.g., serial publications, government documents, publications of religious bodies, anonymous classics, music and maps; to amplify existing rules to cover specific cases of frequent occurrence; to provide better examples and more adequate definitions. It was divided into two parts: "Part I. Entry and heading;" "Part II. Description of book." As certain parts of the rules were criticized as being overelaborate and likely to make cataloging unduly expensive, a Committee on the Use of the Code was appointed to consider the various points of view and to make recommendations bearing on further revision. This committee, in 1944, submitted its report[3] to the Executive Board of the American Library Association, which accepted the recommendations of the Committee and instructed the Catalog Code Revision Committee to proceed with the revision of Part I in the light of the criticism available. Further work on Part II was deferred.

As the Catalog Code Revision Committee had no funds at its disposal little could be done before 1946, when it received a grant from the American Library Association. By direction of the American Library Association Council, the Catalog Code Revision Committee, which was an Executive Board committee, was discontinued and the responsibility for the revision of Part I placed with the A. L. A. Division of Cataloging and Classification.

The revised edition.—In July, 1946, an editor, Clara Beetle, was appointed by the Division of Cataloging and Classification, and, having been granted six months' leave from the Library of Congress, she began the editorial revision of Part I on September 1, 1946. She was guided in her work by the suggestions and criticisms already available, some sent to

---

[3] *A. L. A. bulletin*, v. 38. Oct. 1, 1944.

the editor of the 1941 edition and some in print, and by the aid and counsel of an Advisory Board. The Board, appointed by the Division of Cataloging and Classification, was composed of the following members: Rudolph Gjelsness, Evelyn M. Hensel, M. Ruth MacDonald, Harriet D. MacPherson, Mary Hays Marable, Lucile M. Morsch and Arnold H. Trotier. Many others were consulted by the Board or by the editor on both general and specific questions raised by the comments on the preliminary edition.

The chief changes from the preliminary edition are a rearrangement of the material to emphasize the basic rules and subordinate their amplifications, and to make the sequence of rules logical so far as possible; reduction of the number of alternate rules; omission of rules of description; rewording to avoid repetition or to make the meaning clearer; and revision, where possible, of rules inconsistent with the general principles.[4]

Acknowledgements.—It is impossible to list all the individuals who assisted in one way or another in the preparation of the preliminary edition (1941). The editors had the cooperation not only of the members of the committee, the chairmen of subcommittees, editors of sections, and members of the editorial subcommittee, but also of a large advisory committee. Other individuals whose assistance should be acknowledged are Catharine Keyes Miller and Richard S. Angell, in connection with the music rules; Margaret B. Stillwell and Dean P. Lockwood with the incunabula rules; Leon Nemoy, especially on Oriental names, Shio Sakanishi, Naomi Fukuda, and Da-June Lu on Japanese and Chinese names; David J. Haykin, especially in preparing the transliteration tables; and Horatia Corbin, in preparation of the Index. Assistance or criticism of the tentative revisions was given by W. W. Bishop, Susan Grey Akers, Alice Charlton, Jens Nyholm, Andrew D. Osborn, and Esther A. Smith, and by Charles Harris Hastings, Jessie McL. Watson and other members of the Library of Congress staff.

In the preparation of the revised edition, the editor had the assistance not only of the Advisory Board, but also of members of the former committee, especially the editors of sections. Thanks are due particularly to Amelia Krieg, Julia Pettee and Harriet W. Pierson, and also to members of the Library of Congress staff who answered questions and prepared or criticized drafts of rules in their special fields. Mrs. Clara Newth de Villa S.'s offer to undertake revision of the Glossary was most gratefully accepted. The definitions and rules for music were prepared by a joint committee of the A. L. A. Division of Cataloging and Classification

---

[4] Cf. "Progress report on the editing of Part I of the A. L. A. catalog rules," *News notes of the Board of Directors* (A. L. A. Division of Cataloging and Classification, 1947) v. 3, no. 2, p. 4–8.

ix

and the Music Library Association, with Mrs. Virginia Cunningham as chairman.

The British Committee, whose cordial cooperation was interrupted in 1939 by the outbreak of war, has been kept informed of progress and general agreement is assured. The work on the preliminary edition profited throughout from suggestions that came through the Honorary Secretary, H. S. Acomb, Librarian of Durham University, reporting on sections of the tentative rules as they passed through the hands of the British Committee.

RUDOLPH GJELSNESS, *Chairman*
A. L. A. Catalog Code Revision Committee

Contents

Rules of Entry and Heading

I. Choice of Main Entry

Works of Special Type

CONTENTS

Government Publications

Societies and Institutions

IV. Geographic Headings

V. Added Entries. References

Appendixes

CONTENTS

Introduction

The A. L. A. CATALOGING RULES are intended to represent the best or the most general current practice in cataloging of the libraries of the United States. The rules are not few nor are they, in total, simple, for the material to which they are to be applied is almost as multitudinous and complicated as humanity itself. The world may have become one world, but we certainly do not yet speak with one tongue nor even write our various languages in one alphabet. Our names are formed differently, our governments and institutions are variously organized, our ways of publishing are not the same.

Whether books are to be read from the left or the right, the top or the foot of the page, whether authorship is individual or collective, all books are written to express man's ideas and libraries are formed because other men wish to read and study those ideas.

The cataloger's main business is to make the collection of books and other materials accessible to all who have a legitimate claim on its resources. These persons include not only readers and research workers, but members of the administrative, order, reference and cataloging staffs of the library itself. Determination of the extent, nature and fullness of cataloging needed for various types of material and by any particular library should be reached through study of the needs of all these groups.

The A. L. A. CATALOGING RULES, however, are intended neither as a handbook of cataloging nor as a manual of procedure. They give no instructions on the selection of material for cataloging, nor on research methods; only incidentally do they list any bibliographical aids to research. After decision to catalog a work has been made and the necessary information in regard to its authorship has been obtained, these rules aid the cataloger in the choice of entry and form of the heading so that a reasonable degree of standardization and uniformity may prevail, not only within one catalog, but especially in enterprises such as centralized and cooperative cataloging, the making of union catalogs and the compiling of bibliographies. Such uniformity makes the use of a catalog easier, since the user learns what to expect. It helps both research workers and library workers who go from one library to another to find that the same rules have been applied in the making of the catalogs.

As the catalogs of most American libraries are dictionary card catalogs, the rules are prepared with that type particularly in mind. These rules, however, are restricted primarily to author and title entry. Subject headings are mentioned only where they bear an important relationship to the choice of main entry or where there would be a choice between a subject entry and some other form of added entry.

The principle on which the cataloging is planned is the use as main entry of the author, personal or corporate, considered to be chiefly responsible for the creation of the intellectual content of the work.[1] Thus the finding list function of the catalog is extended beyond what is required for location of a single book to the location of literary units[2] about which the seeker has less precise information. Added entries provide alternative means of approach to help those who lack complete knowledge of a specific work desired or those who lack sufficient acquaintance with the rules of entry to enable them to reach quickly the heading chosen as the main entry. Added entries serve also to complete the assembling of related material as part of a literary unit.

In establishing headings, preference is usually given to authoritative forms: to full names and real names of persons, to full legal names of corporate bodies, to the use of the vernacular in both personal and corporate names. Exceptions are made to allow use of shorter or different forms made familiar by an author's consistent use or by literary custom. Names of corporate bodies also may be used in a shortened form when the full corporate name is so little used as to be practically unknown. Preference is given to English when an international organization has its name in many languages. Geographic names are given in English when that is a well-established usage. In all cases, references from forms not used lead to the established heading.

Similarly, exceptions or qualifications are made when too strict an application of a general rule[3] would result in a heading not giving the most direct approach. Perhaps there should be other similar modifications, but they could be made wisely only on the basis of many more studies of reader approach and catalog use than are now available.

The exceptions to the general principles and to the general rules result from practical experience and make the rules, not arbitrary decisions reached by a theoretical plan alone, but decisions sufficiently flexible to require the exercise of sound judgment on the part of the catalogers

---

[1] Wyllis E. Wright, "Some fundamental principles in cataloging," *Catalogers' and classifiers' yearbook* no. 7 (1938), p. 26–39.

[2] Julia Pettee, "The development of authorship entry," *Library quarterly*, v. 6 (1936), p. 270–290.

[3] Cf. C. A. Cutter, *Rules for a dictionary catalog* (4th ed., rewritten, Washington, Govt. Print. Off., 1904), p. 6.

interpreting and applying them. Similar good judgment is needed in extending and adapting the general rules to problems not specifically covered.

Examples are given to aid in understanding and interpreting the rules, but they are illustrative only of the points of entry and heading covered by the rules. None are complete catalog entries. No attempt should be made to use them as examples for description of the book, nor to derive rules of description from them.

The cataloger must determine for each work cataloged: (1) what the author or main entry should be; (2) what the form of the heading should be—in what language, under what part of a name, whether corporate bodies should be entered under their names directly or as subheadings under country, state or city, etc.; (3) what references should be made to lead to the heading chosen; (4) what added entries should be made. These decisions should be made within the framework of the rules, unless the library has determined a different policy.

Since promoting increased uniformity and standardization is an important purpose of the rules, few alternative rules have been suggested. It is recognized, however, that some other variations may be justifiable. For example, libraries which provide material for general reading rather than for research work may prefer to use an English form of name instead of the recommended vernacular or classical form, or a well-known pseudonym instead of the real name; the fullness of name entries may be reduced; the subdivision of the author entry need not be so minute.[4] It should be emphasized, however, that such deviation should be made only to gain some distinct advantage, since libraries benefit most from the work of other libraries when all conform to standard practice.

In the present edition, an effort has been made to bring the rules abreast of practice that has changed since 1941 and to fill any notable gaps in the rules as given in the preliminary edition. There can, however, be no expectation that provision has been made for all contingencies nor that changes and modifications will not be required by future developments, either in publishing fields or in library administration.

CLARA BEETLE, *Editor*
Second edition

[4] Cf. Susan G. Akers, *Simple library cataloging* (3d ed.; Chicago, American Library Association, 1944).

Rules of
Entry and Heading

I. Choice of Main Entry

1. General rule.

Enter a work under the name of its author whether personal or corporate.

The author is considered to be the person or body chiefly responsible for the intellectual content of the book, literary, artistic or musical. (2, 6-19) When that responsibility is divided, the choice of main entry may be the first author mentioned, as with joint authors, or if there are many contributors, the collector or editor of the material may be considered the author. (3-4) The work of many contributors issued serially or in many volumes or editions is usually entered under title, since the editors may vary. (5)

When authorship is undeterminable, entry is made under a heading substituted for an author's name (as a pseudonym) (30, 31C) or under title. (32-35)

Governments, societies, institutions, and other organizations are to be regarded as the authors of the publications for which they as corporate bodies are responsible, but the papers, addresses, etc., of their officials, members or employees as individuals, are entered under personal author, even though issued by the corporate body. (Cf. III. CORPORATE BODIES AS AUTHORS.)

A form subdivision is sometimes added to the heading to assemble material in a group or in a desired order. (Cf. 31, 33A(1), 85-88, 116-118.)

2. Individual author, Works by.

Enter a work under the name of its author, when known, whether or not his name appears in the publication. (Cf. 32.) Enter revisions and other modifications under the original author whenever the work remains substantially his, especially if the book purports to be an edition of the original work. (Cf. 20-22.)

> **Holbrook, Stewart Hall,** 1893–
> Lost men of American history, by Stewart H. Holbrook.
> ɪ. Title.

> ₍**Blunden, Edmund Charles**₎ 1896–
> De bello Germanico, a fragment of trench history, written in 1918 by the author of Undertones of war.
> ɪ. Title.

₍Kerr, Doris Boake₎ 1893–
The twig is bent, by Capel Boake ₍pseud.₎
I. Title.

Riemann, Hugo, 1849–1919.
Hugo Riemanns Musik-Lexikon. 11. Aufl. bearbeitet von Alfred Einstein.
I. Einstein, Alfred, 1880–

Adler, Alfred, 1870–1937.
Understanding human nature . . . translated by Walter Béran Wolfe.
I. Wolfe, Walter Béran, 1900–1935, tr. II. Title.

3. Joint authors, Works by.

A. Enter under the first author mentioned on the title page a work produced jointly by two or more authors in which the contribution of each is not a separate and distinct part of the whole. Make added entry[1] with designation JOINT AUTHOR for any author after the first whose name is included in transcribing the title.

Nichols, Roy Franklin, 1896–
America yesterday, by Roy F. Nichols, William C. Bagley and Charles A. Beard, with drawings by George M. Richards.
I. Bagley, William Chandler, 1874–   joint author. II. Beard, Charles Austin, 1874–   joint author. III. Title.

B. In a work of joint authorship in which the chief responsibility rests with one author, but the title page reads "with the collaboration of . . ." or words to that effect, the making of added entries for the collaborators will depend on (1) the nature of the work; (2) the number of collaborators and the importance of their contribution.

Warden, Carl John, 1890–
Animal motivation; experimental studies on the albino rat, by C. J. Warden . . . with the collaboration of T. N. Jenkins, Marion Jenkins, L. H. Warner, E. L. Hamilton ₍and₎ H. W. Nissen.
"Prepared under the auspices of Columbia University Council for Research in the Social Sciences."
I. Columbia University. Council for Research in the Social Sciences. II. Title.

C. If in a work of more than one volume, the names of the joint authors do not appear in the same order on the title pages of the different volumes, enter under the name which appears first on the title page of the first volume and give variation in a note.

Woody, Clifford, 1884–
Child-life arithmetics . . . three book series, by Clifford Woody . . . Frederick S. Breed . . . ₍and₎ James R. Overman . . .
Book two, by Frederick S. Breed, James R. Overman and Clifford Woody; book three, by James R. Overman, Clifford Woody and Frederick S. Breed.
I. Breed, Frederick Stephen, 1876–   joint author. II. Overman, James Robert, 1888–   joint author. III. Title.

---

[1] Cf. Added entries (157). In the examples, the typography of the heading (APPENDIX III C) is not shown in the tracing for the added entries.

D. If on the title page of a second or later edition, **the order of** the joint authors has been changed, enter under the name which appears first on the earliest edition and add an explanatory note.

> **Blackmar, Frank Wilson,** 1854-1931.
> Outlines of sociology, by John Lewis Gillin . . . and Frank W. Blackmar . . . 3d ed.
> In the earlier editions Blackmar's name appeared first on the title-page.
> ɪ. Gillin, John Lewis, 1871-   joint author.

E. Enter a narrative told by one person to another person (reporter, "ghost writer," etc.) who prepares the matter for publication, under the narrator. Make added entry for the writer.

> **Jewitt, John Rodgers,** 1783-1821.
> The adventures of John Jewitt, only survivor of the crew of the ship, Boston, during a captivity of nearly three years among the Indians of Nootka Sound, in Vancouver Island, edited with an introduction and notes by Robert Brown . . .
> "Written by . . . Richard Alsop . . . ₍who₎ drew from Jewett his story during repeated interviews."—Hist. mag. v. 4, 1860, p. 91.
> ɪ. Alsop, Richard, 1761-1815. ɪɪ. Brown, Robert, 1842-1895, ed.

> **Belmonte y García, Juan,** 1892-
> Juan Belmonte, killer of bulls; the autobiography of a matador . . . as told to Manuel Chaves Nogales. Translated from the Spanish and with a note on bull-fighting by Leslie Charteris.
> ɪ. Chaves Nogales, Manuel, 1897-   ɪɪ. Charteris, Leslie, 1907- tr.

Distinguish from works in which the narrator is the actual author those in which the writer has merely used the narrator form for an original work (e.g., autobiography of a fictitious person, or fictitious memoirs of a real person).

4. Composite works.

Enter composite works (Cf. Glossary.) under the author chiefly responsible for the work, under the author first mentioned on the title page, or under title, according to the specific rules A-B.

A. Collaborators, Works by.

(1) Enter a work produced by the collaboration of two or more authors, in which the contribution of each forms a distinct part or section of a planned whole, under the author chiefly responsible for it. Whenever their contributions warrant, make added entry for each of the other contributors without the designation ᴊᴏɪɴᴛ ᴀᴜᴛʜᴏʀ. If a corporate body is considered to be chiefly responsible for the work, make an added entry for at least the first personal author mentioned on the title page.

> **Dubech, Lucien,** 1882-1940.
> Histoire générale illustrée du théâtre, par Lucien Dubech, avec la collaboration de Jacques de Montbrial et de Madeleine Horn-Monval . . .

"Toute une part du texte, dans chacun des cinq volumes, est de M. Jacques de Montbrial, et toutes les illustrations ont été rassemblées par Mme. Horn."—Préf.

Vols. 3-5 "avec la collaboration de Jacques de Montbrial, de Claire Engel et de Madeleine Horn-Monval."

I. Montbrial, Jacques de. II. Horn-Monval, Madeleine. III. Engel, Claire Eliane.

International Institute of Intellectual Co-operation.
The educational role of broadcasting, by F. W. Beidler-Wagner, Henry Bonnet, Kristine Bonnevie ₍and others₎ . . . Paris, International Institute of Intellectual Co-operation, 1935.

I. Beidler-Wagner, F. W. II. Title.

(2) If origin, chief interest, or responsibility is not clearly identified with or attributable to any one of the contributors, enter under the first-named author[2] if there are not more than three and the title of the whole work is applicable to each of the contributions, with added entry for the other authors. Otherwise, enter under title, with added entry for the first author mentioned and for as many others as the individual case warrants.

Buckley, Homer John, 1879-
Mail-order and trade-paper advertising, by Homer J. Buckley . . . G. D. Crain, Jr. . . . and Maxwell Droke . . .
CONTENTS.—Mail-order advertising, by H. J. Buckley.—Industrial and trade-paper advertising, by G. D. Crain, Jr.—Advertising letters, by Maxwell Droke.

I. Crain, Gustavus D., 1885-   II. Droke, Maxwell, 1896-

Por que ser anti-semita? Um inquerito entre intellectuaes brasileiros; collaboradores: A. C. Pacheco e Silva, Afranio Peixoto, Alfredo Ellis Junior . . . ₍e outros₎

I. Silva, Antonio Carlos Pacheco e. II. Peixoto, Afranio, 1876-
III. Ellis, Alfredo, 1896-

Is unemployment inevitable? An analysis and a forecast; a continuation of the investigation embodied in "The third winter of unemployment," published in 1923.
"This volume is . . . in the form of a series of essays for which the authors alone are responsible, together with an introductory report which represents our views of the questions which our inquiry covers." —Introd. signed: J. J. Astor, A. L. Bowley ₍and others₎.

I. Astor, Hon. John Jacob, 1886-   II. Bowley, Arthur Lyon, 1869-   III. The third winter of unemployment.

B. Debates, conversations, interviews, table-talk.

(1) Enter a **debate, dialogue, conversation,** under the participant whose name appears first on the title page. Make added entry for each name after the first.

Darrow, Clarence Seward, 1857-1938.
Debate, subject, resolved: That the United States continue the policy of prohibition as defined in the eighteenth amendment.

---

[2] Cf. 5A(2). Note that *independent* writings of two or more authors are entered under the first-named author only when there is no collective title.

Clarence Darrow, negative, versus Reverend John Haynes Holmes, affirmative; introduction by Hon. Royal S. Copeland.
   I. Holmes, John Haynes, 1879-

Goethe, Johann Wolfgang von, 1749-1832.
   Conversations of Goethe with Eckermann and Soret. Translated from the German by John Oxenford.
   I. Eckermann, Johann Peter, 1792-1854. II. Soret, Frédéric Jacob, 1795-1877. III. Oxenford, John, 1812-1877, tr.

(2) Enter an **interview** under the person interviewed if his ideas only are presented; enter under the interviewer if he has added comment and interpretation or if he has interviewed several persons.

MacVeagh, Franklin, 1837-1934.
   Interview, concerning the proposed changes in design and size of paper money, of the Honorable Franklin MacVeagh, Secretary of the Treasury, September 10, 1910.

(3) Enter **table-talk** under the talker with added entry under the compiler.

Selden, John, 1584-1654.
   The table-talk of John Selden; edited with an introduction and notes by Samuel Harvey Reynolds . . .
   Originally recorded by Richard Milward, Selden's secretary.
   I. Milward, Richard, 1609-1680. II. Reynolds, Samuel Harvey, 1831-1897, ed.

5. Collections and serials.

Specification.—This group of rules applies to material in which the responsibility for the intellectual content is so divided that no one of the contributors can be considered the chief author. The choice then is between entry under the agency responsible for editing, assembling or issuing the material, as a government agency, society, institution (Cf. 71.), a personal editor, a publisher, etc., or entry under title. Preference is given to entry under title when it is distinctive or when it is the least variable element and it is, of course, the only possible entry when no editorial or publishing responsibility is apparent.

A. Collections.

(1) With collective title. Enter under the compiler or editor, individual or corporate, a collection of independent works by various authors, artists, composers, etc., issued with a collective title, except as noted in (a) to (c) below.

Chandler, Frank Wadleigh, 1873-   *ed.*
   Twentieth century plays, edited by Frank W. Chandler . . . and Richard A. Cordell . . .
   I. Cordell, Richard Albert, joint ed. II. Title.

Schering, Arnold, 1877-1941, *ed.*
   Geschichte der Musik in Beispielen; dreihundertfünfzig Tonsätze aus neun Jahrhunderten, gesammelt, mit Quellenhinweisen versehen und herausgegeben von Arnold Schering.
   I. Title.

7

> **Muratori, Lodovico Antonio,** 1672-1750, *ed.*
> Rerum Italicarum scriptores ab anno Æræ Christianæ quin-
> gentesimo ad millesimum quingentesimum quorum potissima
> pars nunc primum in lucem prodit ex Ambrosianæ, Estensis,
> aliarumque insignium bibliothecarum codicibus. Ludovicus
> Antonius Muratorius . . . collegit, ordinavit, & præfationibus
> auxit . . .
>> Edited by F. Argellati.
>> I. Argellati, Filippo, 1685-1755, ed.

(a) Enter such collections under title if the work of the editor or
editing body seems to be but slight and their names do not appear
prominently in the publication or if there are frequent changes of
editor. Make added entry under editor.

> **Galleria** delle più belle incisioni in acciaro. Prima versione dall'
> inglese, col testo a fronte, arricchita di scritti originali sopra i
> soggetti italiani. Dai signori: Giacinto Battaglia, Giambattista
> Bazzoni . . . ecc. . . .

> A **Book** of broadsheets, with an introduction by Geoffrey Daw-
> son . . . 2d ed.
>> Selections from the pocket literature provided by the Times, and
>> originally printed in 1915 in the form of broadsheets for distribution to
>> the men in the trenches. *cf.* Introd.
>> I. Dawson, Geoffrey, 1874-   II. The Times, London. III. Title:
>> Broadsheets.

> A **Second** book of broadsheets, with an introduction by Geoffrey
> Dawson . . .
>> Selections from the pocket literature provided by the Times, and
>> originally printed in 1915 in the form of broadsheets for distribution
>> to the men in the trenches. *cf.* Introd.
>> I. Dawson, Geoffrey, 1874-   II. The Times, London. III. Book
>> of broadsheets. IV. Title: Broadsheets, A Second book of.

(b) Enter under title such compilations as **monumenta, scriptores,
anecdota,** etc., when they are generally referred to by title. Make
added entry under editor.

> . . . **Monumenta** minora saeculi secundi. Ed. altera emendata.
> Edited by Gerhard Rauschen.
>> I. Rauschen, Gerhard, 1854-1917, ed.

> **Scriptores** rerum Svecicarum Medii Ævi, ex schedis praecipue
> Nordinianis collectos, dispositos ac emendatos, edidit Ericus
> Michael Fant . . .
>> Vol. 2: "Jussu regis augustissimi post D. Ericum Michaëlem Fant
>> ediderunt ac illustrarunt Ericus Gustavus Geijer . . . et Johannes
>> Henricus Schröder"; v. 3: "Edidit et illustravit Claudius Annerstedt."
>> I. Fant, Erik Mikael, 1754-1817, ed. II. Geijer, Erik Gustaf, 1783-
>> 1847, ed. III. Schröder, Johan Henrik, 1791-1857, ed. IV. Annerstedt,
>> Claes, 1839-1922, ed. V. Nordin, Carl Gustaf, 1749-1812.

> **Corpus** scriptorum ecclesiasticorum Latinorum. Editum consilio
> et impensis Academiae Litterarum Caesareae Vindobonensis
> . . .
>> I. Akademie der Wissenschaften, Vienna.

Anecdota varia Graeca et Latina, ediderunt Rud. Schoell et Guil. Studemund . . .
    i. Schoell, Rudolf, 1844-1893, ed. ii. Studemund, Wilhelm Friedrich Adolf, 1843-1883, joint ed.

(c) Enter **festschriften**[3] and similar collections published by a society or an institution in honor of a person, or to celebrate an anniversary, under the society or institution. When not published by a society or an institution, enter under editor, if the editor's name appears prominently in the publication; otherwise enter under title. In any case, make added entry under editor or distinctive title when not main entry, and make subject entry under the person in whose honor the collection is published.

Germania Männerchor, *Baltimore.*
    Festschrift zum goldenen Jubiläum 10. Oktober 1906 des Germania Männerchor von Baltimore, Md., gegründet am 10. Oktober 1856. Im Auftrage des Ausschusses für Vereinsgeschichte zusammengestellt von Carl Laegeler.
    i. Laegeler, Carl.

Lille. Facultés catholiques. *Faculté des lettres.*
    . . . Mélange de philologie et d'histoire, publiés à l'occasion du cinquantenaire de la Faculté des lettres de l'Université catholique de Lille.
    CONTENTS.—

Frankfurter, Felix, 1882-   *ed.*
    Mr. Justice Holmes; contributions by Benjamin N. Cardozo, Morris R. Cohen, John Dewey [and others] . . . edited by Felix Frankfurter.
    Published on the occasion of the ninetieth birthday of Oliver Wendell Holmes, March 8th, 1931.
    CONTENTS.—
    1. Holmes, Oliver Wendell, 1841-1935. i. Title.

Festschrift Alexander Cartellieri, zum sechzigsten Geburtstag dargebracht von Freunden und Schülern.
    CONTENTS.—
    1. Cartellieri, Alexander, 1867-

Essays in biology in honor of Herbert M. Evans, written by his friends.
    CONTENTS.—
    1. Evans, Herbert McLean, 1882-

---

[3] This rule concerns only festschriften that fall into the category of "collections." A festschrift consisting of an edition of the works of one author, or of a single work to which definite authorship can be assigned, or for which a specific heading is appropriate, such as an anonymous classic, is of course cataloged as any other publication of the same nature.

    Margaret, *Saint.* **Legend.**
      Acta S. Marinae et S. Christophori; edidit Hermannus Usener. [Bonn, Universitäts-Buchdruckerei von C. Georgi, 1886]
      Added title-page: Festschrift zur fünften Säcularfeier der Carl-Ruprechts-Universität zu Heidelberg, überreicht von Rector und Senat der Rheinischen Friedrich-Wilhelms-Universität.
      1. Heidelberg. Universität. i. Bonn. Universität. [and other added entries]

(2) Without collective title. Enter two or more writings by different authors, published together but having no collective title, under the one named first on the title page, or lacking such indication, under the heading appropriate to the first work in the collection. Make added entries for other works mentioned on the title page and for the editor.

> **Lowell, James Russell,** 1819-1891.
> . . . The vision of Sir Launfal, by James Russell Lowell; The courtship of Miles Standish, by Henry Wadsworth Longfellow; Snow-bound, by John Greenleaf Whittier; edited with an introduction and notes, by Charles Robert Gaston . . .
> ɪ. Longfellow, Henry Wadsworth, 1807-1882. The courtship of Miles Standish. ɪɪ. Whittier, John Greenleaf, 1807-1892. Snowbound. ɪɪɪ. Gaston, Charles Robert, 1874-   ed.

B. Encyclopedias and dictionaries. Enter encyclopedias and dictionaries under title unless decidedly better known by the name of their editors. In either case make added entry under the form not chosen for main entry, and for the publisher if the work is likely to be referred to by his name.

> **Cyclopedia** of American government, edited by Andrew C. McLaughlin . . . and Albert Bushnell Hart . . .
> ɪ. McLaughlin, Andrew Cunningham, 1861-   ed. ɪɪ. Hart, Albert Bushnell, 1854-1943, joint ed.

> **Larousse, Pierre,** 1817-1875.
> Grand dictionnaire universel du xɪxᵉ siècle, français, historique, géographique, mythologique, bibliographique, littéraire, artistique, scientifique, etc. . . . par Pierre Larousse . . .
> ɪ. Title.

> **Heath's** standard French and English dictionary, edited by J. E. Mansion . . .
> London edition (G. G. Harrap & company, ltd.) has title: Harrap's standard French and English dictionary.
> ɪ. Mansion, Jean Edmond, ed.

C. Periodicals[4] and newspapers.

(1) Enter a periodical (Cf. GLOSSARY.) under its latest title. Make a reference or an added entry for any earlier title or titles under which the periodical may have been issued. In the case of a periodical which has ceased publication, make exception in favor of entry under an earlier title used for a much longer period than the later title. A publication which does not continue the volume numbering of an earlier publication is usually considered a new periodical, and should have separate entry.

A periodical issued by a society, institution, or government body

---

[4] The rules for cataloging periodicals as stated here are based on U. S. Library of Congress, Catalog Division, *Guide to the cataloguing of periodicals* (3d ed. Prepared by Mary Wilson MacNair; Washington, Govt. Print. Off., 1925). Reprinted 1938. For alternative treatment, cf. C. A. Cutter, *Rules for a dictionary catalog* (4th ed., rewritten; Washington, Govt. Print. Off., 1904), sec. 133, p. 59 and sec. 145, p. 62.

is ordinarily to be entered under its title (especially if this is distinctive in character) with added entry for the issuing body. (Cf. 71.)

For the more important periodicals, make added entries for editors included in the title or mentioned in a note; for compilers of indexes when of sufficient importance; and for societies or other bodies of which the periodical is an organ. The name of each editor is followed by the abbreviation ED. not JOINT ED.

> The **Children's** home magazine.
> > Vol. 1, no. 1 has title: The Children's monthly messenger.
> > Merged into Boys' and girls' treasury.
> > *Refer from*
> > The Children's monthly messenger.

> **California** schools; official publication of the state Department of Education.
> > I. California. Dept. of Education.

> The **American** labor legislation review. Published quarterly by the American Association for Labor Legislation.
> > Founded and edited by J. B. Andrews.
> > I. Andrews, John Bertram, 1880-1943, ed. II. American Association for Labor Legislation.

When the title of a periodical begins with the initials of the name of a corporate body, enter under the initials and make added entry or reference under the name of the body for which they stand.

> **A.S.M.E.** news. v.1-
> > *with added entry under*
> > American Society of Mechanical Engineers.

> **AAA** travel . . . v.1-
> > *with added entry under*
> > American Automobile Association.

> . . . **A. and G.** motor vehicle year book.
> > *Refer from*
> > Armstrong and Gans motor vehicle year book.

> **B.-M.** Co's cumulative code annotations and current digest.
> > *Refer from*
> > Bender-Moss Company's cumulative code annotations and current digest.

When the title of a periodical begins with the initials of the forenames of the editor or publisher, omit the initials. Refer from the exact title, and from the title following the name, if distinctive.

> . . . **Case's** botanical index; an illustrated quarterly botanical magazine.
> > Title reads: L. B. Case's botanical index . . .
> > *Refer from*
> > L. B. Case's botanical index.

> . . . **Pepper** piano music magazine.
> > Title reads: J. W. Pepper piano music magazine.

11

Refer from
J. W. Pepper piano music magazine.
Piano music magazine.

When the title begins with a forename, use the forename as **entry** word but refer from other forms of the name, and if necessary, from the part of the title following the personal name.

Carl Hagenbecks illustrierte Tier- und Menschenwelt.
Refer from
Hagenbecks illustrierte Tier- und Menschenwelt.

Justus Liebigs Annalen der Chemie.
Refer from
Liebigs Annalen der Chemie.
Annalen der Chemie.

(2) Enter a **newspaper** under its latest title. Refer from earlier titles, if any, and from catch titles by which the paper may be popularly known. In the case of newspapers which appear in several editions (Sunday, morning, evening, etc.) under slightly varying titles, enter each edition independently, but with added entry under the main title, and reference under the name of the city unless this occurs as the first word of the title.

Boston Evening Transcript.
Refer from
Boston Daily Evening Transcript.
Boston Transcript.
Evening Transcript, *Boston.*
The Transcript, *Boston.*

The **Westminster** Gazette.
Refer from
London. Westminster Gazette.

The **Sunday** Star.
with added entry
The Evening Star, *Washington, D. C.*
and reference from
Washington, D. C. Sunday Star.

(3) If it is desirable to catalog a **special number** of a newspaper or periodical independently, enter it under the name of the newspaper or periodical unless a more definite authorship can be established, in which case make added entry under the name of the newspaper or periodical.

Springfield Daily Times.
The village of Holyoke, Massachusetts . . .
Issued as a special number of the Springfield Daily Times, no. 5, 1894.

L'Illustration.
. . . S. M. la reine Astrid, 1905-1935.
"Album hors série. Juin 1936."

> **Holme, Geoffrey,** 1887–   *ed.*
>   Children's toys of yesterday, edited by C. Geoffrey Holme.
>   "Special winter number of 'The Studio'."
>   I. The Studio.

When the place is not included in the name of a newspaper used as a heading, it is to be added. Add the place of publication to a periodical title used as a heading where necessary to distinguish between two periodicals of the same title.

> **The Times,** *London.*
>   . . . War graves number . . . no. 10, 1928.
>   "The Times . . . no. 45,047."
>
> **Times-Dispatch,** *Richmond.*
>   Annual educational number.
>
> **Life.** *Chicago.*
>   War art.
>
> **Life.** *New York.*
>   Men, women and birth.

For monographs issued as supplements to a periodical or newspaper see 25C-D.

(4) Enter a **collection of extracts** by various authors from a single periodical or newspaper under the name of the periodical or newspaper. Make added entries under the title of the collection and the name of the collector if given.

> **Blackwood's Edinburgh magazine.**
>   Humorous tales from Blackwood.
>   I. Title.
>
> **The Atlantic monthly.**
>   Youth and the new world, essays from the Atlantic monthly, edited by Ralph Boas . . .
>   I. Boas, Ralph Philip, 1889–   ed. II. Title.
>
> **The Sun,** *New York.*
>   Casual essays of the Sun; editorial articles on many subjects, clothed with the philosophy of the bright side of things.
>   I. Title.
>
> **Cassell's magazine.**
>   My aunt's match making, and other stories by popular authors.
>   Running title: Stories from Cassell's.
>   I. Title.

For entry of a collection of extracts by various authors from different periodicals see 5A.

The work of a single author republished from a periodical (entered under the name of the author if known, or under title if anonymous) has no added entry for the *periodical,* but an added entry is usually made under the *newspaper* for the work of a single author republished from it, especially if the author is an editor or official correspondent, or if the article is anonymous.

> **Phelps, William Lyon,** 1865-1943.
> As I like it, by William Lyon Phelps . . .
> Previously published in Scribner's magazine from September 1922 to August 1923.
> ɪ. Title.

> ₍Church, **Francis Pharcellus,** 1839-1906.
> Is there a Santa Claus?
> The text of the editorial by F. P. Church which appeared in the New York Sun, September 21, 1897, together with two letters from Mrs. Virginia O'Hanlon Douglas and a biographical sketch of Mr. Church.
> ɪ. The Sun, New York. ɪɪ. Title.

D. Almanacs, yearbooks, etc. Enter almanacs, general yearbooks and similar serial publications under title.

> The **Aviation** year book . . . 1930-
> Editor: 1930-   C. E. Lee.
> ɪ. Lee, Charles E., ed.

> **Buffalo** Evening News almanac and . . . year book. 1933-

> The **Farmer's** almanack . . .
> 18   by Samuel Burr; 18   by Elisha Dwelle; 18   by Joseph Ray.
> ɪ. Burr, Samuel. ɪɪ. Dwelle, Elisha. ɪɪɪ. Ray, Joseph, 1807-1855.

> **Who's** who in commerce and industry, 1936-

E. Directories.

(1) Enter a directory published serially under the first word of the title not a serial number or the initial of a compiler or publisher.

> The **Post Office** London directory . . . comprising . . . official, streets, commercial . . . parliamentary, postal . . . and banking directories . . .
> Title varies: 18   The Post-Office annual directory . . .
> 18   The Post Office London directory
> 1. London—Direct.

> **Polk's** Crocker-Langley San Francisco city directory . . .
> ₍1895₎-19
> Title varies: 1895, Crocker's San Francisco directory.
>   1896-1919, Crocker-Langley San Francisco directory.
>   1920-29, Crocker-Langley San Francisco city directory.
>   1930-   Polk's Crocker-Langley San Francisco city directory . . .
> 1. San Francisco—Direct.
>   *Refer from*
> Crocker's San Francisco directory.
> Crocker-Langley San Francisco directory.

> **Crockford's** clerical directory . . . being a statistical book of reference for facts relating to the clergy and the church . . .
> Subtitle varies slightly.
> 18   published by H. Cox.
> Supersedes the Clerical directory.

(2) Enter a **nonserial directory** under the name of the compiler if mentioned on the title page. If no compiler is mentioned, enter under title.

> **Cattell, James McKeen,** 1860-1944, *ed.*
> Leaders in education, a biographical directory, edited by
> J. McKeen Cattell . . . 1st ed.
> ɪ. Title.

(3) Enter a **telephone directory** issued by a telephone company under the name of the company.

> **New England Telephone and Telegraph Company.**
> List of subscribers . . . and business directory . . .
> 1. Boston—Direct.—Telephone.

(4) Enter a **telephone directory** issued by a compiler or publisher other than a telephone company under title if published serially. If it is nonserial, enter under compiler if prominently mentioned on the title page, otherwise, enter under title.

> **San Francisco** classified business telephone directory for San
> Francisco and suburbs.
> San Francisco, C. L. Schachtebeck, c18
> 1. San Francisco—Direct.—Telephone.

> **Rothermel (Charles T.) & Co.,** *Chicago.*
> Auxiliary telephone directory of Chicago . . . March, 1896.
> Compiled and published by Chas. T. Rothermel & Co.
> 1. Chicago—Direct.—Telephone.

F. Series. Enter a series under its title except as noted in paragraphs (1) and (2) below. In choosing between varying forms of series title, prefer the title as given on (*1*) added title page; (*2*) title page, unless half title is more exact or gives noteworthy additional information; (*3*) half title; (*4*) cover; (*5*) any other source. Make added entry or reference under name of editor.

(1) Enter under editor or publisher a series which is familiarly known by the name of the editor or publisher. Refer from title.

(2) Enter under the name of a society, institution, or other corporate body, a series issued by it without distinctive title. However, entry under title is preferred for a series whose name begins with the word Biblioteca or its equivalent in other languages,[5] with reference from the society, institution, or periodical issuing it.

> **International** scientific series.

> **Historic** towns.
> Edited by Edward A. Freeman and Rev. William Hunt.
> *Make added entry or reference*
> Freeman, Edward Augustus, 1823-1892, *ed.*
> Hunt, William, 1842-1931, *ed.*

---

[5] To avoid confusion with entry for the library of the organization.

Gröber, Gustav, 1844-1911.
   Grundriss der romanischen Philologie. Neue Folge.
      Refer from title.

Catholic University of America.
   Canon law studies.
      Refer from title.

Toledo University, *Toledo. College of Law.*
   Lectures on the problems of the practicing lawyer.
      Refer from title.

Haskell lectures in comparative religion delivered before the
   University of Chicago.
      Refer from
   Chicago. University.
      Haskell lectures in comparative religion.

Works of Special Type

6. Correspondence and letters.
   A. Enter correspondence between two or more persons under the
first one mentioned on the title page, with added entry for the other
party or parties to the correspondence, and for the editor or compiler.

Terry, *Dame* **Ellen,** 1848-1928.
   Ellen Terry and Bernard Shaw; a correspondence, edited by
Christopher St. John ₍pseud.₎
      ɪ. Shaw, George Bernard, 1856-   ɪɪ. Marshall, Christabel, ed.

   B. Enter collected letters of one writer under the writer with added
entry under the editor or compiler.

Sedgwick, Anne Douglas, 1873-1935.
   Anne Douglas Sedgwick; a portrait in letters, chosen and
edited by Basil de Sélincourt.
      ɪ. De Sélincourt, Basil, 1876-   ed.

   (1) If the letters are all addressed to the same person, make added
entry for the addressee. Extend this treatment to include two writers
or two recipients. When more than two writers are involved apply
rule C, p. 17.

Cobbett, William, 1763-1835.
   Letters from William Cobbett to Edward Thornton, written
in the years 1797 to 1800; edited with an introduction and notes
by G. D. H. Cole . . .
      ɪ. Cole, George Douglas Howard, 1889-   ed. ɪɪ. Thornton, Sir
Edward, 1766-1852.

Browning, Elizabeth (Barrett) 1806-1861.
   Twenty-two unpublished letters of Elizabeth Barrett Brown-

ing and Robert Browning, addressed to Henrietta and Arabella Moulton-Barrett.

    i. Browning, Robert, 1812-1889. ii. Cook, Henrietta (Barrett) d. 1860. iii. Barrett, Arabella, d. 1868.

Hobbs, Mary (Mendenhall) 1852-
    Letters to Gertrude, 1910-1913, edited by Mary I. Shamburger.
    "The letters comprising the present volume were written [by] two Carolina Quakers, Mary Mendenhall and Lewis Lyndon Hobbs . . . to their young daughter in a boarding school near Philadelphia."—Introd.
    i. Hobbs, Lewis Lyndon, 1849- ii. Shamburger, Mary Ina, 1898- ed. iii. Körner, Gertrude Mendenhall (Hobbs) 1896- iv. Title.

(2) When the collected letters of a single writer are accompanied by biographical matter and the whole is entitled "Life and letters," or words to that effect, choice of entry under the writer of the letters or under the author of the biography is governed by the relative extent and importance or interest of the letters as compared with the biography. In case of doubt, prefer entry under the author of the biography. If entry is made under the writer of the letters, make added entry under the author of the biography; if under the author of the biography, make subject entry under the writer of the letters. If the latter is a very voluminous writer, both a subject and an added entry may be made.

    Barrus, Clara, 1864-1931.
        The life and letters of John Burroughs, by Clara Barrus . . .
        1. Burroughs, John, 1837-1921.

    MacCallum, John Bruce, 1876-1906.
        Short years; the life and letters of John Bruce MacCallum, M.D., 1876-1906, by Archibald Malloch.
        "It seemed best to let MacCallum tell his own story through extracts from his letters and his 'Memories' which are preserved in his notebooks. I have added connecting paragraphs and explanations as appeared necessary."—Pref.
        i. Malloch, Archibald, 1887- ed. ii. Title.

C. Enter collected letters by various writers under the compiler or editor. (Cf. 5A.) If the letters are all addressed to the same person, make added entry for the addressee. Extend this treatment to include two recipients. (Cf. B(1) above.)

    Taintor, Sarah Augusta, *comp.*
        The book of modern letters, compiled by Sarah Augusta Taintor and Kate M. Monro; illustrated by W. M. Berger.
        i. Monro, Kate M., joint comp. ii. Title.

7. Expeditions (Reports, etc.).
    Enter official accounts and publications of results of scientific and exploring expeditions as follows:
    A. When the work is clearly the production of one person or of two or more persons working in conjunction, enter under author or compiler.

Wilkes, Charles, 1798-1877.
    Narrative of the United States Exploring Expedition. During
the years 1838, 1839, 1840, 1841, 1842. By Charles Wilkes, u. s. n.,
commander of the expedition . . .
          i. United States Exploring Expedition, 1838-1842.
          [The first five volumes of the official reports of the expedition copy-
              righted and published by the author]

Beebe, Charles William, 1877-
    The Arcturus adventure; an account of the New York Zoolog-
ical Society's first oceanographic expedition, by William Beebe
. . . Published under the auspices of the Zoological Society.
          1. Arcturus (Ship) i. New York Zoological Society.

Hooker, *Sir* **William Jackson,** 1785-1865.
    The botany of Captain Beechey's voyage; comprising an ac-
count of the plants collected by Messrs. Lay and Collie, and other
officers of the expedition, during the voyage to the Pacific and
Behring's Strait, performed in His Majesty's ship Blossom,
under the command of Captain F. W. Beechey . . . in the years
1825, 26, 27, and 28. By Sir William Jackson Hooker . . . and
G. A. Walker Arnott . . .
          1. Blossom (Ship) i. Arnott, George Arnott Walker, 1799-1868, joint
author. ii. Beechey, Frederick William, 1796-1856.

B. When the work consists of contributions by several persons,
choice of heading is governed by the way in which the expedition is
generally designated, or by the prominence given on the title page
to any one of the headings suggested below.[6] In cases of doubt, give
preference to this order.

    (1) The official name of the expedition, followed by the date.

United States Exploring Expedition, 1838-1842.
    United States Exploring Expedition. During the years 1838,
1839, 1840, 1841, 1842. Under the command of Charles Wilkes,
u.s.n. . . .
          i. Wilkes, Charles, 1798-1877. ii. U. S. Congress.
          [The complete report of the expedition (19v.) published under act of
              Congress of Aug. 26, 1842. cf. L. C. card 14-19399]

Navy-Princeton Gravity Expedition to the West Indies, 1932.
    The Navy-Princeton Gravity Expedition to the West Indies in
1932.
          i. U. S. Navy. ii. Princeton University.

    (2) The society, institution, government department, or individual
assuming the responsibility of the expedition and the publication of
the results.

Gesellschaft für Erdkunde zu Berlin. *Grönland-Expedition.*
    Grönland-Expedition der Gesellschaft für Erdkunde zu Berlin,
1891-1893. Unter Leitung von Erich von Drygalski . . .
          i. Drygalski, Erich von, 1865-

---

    [6] In the examples subject entries have been indicated only when the name of the
vessel or of the expedition is involved. Other appropriate subject entries would of
course be necessary.

Pennsylvania. University. *Babylonian Expedition.*
The Babylonian Expedition of the University of Pennsylvania. Series D: Researches and treatises, edited by H. V. Hilprecht.

I. Hilprecht, Hermann Vollrat, 1859-1925, ed. II. Pennsylvania. University. Dept. of Archaeology.

Gt. Brit. *Challenger Office.*
Report on the scientific results of the voyage of H.M.S. Challenger during the years 1873-76 under the command of Captain George S. Nares . . . and the late Captain Frank Tourle Thomson, R. N. Prepared under the superintendence of the late Sir C. Wyville Thomson . . . and now of John Murray . . . Published by order of Her Majesty's government.

1. Challenger Expedition, 1872-1876. I. Thomson, Sir Charles Wyville, 1830-1882. II. Murray, Sir John, 1841-1914. III. Nares, Sir George Strong, 1831-1915. IV. Thomson, Frank Tourle. V. Gt. Brit. Admiralty. VI. Royal Society of London. Circumnavigation Committee.

Albert I, *Prince of Monaco,* 1848-1922.
Résultats des campagnes scientifiques accomplis sur son yacht par Albert Ier, prince souverain de Monaco. Publiés sous sa direction avec le concours du baron Jules de Guerne.

1. Hirondelle (Yacht) I. Guerne, Jules de, baron, 1855-

(3) The commander of the expedition, especially when he edits the results.

Beechey, Frederick William, 1796-1856, *ed.*
The zoology of Captain Beechey's voyage; compiled from the collections and notes made by Captain Beechey, the officers and naturalist of the expedition during a voyage performed in His Majesty's ship Blossom under the command of Captain F. W. Beechey . . . in the years 1825, 26, 27, and 28 . . . Published under the authority of the lords commissioners of the Admiralty.

1. Blossom (Ship) *and* added entries I-X for the ten members of the expedition whose contributions are shown in the Contents note, *and* XI. Gt. Brit. Admiralty.

(4) The editor of the results.

Adams, Arthur, 1820-1878, *ed.*
The zoology of the voyage of H.M.S. Samarang; under the command of Captain Sir Edward Belcher . . . during the years 1843-1846 . . . edited by Arthur Adams . . . Published under the authority of the lords commissioners of the Admiralty.

1. Samarang (Ship) *and* added entries I-IV for the four members of the expedition whose contributions are shown in the Contents note *and* V. Gt. Brit. Admiralty.

(5) The name of the vessel, followed by the date of the expedition. If more than one vessel participates, enter under the first-named vessel, with added entry for the others.

Scotia *(Ship)* 1913.
Ice observation, meteorology and oceanography in the North Atlantic Ocean. Report on the work carried out by the S.S. "Scotia" in 1913.

Expense of the expedition shared by the Board of Trade and the shipowners concerned.

Added entries for authors of special reports mentioned in Contents note *and* Gt. Brit. Board of Trade.

(6) The first word of the title.

Exploration scientifique de l'Algérie pendant les années 1840, 1841, 1842. Publiée par ordre du Gouvernement . . .
    i. France. Ministère de la Marine.

In all cases make added entries freely for government departments, names of vessels, commanders, societies, editors, etc.

8. Inscriptions.
    A. Enter a single inscription of unknown authorship under the editor unless it is generally known and referred to by a distinctive name, in which case enter under that name as a uniform heading.

Comparetti, Domenico Pietro Antonio, 1835-1927, *ed.*
    Iscrizione arcaica del Foro romano, edita ed illustrata da Domenico Comparetti.
but
Moabite stone.
    The Moabite stone; a facsimile of the original inscription, with an English translation, and a historical and critical commentary . . .

B. Enter a collection of inscriptions ordinarily under the editor or compiler; however, if the editorial work is slight, or if the collection is better known by title or by some distinctive name, enter under title or distinctive name with added entry for editor or compiler; or, if the collection is the property of a private individual or of a corporate body, entry under the name of the owner may be preferred. (Cf. 5A.)

Hughes Clarke, Arthur William, 1873-
    Monumental inscriptions in the church and churchyard of St. Mary's, Wimbledon, transcribed and annotated by A. W. Hughes Clarke . . .
    1. Wimbledon, Eng. St. Mary's Church.

Inscriptiones Graecae, consilio et avctoritate Academiae Litterarvm Regiae Borvssicae editae . . .
    i. Akademie der Wissenschaften, Berlin.

Tell el-Amarna tablets.
    . . . Oriental diplomacy: being the transliterated text of the cuneiform despatches between the kings of Egypt and Western Asia in the xvth century before Christ, discovered at Tell el-Amarna . . .

British Museum. *Dept. of Egyptian and Assyrian Antiquities.*
    Coptic and Greek texts of the Christian period from ostraka, stelae, etc., in the British Museum. By H. R. Hall. London, Printed by order of the Trustees, 1905.
    i. Hall, Harry Reginald Holland, 1873-1930.

20

9. Manuscripts.[7]

A. Manuscripts and facsimiles of manuscripts. Enter a manuscript or the facsimile of a manuscript according to the rules for printed books. Make the usual added entries for editors, compilers, titles, etc., and in addition, make added entry for the manuscript as such, if it belongs to a collection of manuscripts or has a distinctive name. The added entry may be for the collection, followed by the abbreviation Mss. and the name or number of the manuscript or it may be the name of the manuscript, if distinctive. If the two are equivalent, make a reference from one to the other rather than two added entries.

If the main entry heading is one under which there are likely to be many entries, make an assembling added entry consisting of the heading followed by the abbreviation Mss. and the particular designation of the manuscript if it has one. For exception to this treatment see A (1), p. 22.

For every manuscript or facsimile of a manuscript make a form subject heading: MANUSCRIPTS, [LANGUAGE] or MANUSCRIPTS, [LANGUAGE]—FACSIMILES, e.g., MANUSCRIPTS, FRENCH, or MANUSCRIPTS, FRENCH—FACSIMILES.

Homerus.
Homeri Ilias cùm scholiis. Codex Venetus A, Marcianus 454 phototypice editus . . .

1. Manuscripts, Greek—Facsimiles. i. Venice. Biblioteca nazionale marciana. Mss. (454) ii. Homerus. (Codex Venetus A)

Ẕu'l-Faḳār, Ḳiwām ul-Dīn Ḥusain ibn Ṣadr ul-Dīn 'Alī *Shir-wānī, 13th cent.*
. . . A facsimile of the manuscript (Or. 9777) of Dīwān i Ẕu'l-Faḳār, the collected poems of Ẕu'l-Faḳār Shirwānī . . .

1. Manuscripts, Persian—Facsimiles. i. British Museum. Mss. (Oriental 9777) ii. British Museum. Dept. of Oriental Printed Books and Manuscripts. iii. Title: Dīwān i Ẕu'l-Faḳār.

Chaucer, Geoffrey, *d.* 1400.
The Cambridge ms (University Library, Gg. 4.27) of Chaucer's Canterbury tales . . .

1. Manuscripts, English—Facsimiles. i. Cambridge. University. Library. Mss. (Gg. 4.27) ii. Chaucer, Geoffrey. Mss.

---

[7] The rules presented under this heading are based on the cataloging of manuscripts occurring most frequently in the average library in the form of facsimiles.
In cataloging manuscripts, the following points should be kept in mind:
(1) The designation for a manuscript whether added to the main entry or used as an added entry requires that the work be either the original manuscript or a facsimile. If a facsimile, the reproduced text should constitute a considerable part of the entire manuscript (as preserved) or be arranged to read consecutively.
(2) If the reproductions are interspersed as facsimile pages through a work which deals with the manuscript, make subject entry under the heading appropriate to the entire manuscript rather than main or added entry.
(3) A text *edited* from a manuscript for which the *main entry* is its name or designation, may (even though not a reproduction) be entered under the same heading, but without use of the form subject heading MANUSCRIPTS [LANGUAGE]—FACSIMILES.

Keats, John, 1795-1821.
Hyperion, a facsimile of Keats's autograph manuscript . . .
1. Manuscripts, English—Facsimiles. ɪ. Keats, John, 1795-1821. Mss.

Villon, François, b. 1431.
Deux manuscrits de François Villon (Bibliothèque nationale,
Fonds français 1661 et 20041) reproduits en phototypie . . .
1. Manuscripts, French—Facsimiles. ɪ. Paris. Bibliothèque nationale.
Mss. (Fr. 1661) ɪɪ. Paris. Bibliothèque nationale. Mss. (Fr. 20041)

A **Coptic** gnostic treatise contained in the Codex Brucianus
< Bruce ms. 96. Bod. Lib. Oxford > . . .
1. Manuscripts, Coptic—Facsimiles. ɪ. Oxford. University. Bodleian
Library. Mss. (Bruce 96) ɪɪ. Codex Brucianus.

Orthodox Eastern Church. *Liturgy and ritual. Menologion.*
Il menologio di Basilio ɪɪ (Cod. vaticano greco 1613) . . .
1. Manuscripts, Greek—Facsimiles. ɪ. Vatican. Biblioteca vaticana.
Mss. (Graec. 1613)

Edda Snorra Sturlusonar.
Codex Wormianus (The Younger Edda) Ms. no. 242 fol. in
the Arnamagnean collection in the University Library of Copenhagen . . .
1. Manuscripts, Icelandic and Old Norse—Facsimiles. ɪ. Copenhagen.
Universitet. Bibliotek. Mss. (Arnamag. 242f)
with reference Codex Wormianus *see* Copenhagen. Universitet.
Bibliotek. Mss. (Arnamag. 242f)

(1) Enter a manuscript or the facsimile of a **manuscript of the
Bible** or parts thereof under Bɪʙʟᴇ, followed by the word Mᴀɴᴜsᴄʀɪᴘᴛs,
the language of the text, and by further designations appropriate to
the heading for the work concerned. (Cf. 34.) If the manuscript has
a particular name, add it at the end of the heading in parentheses.[8]
When a manuscript is known by a distinctive name and also by a letter
or number,[9] prefer the name in the heading. Make added entry under
the collection or collections to which the manuscript belongs, and
make added entry or reference under the particular name of the
manuscript.

Bible. *Manuscripts, Greek (Codex Alexandrinus)*
. . . The Codex Alexandrinus (Royal ms. 1 ᴅ v-vɪɪɪ) in reduced
photographic facsimile . . .
1. Manuscripts, Greek—Facsimiles. ɪ. British Museum. Mss. (Royal
1ᴅ v-vɪɪɪ)
with reference Codex Alexandrinus *see* Bible. *Manuscripts, Greek
(Codex Alexandrinus)*

Bible. *Manuscripts, Greek. O. T. Genesis (Wiener Genesis)*
Die Wiener Genesis . . .

---

[8] Library of Congress does not use parentheses for Bible manuscripts.
[9] Cf. K. W. Clark, *A descriptive catalogue of Greek New Testament manuscripts in
America* (Chicago, Univ. of Chicago Press, ᶜ1937) and C. R. Gregory, *Die griechischen
Handschriften des Neuen Testaments* (Leipzig, Hinrichs, 1908.) For a manuscript
without a distinctive name, use the number from Gregory in the heading, e.g., Bɪʙʟᴇ.
Mᴀɴᴜsᴄʀɪᴘᴛs, Gʀᴇᴇᴋ. N. T. Gᴏsᴘᴇʟs. (Cᴏᴅᴇx 538 (Gʀᴇɢᴏʀʏ))

1. Manuscripts, Greek—Facsimiles. I. Vienna. Nationalbibliothek. Mss. (Theol. Graec. 31)

with reference Wiener Genesis *see* Bible. *Manuscripts, Greek. O. T. Genesis (Wiener Genesis)*

(2) For manuscripts in two languages, make the main entry for the principal language, with added entry for the other.

Bible. *Manuscripts, Greek. N. T. Epistles of Paul (Codex Bœrnerianus)*
Der Codex Bœrnerianus der Briefe des Apostels Paulus (Msc. Dresd. A 145ᵇ) . . .
Greek with Latin interlinear translation.
1. Manuscripts, Greek—Facsimiles. 2. Manuscripts, Latin—Facsimiles. I. Bible. Manuscripts, Latin. N. T. Epistles of Paul (Codex Bœrnerianus) II. Dresden. Sächsische Landesbibliothek. Mss. (A 145ᵇ)
with reference Codex Bœrnerianus *see* Bible. *Manuscripts, Greek. N. T. Epistles of Paul (Codex Bœrnerianus)*

(3) Enter a manuscript which has neither author nor title under the name by which it is generally known; or, lacking a name, under the collection to which it belongs followed by the specific designation of the manuscript.

Book of Leinster.
The Book of Leinster, sometime called the Book of Glendalough, a collection of pieces (prose and verse) in the Irish language . . .
1. Manuscripts, Irish—Facsimiles. I. Dublin. University. Trinity College. Library. Mss. (H.2.18)

Edwin Smith surgical papyrus.
. . . The Edwin Smith surgical papyrus . . .
The papyrus is named after Edwin Smith, who purchased the document in January 1862 during his stay at Thebes. After his death in 1906 it was presented to the New York Historical Society. *cf.* General introduction.
I. New York Historical Society. Library. Mss.

Codex Fejérváry-Mayer.
Codex Fejérváry-Mayer: an old Mexican picture manuscript in the Liverpool Free Public Museums 12014.
M
1. Manuscripts, Mexican—Facsimiles. I. Liverpool. Public Libraries, Museums and Art Gallery. Museum. Mss. (M. 12014)

Paris. Bibliothèque nationale. *Mss. (Fr. 19152)*
. . . Le manuscrit 19152 du Fonds français de la Bibliothèque nationale . . .
Anonymous anthology (without title) of 61 poems.
1. Manuscripts, French—Facsimiles.

(4) Enter reproductions of initials, miniatures, or other ornamentations without text, under the artist if known, with subject entry under the heading appropriate to the entire manuscript. If the artist is unknown, enter under compiler or editor.

23

> **Huntington, Archer Milton,** 1870-   *ed.*
> Initials and miniatures of the ixth, xth, and xith centuries from the Mozarabic manuscripts of Santo Domingo de Silos in the British Museum; with introduction by Archer M. Huntington . . .
>> From British Museum Additional mss. 30844-48, 30850-55 ("Visigothic codices")
>> i. British Museum. Mss. (Additional 30844-30855) ii. Title. iii. Title: Visigothic codices.

(5) Treat a collection of facsimiles of manuscripts like other collections. **(5A)** Make added entry under the library or other institution to which the originals belong.

> **Budge, Ernest Alfred Thompson Wallis,** 1857-   *ed and tr.*
> Miscellaneous Coptic texts . . .
>> 1. Manuscripts, Coptic—Facsimiles. 2. Manuscripts, Ethiopic—Facsimiles. i. British Museum. Mss. (Oriental)

(6) If such a collection is published by the library owning the manuscripts, enter under the name of the library, without subheading Mss., or, if the library has a special department to which the collection belongs, e.g., Department of Manuscripts, enter under the name of the library with the name of the department as subheading. If the collection is limited to manuscripts in a specified group make added entry under the name of the library with subheading Mss. followed by the name of the group in parentheses.

> **British Museum.** *Dept. of Manuscripts.*
> Facsimiles of . . . manuscripts in the Stowe collection.
>> i. British Museum. Mss. (Stowe)

> **Paris. Bibliothèque nationale.** *Département des manuscrits.*
> . . . Fac-similés de manuscrits grecs, latins et français du ve au xive siècle exposés dans la Galerie mazarine . . .

Prefer the Latin form when the word CODEX or its equivalent occurs at the beginning of a uniform heading. Refer from other forms.

> **Codex Ramirez**
>> *Refer from*
>> Códice Ramirez.

> **Codex Mariano Jiménez**
>> *Refer from*
>> Códice Mariano Jiménez.

Make a general reference from the department heading to individual manuscripts.

> **British Museum.** *Dept. of Manuscripts.*
> For individual manuscripts see under

> **British Museum.** *Mss.* (subdivided by the designation of the particular manuscript, *e.g.,* British Museum. *Mss.* (*Harleian 126*)

(7) Treat a single manuscript or facsimile of a manuscript comprising a miscellaneous collection as a single work, not as a collection.

> **Walters Art Gallery,** *Baltimore. Mss. (514)*
> Proverbes en rimes; text and illustrations of the fifteenth century from a French manuscript in the Walters Art Gallery, Baltimore, by Grace Frank and Dorothy Miner.
> "The manuscript bears no title and that adopted by us, Proverbes en rimes, is the one given the related collection, now in the British Museum, by the cataloguers of the Bibliothèque A. Firmin-Didot. There is nothing to indicate whether the manuscript is complete or not."—Introd., p. 26.
> 1. Manuscripts, French—Facsimiles. i. Frank, Grace, ed. ii. Miner, Dorothy Eugenia, ed. iii. Title.

> **Paris. Bibliothèque nationale.** *Mss. (Fr. 837)*
> Fabliaux, dits et contes en vers français du xiiie siècle; fac-similé du manuscrit français 837 de la Bibliothèque nationale, publié sous les auspices de l'Institut de France (Fondation Debrousse) par Henri Omont . . .
> 1. Manuscripts, French—Facsimiles. i. Omont, Henri Auguste, 1857-1940. ii. Institut de France, Paris. Fondation Debrousse. iii. Title.

B. Calendars of manuscripts. Enter calendars of collections of manuscripts under the person or corporate body responsible for their preparation. This may be the owner of the collection who prepares or causes the calendar to be prepared, or an independent person or body for whose work the owner has no responsibility.

When entry is under owner, make added entry for the person who does the actual work of preparing the calendar; when entry is under the compiler, make added entry under the owner of the collection. If a collection has changed hands but continues to be known by the name of the original collector, make added entry under that name also.

In the case of a calendar of the collected manuscripts of one person, make subject entry under the author.

Enter the calendar of a single document under the heading appropriate for the document itself.

Enter all calendars of court records, by whomsoever prepared, under the name of the court.

> **Wisconsin State Historical Society.** *Library.*
> The Preston and Virginia papers of the Draper collection of manuscripts.
> "The work of calendaring the volume has been performed by Miss Mabel Clare Weaks."—Prefatory note.
> 1. Preston, William, 1729-1783. i. Draper, Lyman Copeland, 1815-1891. ii. Weaks, Mabel Clare.

> **Chapman, Charles Edward,** 1880-
> Catalogue of materials in the Archivo General de Indias for the history of the Pacific Coast . . . by Charles E. Chapman.
> i. Spain. Archivo General de Indias, Seville.

Carnegie Institution of Washington. *Dept. of Historical Research.*

Calendar of manuscripts in Paris archives and libraries relating to the history of the Mississippi Valley to 1803. Edited by N. M. Miller Surrey (Mrs. F. M. Surrey) . . . Privately printed ₍Washington, D. C.₎ Carnegie Institution of Washington, Department of Historical Research, 1926-28.

    I. Surrey, Nancy Maria (Miller) ed.

Gormanston register.

Calendar of the Gormanston register, from the original in the possession of the Right Honourable the Viscount of Gormanston. Prepared and edited by James Mills . . . and M. J. McEnery.

    Printed for the Royal Society of Antiquaries of Ireland.

    The ancient register book of the Lords of Gormanston seems to have been prepared or begun in 1397-8 for the purpose of registering the title-deeds of the property inherited or acquired by Sir Christopher Preston.

    I. Gormanston, Christopher Preston, 2d baron, d. 1422. II. Royal Society of Antiquaries of Ireland. III. Mills, James, 1849-1914, ed. IV. McEnery, Michael Joseph, ed.

Chichester, *Eng. (Diocese) Consistory Court.*

    . . . Calendar of wills in the Consistory Court of the Bishop of Chichester, 1482-1800. By Edward Alexander Fry.

    I. Fry, Edward Alexander.

10. Maps[10] and atlases.

A. Enter a **map** under the name of the person or corporate body responsible for the content of the map, as, cartographer, editor, publisher, government bureau, society or institution.[11] Preference should be given to *(1)* the person or corporate body stated in the title to be responsible; *(2)* cartographer; *(3)* engraver, if known to be a map maker; *(4)* publisher; *(5)* copyright claimant. If responsibility cannot be determined, enter under title.

Early maps are usually known as the work of the individual cartographer, engraver, or surveyor; **recent maps** are in most cases issued by a publishing house or government bureau which assumes full responsibility for the production.

---

[10] For assistance in the technical problems which arise in connection with maps, and cannot be cared for in a statement of rules, catalogers are referred to A. R. Hinks, *Maps and survey* (Cambridge, University Press, 1913); S. W. Boggs and Dorothy C. Lewis, *The classification ·and cataloging of maps and atlases* (New York, Special Libraries Association, 1945); L. A. Brown, *Notes on the care & cataloguing of old maps* (Windham, Conn., Hawthorn House, 1940) and Walter Thiele, *Official map publications* (Chicago, American Library Association, 1938). The last three contain additional references. Maps reprinted or extracted from atlases often can be identified through indexes in U. S. Library of Congress, Division of Maps, *A list of geographical atlases in the Library of Congress* . . . Compiled under the direction of Philip Lee Phillips (Washington, Govt. Print. Off., 1909-20).

[11] Entry under individual or corporate author is consistent with the usage established for book cataloging and makes possible one catalog for both books and maps. Small libraries may, however, find that an entry under subject (i.e., area mapped) is all that is necessary (Cf. American Library Association, *Pamphlets and minor library material* (Chicago, American Library Association Publishing Board, 1917).) and special collections may prefer a main entry under area, a scheme for which is worked out in the Boggs and Lewis Manual.

Make added entries for publisher and editor if not the main entry, for engraver if important, and title if distinctive.

U. S. *Bureau of Insular Affairs.*
Map of the Philippines, prepared in the Bureau of Insular Affairs, War Department. September 1902. Washington, D. C. ₁1902₁

Rocque, Jean, *d.* 1762.
Rocque's map of London, 1746. Published by John Pine & John Tinney in October 1746 according to act of Parliament. London, London Topographical Society, 1913-19.

Canada. *Dept. of Crown Lands.*
. . . Map of the counties of Gaspé and Bonaventure; exhibiting the lands adjudicated, unsurveyed, clergy reserves, &c . . . Reduced and compiled from original surveys, by G. G. Dunlevie . . .
1. Gaspé Co., Quebec—Descr. & trav.—Maps. 2. Bonaventure Co., Quebec—Descr. & trav.—Maps. I. Dunlevie, G. G.

American Geographical Society of New York.
Physical map of the Arctic.
Translated and revised by the American Geographical Society of New York from map in Andree's Hand atlas, 8th ed., 1924.
1. Arctic regions—Descr. & trav.—Maps. I. Andree, Karl Theodor, 1808-1875.

B. Enter **atlases** under the person or corporate body responsible for their production: cartographer, publisher, government bureau, society, or institution. If responsibility cannot be determined, or if the work is familiarly known by title, enter under title. Make added entry for any person or corporate body, other than the one chosen for main entry, who has had any significant share in or responsibility for the work. For comprehensive works, make form subject entry under the form heading ATLASES.

Paullin, Charles Oscar.
Atlas of the historical geography of the United States by Charles O. Paullin . . . edited by John K. Wright . . . ₁Washington, D. C., New York₁ Published jointly by Carnegie Institution of Washington and the American Geographical Society of New York, 1932.
1. Atlases. I. Wright, John Kirtland, 1891-   ed. II. Carnegie Institution of Washington. Division of Historical Research. III. American Geographical Society of New York. IV. Title.

U. S. *Geological Survey.*
. . . World atlas of commercial geology . . .
1. Atlases. I. Title.

Ogle (George A.) & Co., *pub.*
Standard atlas of Ford County, Illinois, including a plat book of the villages, cities and townships of the county . . .

The **People's** illustrated & descriptive family atlas of the world, indexed.
Maps by George F. Cram.
1. Atlases. I. Cram, George Franklin, 1841-1928.

11. Mediumistic writings.

Enter a work received through a medium (automatic writing, table rapping, ouija board, etc.) under the medium with added entry for the purported author.

> **Ramsdell, Sarah A.**
> Food for the million; or, Thoughts from beyond the borders of the material. By Theodore Parker, through the hand of Sarah A. Ramsdell, medium.
> I. Parker, Theodore, 1810-1860. II. Title.

> **Livingston, Marjorie (Prout)** 1893-
> . . . The new Nuctemeron (the twelve hours of Apollonius of Tyana) preface by Sir Arthur Conan Doyle, and explanatory note by the amanuensis.
> "This remarkable script purports to be produced under the direct inspiration of Apollonius of Tyana."
> I. Apollonius, of Tyana. II. Title.

12. Music.[12]

A. Enter a single musical work or the collected works of one composer under the name of the composer. Make added entries for arrangers and editors, and if there is text, make added entry for its author and title. When several authors are represented, make added entries as necessary.

Instrumental work:

> **Elgar,** *Sir* **Edward William,** 1857-1934.
> . . . Introduction and allegro for strings (quartet and orchestra) composed by Edward Elgar. (Op. 47) . . .

Song:

> **Homer, Sidney,** 1864-
> . . . Sing to me, sing; song with piano accompaniment. Poem from "Hawthorn and lavender," by W. E. Henley . . .
> I. Henley, William Ernest, 1849-1903. Sing to me, sing.

Collection of songs by one composer:

> **Elgar,** *Sir* **Edward William,** 1857-1934.
> . . . Sea pictures, a cycle of five songs for contralto . . . The music by Edward Elgar. Op. 37 . . . The words by Raden Noel, C. A. Elgar, Elizabeth Barrett Browning, Richard Garnett, Adam Lindsay Gordon.
> ⌊*Added entries are not made for the authors in this case*⌋

Opera:

> **Parker, Horatio William,** 1863-1919.
> Mona, an opera in three acts, the poem by Brian Hooker,

---

[12] In cataloging music it is frequently necessary to establish a conventional or standard title. This title occupies the line between the author entry and the title as it is transcribed from the work in hand. In the examples the conventional title is not shown, nor are title added entries indicated. In preparing cards for the catalog, if for any reason the conventional title is not given, a line should be left blank for its insertion.

the music by Horatio Parker . . .
    I. Hooker, Brian, 1880-1946. Mona.

(1) Enter a **folk song or traditional melody** under the composer responsible for the arrangement in hand, with added entry for the title. If the composer is not known, enter under title.[13]

> **Gould, Morton, 1913-**
> Sometimes I feel like a motherless child, Negro spiritual; A Morton Gould string choir arrangement.

(2) Enter a **libretto** of an opera, oratorio, masque or other dramatic work under the composer of the music, with added entry for the librettist and the title. If the same text is published as a literary work rather than as a libretto, or if there is no ascertainable connection between the text and a particular composer or performance, enter under the author of the text. If an earlier work, such as a novel, drama or poem has been adapted, make added entry under the author and title of the original work.[14]

Composer and librettist named on title page:

> **Gruenberg, Louis, 1883-**
> Jack and the beanstalk, a fairy opera for the child-like, by John Erskine; for music by Louis Gruenberg.
>   I. Erskine, John, 1879-   Jack and the beanstalk.

Composer not named on title page; named in dedication:

> **Purcell, Henry, 1658 *or* 9-1695.**
> King Arthur; or, The British worthy. A dramatick opera. Perform'd at the Qveens Theatre by Their Majesties servants. Written by Mr. Dryden.
>   I. Dryden, John, 1631-1700. King Arthur.

Performance mentioned; composer not named:

> **[Monsigny, Pierre Alexandre de] 1729-1817.**
> Le deserteur, drame en trois actes, en prose, mêlé de musique;

---

[13] The title may take the form of a uniform heading following the rule for anonymous classics. (33)

[14] Alternative: Enter a libretto under the librettist, with added entry under the composer and title of the work. If the author is not known, enter under title.

Composer and librettist named on title page:

> **Erskine, John, 1879-**
> Helen retires; an opera in three acts, by John Erskine; for music by George Antheil.
>   I. Antheil, George, 1900-   Helen retires.

Composer named; libretto anonymous:

> La **finta** giardiniera. Dramma giocoso da rappresentarsi in Prato nel carnevale dell' anno 1775-nel teatro pubblico dei Nobili Accademici Semplici . . .
>   I. Anfossi, Pasquale, 1727-1797. La finta giardiniera.

par M. Sedaine. La musique par M.*** Représenté à Paris pour
la premiére fois par les Comédiens italiens ordinaires du Roi,
le lundi 6 mars 1769.

    i. Sedaine, Michel Jean, 1719–1797. Le déserteur.

No mention of composer or of performance:

Zeno, Apostolo, 1668–1750.
    Merope.
    (*In his* Poesie drammatiche, Venezia, 1774, t. 1, p. 81–171)
    [*No composer is mentioned. The libretto was set to music by various
composers*]

Libretto adapted from earlier work:

Thomas, Ambroise, 1811–1896.
    Hamlet, opéra en cinq actes par Michel Carré et Jules Barbier,
musique de Ambroise Thomas.
    Adapted from Shakespeare's Hamlet.
    i. Carré, Michel, 1819–1872. Hamlet. ii. Barbier, Jules, 1825–1901.
Hamlet. iii. Shakespeare, William. Hamlet.

Identical text published as a literary work and as a libretto:

Millay, Edna St. Vincent, 1892–
    The King's henchman; a play in three acts . . .

Taylor, Deems, 1885–
    The King's henchman, lyric drama in three acts; book by
Edna St. Vincent Millay, music by Deems Taylor.
    i. Millay, Edna St. Vincent, 1892–   The King's henchman.

    [*The examples given below show the kind of references which may
be used to connect entries under both librettist and composer*]

Millay, Edna St. Vincent, 1892–
    The King's henchman.
    Editions of this work published as librettos of the opera by Deems
Taylor are entered under the name of the composer.

Taylor, Deems, 1885–
    The King's henchman.
    Editions without the music, published as literary works rather than
as librettos, are entered under the name of the dramatist, Edna St.
Vincent Millay.

(3) Enter a **pasticcio** under the name of the person responsible for
the arrangement of the material in this form. If, however, there is
difficulty in determining which of several persons would have the
status of author or editor, enter under title. Make added entries as
necessary for the composers and librettists whose work is adapted or
parodied, for the author of the new libretto, and for any others who
have contributed important work.

    Bishop, *Sir* **Henry Rowley,** 1786–1855.
      Faustus, a musical romance . . . composed by T. Cooke, Charles
E. Horn, and Henry R. Bishop . . .
      i. Cooke, Thomas Simpson, 1782–1848. Faustus. ii. Horn, Charles
Edward, 1786–1849. Faustus.

[*A collection of musical numbers with very slight plot and little reference to Faust. Bishop's name, although third on the title-page, is
printed in larger letters than those of the others; he contributed six
of the twelve numbers, Horn, three, Cooke, one*]

(4) For **incidental music,** make added entry under the author and
title of the play for which the music was composed.

Sharp, Cecil James, 1859-1924.
The songs and incidental music arranged and composed by
Cecil J. Sharp for Granville Barker's production of A mid-
summer night's dream at the Savoy Theatre in January, 1914 . . .
   I. Shakespeare, William. A midsummer night's dream.

(5) For **ballets, pantomimes and other dance compositions,** make
added entry for the author and title of the scenario or program, and
for the choreographer if his work is represented. Where the scenario
or choreography is published apart from the music, enter under its
own author, with added entry for the composer and title of the work.
   Score:

Falla, Manuel de, 1876-1946.
El sombrero de tres picos. Le tricorne. The three-cornered
hat. Ballet de G. Martínez Sierra d'après le roman de P. A. de
Alarcón. Musique de Manuel de Falla.
   I. Martínez Sierra, Gregorio, 1881-   El sombrero de tres picos.
   II. Alarcón, Pedro Antonio de, 1833-1891. El sombrero de tres picos.

   Scenario:

Rosato, Arturo.
Castello nel bosco, azione coreografica in un quadro, per la
musica di Franco Casavola.
   I. Casavola, Franco, 1892-   Castello nel bosco.

(6) **Liturgical music.** Enter music officially prescribed by a church,
or music authorized by a church council or other governing body,
under the name of the church, with an appropriate subheading, if
needed. (Cf. rules 116F and 120G.)

Catholic Church. *Liturgy and ritual. Hymnary.*
The hymns of the Dominican missal and breviary, edited with
introduction and notes by Aquinas Byrnes . . .
   I. Catholic Church. Liturgy and ritual. Dominican. II. Byrnes,
Aquinas, ed.

Catholic Church. *Liturgy and ritual. Psalter.*
The Psalms with Gregorian notation for Sundays and feast-
days at vespers and compline.
   I. Bible. O. T. Psalms. Latin. Selections. 1938.

Presbyterian Church in the U. S. A.
The hymnal; published by the authority of the General
Assembly of the Presbyterian Church in the United States of
America, 1933.
   Clarence Dickinson, editor; C. W. Laufer, assistant editor. *cf.* p. [1]
   I. Dickinson, Clarence, 1873-   ed. II. Laufer, Calvin Weiss, 1874-
1938, joint ed.

31

(7) Enter a musical setting of a **mass, requiem or other text for church use** under the composer. Prefer a subject (or form) heading to which a general reference is made from the church heading, to added entry for the text under the name of the church.

Beethoven, Ludwig van, 1770-1827.
Messe (Missa solemnis) für 4 Solostimmen, Chor und Orchester von L. van Beethoven.
1. Masses.

Make general reference:

Catholic Church. *Liturgy and ritual. Missal.*
For musical settings of the mass see entries under the subject heading, Masses.

Yon, Pietro Alessandro, 1886-1943.
Missa "Regina Pacis" in honor of St. Vincent Ferrer.
1. Masses.
[*Added entry not made for the person honored*]

Bruckner, Anton, 1824-1896.
. . . Te Deum laudamus, for chorus, soli and orchestra by Anton Bruckner . . .
1. Te Deum laudamus.

(8) Enter a **psalter** with music by one composer under the composer. For psalters officially prescribed for church use, see (6) above. If the composer is unknown or if there are several composers, enter under the heading for the text. (Cf. 34.)

Playford, John, 1623-1686?
Psalms & hymns in solemn musick of foure parts on the common tunes to the Psalms in metre: used in parish-churches . . . By John Playford.
ɪ. Bible. O. T. Psalms. English. Paraphrases. 1671. Sternhold and Hopkins.

Bible. *O. T. Psalms. French. Paraphrases. 1920.*
. . . Psaumes, avec les mélodies.
Translator's name, Clément Marot, at head of title.
"Introduction" signed: Théodore Gerold.
ɪ. Marot, Clément, 1495?-1544, tr. ɪɪ. Gerold, Théodore, 1866-   ed.

(9) Enter a **cadenza** under the composer of the concerto or other work with which it is associated, with added entry under the composer of the cadenza.

Mozart, Wolfgang Amadeus, 1756-1791.
Cadenzas for the flute concerto in G major (K.313) by Mozart . . . [By] Georges Barrère.
ɪ. Barrère, Georges, 1876-1944.

(10) Enter **arrangements, transcriptions, paraphrases** and other compositions in which the work of the original composer has been changed, extended, or used in a new context under the original composer or under the arranger, depending on the extent of new composition involved. Criteria for determining whether a composition is a new work are: marked difference in length, introduction of new thematic material, marked differences in harmonization. The mere addition of embellishments (trills, runs, and passage work) does not constitute a new work. In case of doubt, enter under the original composer.

Arrangement:

> **Schubert, Franz Peter,** 1797-1828.
> . . . Franz Schubert's Märsche für das Orchester übertragen von F. Liszt . . . Partitur.
> i. Liszt, Franz, 1811-1886, arr.

Transcription, not constituting new work:

> **Beethoven, Ludwig van,** 1770-1827.
> Adelaide de Beethoven, transcrite pour piano par H. Cramer.
> i. Cramer, Heinrich, b. ca. 1818, arr.

Transcription, constituting new work:

> **Respighi, Ottorino,** 1879-1936.
> "Rossiniana": suite for orchestra, from "Les riens" of G. Rossini. Freely transcribed by Ottorino Respighi.
> i. Rossini, Gioacchino Antonio, 1792-1868. Les riens.

Paraphrase:

> **Liszt, Franz,** 1811-1886.
> . . . Concert-Paraphrasen über Verdi's Rigoletto, Trovatore, Ernani, für Pianoforte von Franz Liszt.
> i. Verdi, Giuseppe, 1813-1901.

Opera adaptation:

> **Bizet, Georges,** 1838-1875.
> Carmen Jones, by Oscar Hammerstein ii, based on Meilhac and Halévy's adaptation of Prosper Merimée's Carmen.
> i. Hammerstein, Oscar, 1895-   Carmen Jones. ii. Meilhac, Henri, 1831-1897. Carmen. iii. Halévy, Ludovic, 1834-1908. Carmen.

(11) Enter **fantasias, rhapsodies, caprices, medleys, potpourris, variations,** etc., under the composer of the medley, unless it is made up of excerpts from the work of one composer. In such cases enter under the original composer. If the title indicates the use of borrowed thematic material, make added entry for the composer whose work has been borrowed. **(Cf. 22.)**

Fantasia:

> **Smith, Edward Sydney,** 1839-1889.
> . . . Fra Diavolo, fantaisie brillante pour piano sur l'opéra comique d'Auber par Sydney Smith. Op.67 . . .
> i. Auber, Daniel François Esprit, 1782-1871. Fra Diavolo.

Composition on borrowed theme:

> **Rachmaninoff, Sergei,** 1873-1943.
> . . . Rapsodie sur un thème de Paganini, op.43, pour piano
> et orchestre . . .
>   I. Paganini, Nicolò, 1782-1840.

Work modelled upon the style of another composer:

> **Tausig, Karl,** 1841-1871.
> Nouvelle soirées de Vienne. Valses-caprices d'après J. Strauss
> [par] Ch. Tausig . . .
>   I. Strauss, Johann, 1825-1899.

Medley:

> **Paul, S   T**
> "Hodge podge," medley . . . Two-part chorus for female
> voices. Arranged by S. T. Paul.
>   Works included: Waltz from Faust (Gounod); Soft and light as
> mists of the morning; Jingle bells (J. S. Pierpont); Old folks at home
> (S. C. Foster); The rally (S. T. Paul); Nelly Gray (B. R. Hanby);
> Kentucky home (S. C. Foster); The flag of freedom.

Potpourri, from one composer:

> **Strauss, Johann,** 1825-1899.
> Streifzug durch Johann Straussche Operetten. Potpourri für
> kleines Orchester, von Ludwig Schlögel.
>   I. Schlögel, Ludwig.

B. If the composer is not known, enter the work under title.
(Cf. 32.)

> Les **amusements** d'Orphée. Menuet italien pour les violons,
> flûte et hautbois.

C. Enter a **spurious work** or a work of doubtful authorship (Cf.
31.) under the name of the composer to whom it has been generally
attributed, followed by the designation SUPPOSED COMPOSER. The
designation is used in an added entry as well as in main entry.

D. Enter a composition written by **two or more composers** in collaboration under the one first mentioned on the title page, with composer and title added entries under the others.

> **Schumann, Robert Alexander,** 1810-1856.
> F. A. E. In Erwartung der Ankunft des verehrten und gelieb-
> ten Freundes Joseph Joachim schrieben diese Sonate Robert
> Schumann, Albert Dietrich und Johannes Brahms . . .
>   I. Dietrich, Albert Hermann, 1829-1908. F. A. E. II. Brahms, Jo-
> hannes, 1833-1897. F. A. E.

E. Enter **collections** of compositions by several composers under
the compiler or editor. If, in the case of collections containing both
text and music, the work of the editor of the text seems to be more
important than that of the compiler or the editor of the music, enter

under the editor of the text. If the work of the editor or editing body appears to be slight, enter under the title, with added entry for the editor.

> **Hughes, Robert.**
> Songs from the hills of Vermont, sung by James and Mary Atwood and Aunt Jenny Knapp. Texts collected and edited by Edith B. Sturgis. Tunes collected and piano accompaniment arranged with historical notes by Robert Hughes.
> i. Sturgis, Edith B.

> **Friedlaender, Max,** 1852-1934, *ed.*
> Gedichte von Goethe in Compositionen . . . Herausgegeben von Max Friedlaender.
> i. Goethe, Johann Wolfgang von, 1749-1832.

> **Larkin, Margaret,** 1899-   *comp.*
> Singing cowboy; a book of Western songs, collected and edited by Margaret Larkin; arranged for piano by Helen Black.
> i. Black, Helen, 1890-   arr.

> **Bing Crosby's** album of song souvenirs . . . with arrangements of the . . . songs for all B$\flat$ and E$\flat$ instruments . . .
> i. Crosby, Bing, 1901-

F. Enter a **thematic catalog** under the compiler, if known, otherwise under the publisher. Make subject entry for the composer.

> **Köchel, Ludwig Alois Friedrich,** *Ritter* **von,** 1800-1877.
> Chronologisch-thematisches Verzeichnis sämtlicher Tonwerke Wolfgang Amadeus Mozarts . . . von Dr. Ludwig Ritter von Köchel. 3. Aufl. bearbeitet von Alfred Einstein.
> 1. Mozart, Wolfgang Amadeus—Thematic catalogs. i. Einstein, Alfred, 1880-   ed.

> **Breitkopf & Härtel,** *Leipzig, pub.*
> Thematisches Verzeichnis sämtlicher in Druck erschienenen Werke von Ludwig van Beethoven.
> 1. Beethoven, Ludwig van—Thematic catalogs.

13. Private collections (Catalogs).

A. Enter catalogs, lists, etc., of private collections (libraries, art galleries, numismatic cabinets, stamp collections, etc.) under the name of the owner of the collection, with added entry under the name of the author (compiler) of the work, and under place when known also by the latter.

> **Walters, William Thompson,** 1820-1894.
> Oriental collection of W. T. Walters, 65 Mt. Vernon Place, Baltimore.

> **Brinley, George,** 1817-1875.
> Catalogue of the American library of the late Mr. George Brinley . . .
> Compiled by J. H. Trumbull.
> i. Trumbull, James Hammond, 1821-1897.

B. When a private collection has passed into the possession of some institution, society, or other body, entry for all subsequent publications is to be made under the name of that body, with added entry under the name of the collection and the original collector. Publications issued before the change of ownership are to have added entry under the name of the institution or other body into whose possession the collection has passed.

> **Boston. Public Library.** *Prince collection.*
> The Prince library. A catalogue of the collection of books and manuscripts which formerly belonged to the Reverend Thomas Prince, and was by him bequeathed to the Old South Church, and is now deposited in the Public Library of the city of Boston.
> I. Boston. Old South Church. II. Prince, Thomas, 1687-1758.

> **Crace, Frederick,** 1779-1859.
> A catalogue of maps, plans, and views of London, Westminster & Southwark collected and arranged by Frederick Crace; edited by his son John Gregory Crace. London, 1878.
> Collection purchased by the British Museum in 1880.
> I. Crace, John Gregory. II. British Museum. Dept. of Printed Books. Map Room.

C. Enter under the name of the compiler unofficial catalogs of books or other objects in libraries, exhibitions, galleries, museums, etc., private or public; i.e., catalogs which are not issued as publications under the auspices of the owners or custodians of the collections concerned, though possibly with their approval. Make added entry under the name of the personal or institutional owner.

> **Daley, Charles Marie,** 1897-
> Incunabula of Albert Magnus in the Library of Congress, by Rev. Charles M. Daley.
> I. U. S. Library of Congress.

D. Enter dealers' sales catalogs limited to an individual collection under the name of the collector (individual, association, institution, or firm).

> **Thomas, George Clifford,** *d.* 1909.
> . . . Autographs, rare books and fine bindings, the collection of the late George C. Thomas, to be sold . . . November 18 . . . and . . . November 19, 1924 . . . in our art galleries . . . under the management of Samuel T. Freeman & Co., auctioneers . . .

If the catalog covers several collections, one of which is the principal or featured collection, enter under the name of the principal collector.

> **Salter, Allen,** 1864-1933.
> . . . The renowned medical library of Allen Salter, M.D., of Ill., with a few additions, for sale by Argosy Book Stores, inc.

Unidentified collections and miscellaneous sales catalogs are entered under the name of the dealer.

> **Maggs Bros.,** *London.*
> . . . English literature of the 19th & 20th centuries, being a selection of first and early editions of the works of esteemed authors & book illustrators, together with books on sports and pastimes . . .

14. Radio scripts.

A. Enter a radio script or series of scripts under the author, when known. If all of the series were written for a named program or for a single broadcasting company, make added entry under the name of the program followed by RADIO PROGRAM in parentheses, or under the name of the broadcasting company.

> **Corwin, Norman Lewis,** 1910-
> Thirteen by Corwin, radio dramas.

> **Fane, Guy.**
> Over the garden wall (Mrs. "H." and Mrs. "C." gossip, as broadcast in "Monday night at seven") A series of comedy episodes, by Guy Fane.
> i. Monday night at seven (Radio program)

B. Enter a single script, when no author is named, under a named program or a broadcasting company or station, if any is mentioned; otherwise under title.

> **Columbia Broadcasting System.**
> CBS open letter on race hatred. Saturday, July 24th, 1943 (as broadcast)
> i. Title.

C. Enter collections of radio scripts by different authors or by unnamed authors under editor or under title. However, if all were written for a named program or broadcast by a single company or station, enter under the name of the program or the name of the company or station, giving preference to the name of the program, if distinctive. Make added entry for the name of the company.

> **Rees, Leslie,** 1905-   *ed.*
> Australian radio plays, edited by Leslie Rees.

> **Americans at work** (*Radio program*)
> Americans at work. May 20, 1939-
> i. Columbia Broadcasting System.

> **The family hour** (*Radio program*)
> United nations; six radio dramatizations presented on "The family hour," starring Gladys Swarthout, Deems Taylor and Al Goodman.

> **Amigos inolvidables** (*Radio program*)
> Amigos inolvidables; recopilación de los folletos correspondientes a la . . . serie de audiciones del programa "Amigos inolvidables," auspiciado por la Asociación de Difusión Interamericana, transmitido por LRl, Radio El Mundo y la Red azul y blanca, Buenos Aires.

National Broadcasting Company, inc.
These four men; radio biographies of the four most talked-about men in the world, Winston Churchill, Joseph Stalin, Adolf Hitler, Franklin D. Roosevelt, presented by the National Broadcasting Company.

15. Scenarios (Motion picture).

Enter scenarios of motion pictures under the title of the picture, with explanatory phrase MOTION PICTURE added in parentheses to the heading.

Elephant boy (*Motion picture*)

16. Ships' logs.

Enter the official log of a ship under the name of the ship. Make added entry for the commanding officer if his name appears prominently on the title page.

Gloucester (*U. S. gunboat*)
Log of the U. S. gunboat Gloucester, commanded by Lt.-Commander Richard Wainwright, and the official reports of the principal events of her cruise during the late war with Spain.
ɪ. Wainwright, Richard, 1849-1926.

Bon Homme Richard (*Ship*)
The log of the Bon Homme Richard; with introduction by Louis F. Middlebrook.
Includes the account by Nathaniel Fanning of the sea battle of September 23, 1779 (p. 49-61)
ɪ. Fanning, Nathaniel, 1755-1805. ɪɪ. Middlebrook, Louis Frank, 1866-

Ariel (*Steam yacht*)
Log of the "Ariel" in the gulf of Maine.

17. Theses and dissertations.[15]

A. Enter under the author theses and dissertations issued after 1800 with the exceptions noted in C, p. 39.

B. Enter under praeses dissertations issued before 1800 at continental European universities and faculties. Make added entry under the respondent. Include the word PRAESES or RESPONDENT in the heading.

Schurtzfleisch, Conrad Samuel, 1641-1708, *praeses.*
. . . Lemmata antiqvitatum francicarum . . .
Diss.—Wittenberg (P. C. Scheibler, respondent)
ɪ. Scheibler, P. C., respondent.

Reinharth, Tobias Jacob, 1684-1743, *praeses.*
. . . De rervm vxoriarvm marito traditarvm favore, et qvibvsdam cavtionibvs earvm cavsa attendis . . .
Diss.—Erfurt (G. L. Hoyer, respondent and author)
ɪ. Hoyer, Georg Leopold, respondent.

---

[15] Cf. H. B. Wheatley, "On the question of authorship in academical dissertations," in his *How to catalogue a library* (London, Stock, 1889), p. 105-121.

Make exception in favor of entry under respondent in cases of well-authenticated authorship.[16] In case of doubt prefer main entry under praeses.

> **Rudolphi, Karl Asmund,** 1771-1832, *respondent and author.*
> Observationes circa vermes intestionales . . .
> Diss.—Greifswald.
> Part 1, Joannes Quistorp, praeses; pt. 2, Chr. Ehrenfr. Weigel, praeses.
> I. Quistorp, Joannes, praeses. II. Weigel, Christian Ehrenfried von, 1784-1831, praeses.

If two respondents are named without a praeses, and without designating the author, enter under the first and make added entry for the second.

C. Treat in the same way as in B, p. 38-39, the later dissertations of certain universities at which the old custom continued after 1800 (e.g., the Swedish and Finnish, and some of the German, particularly Tübingen).

> **Schuebler, Gustav,** 1787-1834, *praeses.*
> Untersuchungen über das specifische Gewicht der Samen und näheren Bestandtheile des Pflanzenreichs . . .
> Inaug.-Diss.—Tübingen (C. F. Renz, respondent)
> I. Renz, Carl Friedrich, respondent.

D. Enter a dissertation consisting of an edition or translation of the work of another under the original author. (Cf. 2.)

> **Alanus** *de Insulis,* d. 1202.
> The Anticlaudian of Alain de Lille; prologue, argument and nine books, translated, with an introduction and notes . . . ₁by₎ William Hafner Cornog.
> W. H. Cornog's thesis (PH.D.)—University of Pennsylvania, 1934.
> I. Cornog, William Hafner, 1909-   tr. II. Title.

E. Enter a **program dissertation** under the author of the dissertation. If a program is accompanied by two or more dissertations, enter each independently. Added entry under the institution (or, if the case require, form subject entry) may be made.

> **Elter, Anton,** 1858-1925.
> . . . De Henrico Glareano geographo et antiquissima forma 'Americae' commentatio.
> Programm—Bonn (Natalicia Gvilelmi II)
> I. Bonn. Universität.

---

[16] The respondent's designation as "auctor" on the title page, however, is not to be accepted as proof of his authorship without other evidence. Concerning the authorship of dissertations entered under the praeses, see the following: Ferdinand Eichler, "Die Autorschaft der akademischen Disputationen," *Sammlung bibliothekswissenschaftlicher Arbeiten,* Hft. 10 (1896), p. 24-37; Hft. 11 (1898), p. 1-40. Ewald Horn, "Die Disputationen und Promotionen an den deutschen Universitäten, vornehmlich seit dem 16. Jahrhundert," *Centralblatt für Bibliothekswesen,* 11. Beiheft (1893) and Georg Kaufmann, "Zur Geschichte der academischen Grade und Disputationen," *ibid.,* XI. Jahrg. (May, 1894), p. 201-225.

Jeitteles, Ludwig Heinrich, 1830-1883.
Ueber einige seltene und wenig bekannte Säugethiere des
südöstlichen Deutschlands . . .
Programm—N. Ö. Landes-Ober-Realschule, St. Pölten.
I. Sankt Pölten, Austria. Landes-Real- und Ober-Gymnasium.

Rydberg, Johannes Robert, 1854-1919.
Fysikens utveckling till allmän tillståndslära . . .
Programm—Lund (with list of doctors' degrees)
1. Lund. Universitet. Doctors' degrees, 1903.

18. Visitations, Heraldic.

Enter heraldic visitations under the name of the herald or king-of-
arms who makes the visitation. Make added entries for other heralds
assisting in or continuing the visitation, for the editor, for the college
or king-of-arms, and make form subject entry under the heading
VISITATIONS, HERALDIC.

Bysshe, *Sir* **Edward,** 1615?-1679.
The visitation of Sussex, anno Domini 1662, made by Sir Edward Bysshe, knt. . . . edited and annotated by A. W. Hughes
Clarke, F. S. A.
1. Visitations, Heraldic—Sussex, Eng. I. Hughes Clarke, Arthur William, 1873-   ed. II. England. College of Arms. III. Title.

19. Works of art.

A. Enter under the artist collections of drawings, or reproductions of drawings, engravings, paintings, sculptures, photographs, or
designs of other art objects, which are the work of a single artist, and
issued without text, with prefatory notice and list of plates only, or
with a brief descriptive or other text of obviously secondary importance. Make added entry for the editor or compiler, personal or
corporate (museum, gallery, association, etc.) as the case may be.

Capon, William, 1757-1827.
Views of Westminster, sketched 1801-1815 and drawn in water-
colours by William Capon. Reproduced from the originals in the
possession of the Society of Antiquaries with Capon's descriptions annotated by Philip Norman . . .
I. Norman, Philip, 1842-1931. II. Society of Antiquaries of London.
III. Title.

Dürer, Albrecht, 1471-1528.
Albrecht Dürers sämtliche Kupferstiche im Grösse der Orig-
inale in Lichtdruck wiedergegeben, nebst einem erläuternden
Vorwort von Dr. Franz Friedrich Leitschuh . . .
I. Leitschuh, Franz Friedrich, 1865-1924, ed.

Brangwyn, *Sir* **Frank,** 1867-
The British Empire panels designed for the House of Lords
by Frank Brangwyn, R. A.; descriptive text by Frank Rutter,
foreword by the Earl of Iveagh.
I. Rutter, Frank Vane Phipson, 1876-1937. II. Title.

Rubens, *Sir* **Peter Paul,** 1577-1640.
The masterpieces of Rubens . . . sixty reproductions . . .
from the original paintings . . .

40

Rodin, Auguste, 1840-1917.
Sculptures de Rodin.

Adams, Ansel Easton, 1902-
The four seasons in Yosemite National Park; a photographic story of Yosemite's spectacular scenery, photographed by Ansel Adams, edited by Stanley Plumb.

ɪ. Plumb, Stanley, ed.

B. Enter **engravings** which reproduce the work of another artist under the original artist with added entry for the engraver, but enter reproductions of the work of several artists by a single **engraver** under the engraver.

Turner, Joseph Mallord William, 1775-1851.
Picturesque views on the southern coast of England, from drawings made principally by J. M. W. Turner, ʀ. ᴀ., and engraved by W. B. Cooke, George Cooke, and other eminent engravers . . .

ɪ. Cooke, William Bernard, 1778-1855, engr. ɪɪ. Cooke, George, 1781-1834, engr. ɪɪɪ. Title.

Feuchère, Léon, 1804-1857.
L'art industriel, recueil de dispositions et de décorations intérieures, comprenant des modèles pour toutes les industries d'ameublement et de luxe . . . 72 planches composées et dessinées par Léon Feuchère . . . gravées par Varin frères et précédées d'une introduction sur l'application de l'art à l'industrie.

ɪ. Varin, Amédée, 1818-1883, engr. ɪɪ. Varin, Eugène Napoléon, 1831- engr.

Finden, William, 1787-1852.
Views of ports and harbours, watering places, fishing villages, and other picturesque objects on the English coast. Engraved by William and Edward Finden, from paintings by J. D. Harding, G. Balmer, E. W. Cooke, T. Creswick and other eminent artists.

Text by W. A. Chatto.

ɪ. Finden, Edward Francis, 1791-1857. ɪɪ. Chatto, William Andrew, 1799-1864, ed. ɪɪɪ. Title.

C. If the drawings, engravings, etc., form part of a work, even a more or less independent part (portfolio, or separate volume or volumes) in conjunction with a substantial text by a person (or persons) other than the artist himself, make the main entry under the author of the text with added entry, or subject (depending on the individual case) under the artist. In case of doubt, prefer main entry under the author of the text, with subject entry under artist.

Hind, Charles Lewis, 1862-1927.
Augustus Saint-Gaudens, by C. Lewis Hind.

1. Saint Gaudens, Augustus, 1848-1907.

ₜ47 *pages of text, 52 plates*₎

41

Horne, Herbert Percy, 1864-1916.
Alessandro Filipepi, commonly called Sandro Botticelli,
painter of Florence, by Herbert P. Horne.
  1. Botticelli, Sandro, 1447?-1510.
  ₍366 *pages of text, 42 plates*₎

D. When an artist and an author collaborate in the production
of a work, enter under the one whose contribution forms the pre-
dominant feature of the work, and make added entry for the other.
In case of doubt, prefer entry under the author of the text.

Smith, Alice Ravenel Huger, 1876-
A Carolina rice plantation of the fifties; 30 paintings in water-
colour, by Alice R. Huger Smith, narrative by Herbert Ravenel
Sass, with chapters from the unpublished memoirs of D. E. Huger
Smith.
  I. Sass, Herbert Ravenel, 1884-   II. Smith, Daniel Elliott Huger.
  III. Title.

Kemble, Edward Windsor, 1861-1933.
Cartoons by E. W. Kemble; limericks by G. Mayo . . .
  I. Mayo, Gertrude, 1879-

Casdorff, Heinz.
Heiteres Capri, von Heinz Casdorff. Mit Bildern von Erica
Casdorff-Westendorff.
  I. Casdorff-Westendorff, Erica, illus. II. Title.

E. When the contribution of the artist is limited to the **illustration**
of a work independently written by another person, make added entry
for the illustrator only if the illustrations are a noteworthy feature
of the work.

Dante Alighieri, 1265-1321.
The Divine comedy of Dante Alighieri, translated by Jeffer-
son Butler Fletcher . . .
  Illustrations from drawings by Botticelli.
  I. Fletcher, Jefferson Butler, 1865-   tr. II. Botticelli, Sandro,
1447?-1510, illus.

Coleridge, Samuel Taylor, 1772-1834.
Rime of the ancient mariner. By Samuel Taylor Coleridge.
With twenty illustrations by J. Noel Paton, R.S.A.
  I. Paton, Sir Joseph Noël, 1821-1901, illus. II. Title.

Barne, Kitty, 1883-
She shall have music, by Kitty Barne; illustrated by Ruth
Gervis . . .
  I. Title. [*No added entry for illustrator*]

But if the illustrations are assembled and published without the
text, enter under the illustrator with subject entry under the **name**
of the author of the text with subheading ILLUSTRATIONS.

Paton, *Sir* Joseph Noël, 1821-1901.
Compositions from Shakespeare's Tempest. Fifteen engrav-
ings in outline. By Sir J. Noel Paton.
  I. Shakespeare, William—Illustrations.

F. Enter **architectural drawings** and plans of buildings under the person (architect) or corporate body responsible for them.

> Burges, William, 1827-1881.
>> The architectural designs of William Burges, A. R. A., edited by Richard Popplewell Pullan, F. R. I. B. A.
>>> I. Pullan, Richard Popplewell, 1825-1888, ed.

> Kaufmann, Oskar, 1873-
>> Der Architekt Oskar Kaufmann; Vorwort von Oscar Bie; mit 140 Abbildungen auf 127 Tafeln und 5 Farbentafeln.
>>> I. Bie, Oskar, 1864-1938.

> Northwestern Lumbermen's Association, *Minneapolis.*
>> Practical small homes. 3d ed. . . . Designs by Northwestern Lumbermen's Ass'n, Minneapolis, Minn.

Works Related to Previous Publications

20. Revisions.

Enter a revision under the name of the original author with added entry for the reviser. (Cf. 2.)

> [Chisholm, George Goudie] 1850-1930.
>> . . . Europe . . . edited by B. C. Wallis . . . London, E. Stanford, ltd. [1924-25?]
>>> The work of G. C. Chisholm in the previous edition, 1899-1902, has been largely retained. It has been brought up to date by B. C. Wallis.
>>> I. Wallis, Bertie Cotterell, ed.

The rule applies as long as the work remains substantially that of the original author, especially if it purports to be an edition of his work. If, however, the revision is substantially a new work, enter it under the reviser with added entry for the author and title of the original work.

> Mudge, Isadore Gilbert, 1875-
>> New guide to reference books, by Isadore Gilbert Mudge . . . Based on the 3d edition of Guide to the study and use of reference books by Alice Bertha Kroeger as revised by I. G. Mudge.
>>> I. Kroeger, Alice Bertha, d. 1909. Guide to the study and use of reference books.

> Seubert, Adolf Friedrich, 1819-1890, *ed.*
>> Allgemeines Künstler-Lexicon; oder, Leben und Werke der berühmtesten bildenden Künstler. 2. Aufl. umgearbeitet und ergänzt von A. Seubert.
>>> Second edition of Friedrich Müller's Die Künstler aller Zeiten und Völker.
>>> I. Müller, Friedrich, d. ca. 1858. Die Künstler aller Zeiten und Völker.

21. Translations.

A. Enter a translation under the author of the original work, with added entry for the translator. (Cf. 32G, 33A.)

> **Maurois, André,** 1885-
> The Edwardian era, by André Maurois; translated by Hamish
> Miles.
> I. Miles, Hamish, 1894-1937, tr. II. Title.

B. Enter translations from various authors by a single **translator,** published as one work, under the translator.

> **Underwood, Edna (Worthley)** 1873-   *tr.*
> Short stories from the Balkans, translated into English by
> Edna Worthley Underwood.
> CONTENTS.—

C. Enter translations from various authors by different translators under the compiler or editor, or under title. (Cf. 5A.)

> **Cohen, Gustave,** 1879-   *ed.*
> . . . La "comédie" latine en France au xIIᵉ siècle; textes
> publiés sous la direction et avec une introduction de Gustave
> Cohen . . . Textes établis et traduits par Marcel Abraham,
> Robert Baschet, André Cordier ₍etc.₎ . . .
> I. Abraham, Marcel, tr. II. Baschet, Robert, tr. III. Cordier, André,
> tr. IV. Title.

> **Specimens** of the German lyric poets: consisting of translations
> in verse, from the works of Bürger, Goethe, Klopstock,
> Schiller, &c., interspersed with biographical notices, and orna-
> mented with engravings on wood . . .

22. Abridgments, adaptations, excerpts.

A. Enter an **abridgment,** epitome, or outline under the same heading as the original work with added entry for the abridger, epitomizer, etc.

> **Scott,** *Sir* **Walter,** *bart.,* 1771-1832.
> Scott's Ivanhoe; modernized and abridged by Carolyn Pulcifer
> Timm . . .
> I. Timm, Carolyn (Pulcifer) II. Title: Ivanhoe.

> **Remarque, Erich Maria,** 1898-
> . . . Im Westen nichts Neues. (Abridged ed.) Prepared with
> introduction, notes and vocabulary by Waldo C. Peebles . . .
> I. Peebles, Waldo Cutler, 1895-   ed. II. Title.

B. Enter an **adaptation,** a paraphrase, or a free translation, as a general rule, under the same heading as the original work with added entry for the adapter, paraphraser, etc. (Cf. 33D.)

> ₍Blackmore, Richard Doddridge₎ 1825-1900.
> Lorna Doone, adapted by Rachel Jordan, A. O. Berglund ₍and₎
> Carleton Washburne, illustrated by Alexander Key.
> I. Jordan, Rachel. II. Berglund, Albert Olaf, 1902-   III. Wash-
> burne, Carleton Wolsey, 1889-   IV. Title.

> **Vergilius Maro, Publius.**
> Stories of old Rome. The wanderings of Æneas and the
> founding of Rome. By Charles Henry Hanson . . .
> "Little more than a simplified paraphrase of the poem."—Pref.
> I. Hanson, Charles Henry. II. Title.

Rosenkranz, Karl, 1805-1879.
   The science of education. A paraphrase of Dr. Karl Rosen-
kranz's Paedagogik als System. By Anna C. Brackett.
   I. Brackett, Anna Callender, 1836-1911, ed. and tr.

However, if the adaptation or paraphrase has been so freely made
as to bear slight kinship with the original work as in the case of many
adaptations for the use of juvenile readers, or if it has become a
classic in its own right, prefer entry under the adapter or paraphraser,
with added entry under the author and title of the original work. In
doubtful cases, prefer entry under heading used for the original work.

When entry is under adapter or paraphraser and the paraphrase
is not limited to a single work, or if the work paraphrased is by a
voluminous author under whose name there is a systematic arrangement of material in the catalog, make added entry under the author's
name with subheading PARAPHRASES, TALES, ETC.

Hosford, Dorothy G.
   Sons of the Volsungs; adapted by Dorothy G. Hosford from
Sigurd the Volsung by William Morris . . .
   I. Morris, William, 1834-1896. The story of Sigurd the Volsung and
the fall of the Niblungs. II. Völsunga saga.

Lamb, Charles, 1775-1834.
   Tales from Shakespeare, by Charles & Mary Lamb; with
sundry pictures and illuminations (now for the first time pub-
lished) both in colour and in line, by Elizabeth Shippen Green
Elliott . . .
   I. Shakespeare, William. Paraphrases, tales, etc. II. Lamb, Mary
Ann, 1764-1847, joint author. III. Elliott, Elizabeth Shippen (Green)
illus. IV. Title.

ₜ**Greene, Edward Burnaby**ₗ d. 1788.
   The Satires of Juvenal paraphrastically imitated, and adapted
to the times. With a preface . . .
   I. Juvenalis, Decimus Junius. Paraphrases, tales, etc.

C. Enter **excerpts** (selections) from a single author under that
author, with added entry under compiler.
   For entry of excerpts, etc., from several authors see 5A.

Plato.
   Gleanings from Plato, being analects selected by J. R. Whit-
well, M. B.
   I. Whitwell, James Richard, ed. II. Title.

Dickens, Charles, 1812-1870.
   Dickens all the year round; a Dickens anthology, arranged by
H. N. Wethered & Charles Turley, with an introduction by
Bernard Darwin.
   I. Wethered, Herbert Newton, 1869-   ed. II. Turley, Charles, joint
ed. III. Title.

23. Dramatizations and novelizations.
   A. Enter a **dramatization** based on a novel, legend, poem or other

45

literary form under the playwright, with added entry under the author
and title of the work upon which the dramatization is based.

> **Howard, Sidney Coe, 1891-1939.**
> Sinclair Lewis's Dodsworth, dramatized by Sidney Howard . . .
> I. Lewis, Sinclair, 1885-   Dodsworth. II. Title: Dodsworth.

> **White, Edward Joseph, 1869-**
> Patient Griselda, a drama of the eleventh century (from
> Chaucer's Canterbury tales) Adapted for the screen. By Edw.
> J. White . . .
> I. Chaucer, Geoffrey. Canterbury tales. Clerk's tale. II. Title.

For musical dramas, see the rule for librettos, 12A (2).

B. Enter a **novelization** based on a play or other literary form under
the novelist, with added entry under the author and title of the work
upon which the novelization is based.

> **Miln, Louise (Jordan) 1864-1933.**
> The green goddess, by Louise Jordan Miln . . . based on the
> play, "The green goddess," by William Archer.
> I. Archer, William, 1856-1924. The green goddess. II. Title.

24. Parodies and imitations.

Enter a parody or an imitation under its own author with subject
entry for the author and title of the work parodied or imitated.

For parodies not limited to a single work or for a parody of a single
work by a voluminous author under whose name in the catalog there
is a systematic arrangement of material, make subject heading under
the name of the author parodied with subheading PARODIES, TRAV-
ESTIES, ETC.

> **Downey, Fairfax Davis, 1893-**
> When we were rather older, by Fairfax Downey . . .
> A parody of "When we were very young," by A. A. Milne.
> 1. Milne, Alan Alexander, 1882-   When we were very young.
> I. Title.

> **Desfontaines, Pierre François Guyot, 1685-1745.**
> O novo Gulliver, ou Viagem de João Gulliver, filho do capitão
> Gulliver. Traduzida de hum manuscrito inglez pelo abbade des
> Fontaines, trasladada do francez . . .
> An imitation of Gulliver's travels by the Abbé Desfontaines.
> 1. Swift, Jonathan, 1667-1745. Gulliver's travels. I. Title.

> **Stevens, Harold Charles Gilbard, 1892-**
> . . . High-speed Shakespeare: "Hamlet," "Julius Caesar,"
> "Romeo and Juliet"; three tragedies in a tearing hurry.
> At head of title: H. C. G. Stevens.
> 1. Shakespeare, William—Parodies, travesties, etc. I. Title.

> **Rice, George Edward, 1822-1861.**
> An old play in a new garb; (Hamlet, Prince of Denmark;) in
> three acts. By Geo. Edward Rice . . .
> 1. Shakespeare, William—Parodies, travesties, etc. I. Title.

25. Continuations (Supplements).

A. Enter a continuation which is in the form of an independent work with author and title differing from that of the original work under its own author. Make added entry under the name of the original author followed by a brief title of his work, or, if preferred, a reference may take the place of an added entry.

> **Donaldson, John William, 1811-1861.**
> A history of the literature of ancient Greece; from the foundation of the Socratic schools to the taking of Constantinople by the Turks. Being a continuation of K. O. Müller's work. By John William Donaldson.
> I. Müller, Karl Otfried, 1797-1840. Geschichte der griechischen Literatur.

or, instead of added entry make reference:

> **Müller, Karl Otfried, 1797-1840.**
> Geschichte der griechischen Literatur . . .
> For a continuation of this work
> *see*
> **Donaldson, John William, 1811-1861.**
> A history of the literature of ancient Greece . . . Being a continuation of K. O. Müller's work.

> **Copinger, Walter Arthur, 1847-1910.**
> Supplement to Hain's Repertorium bibliographicum. Or, Collections towards a new edition of that work. In two parts . . . by W. A. Copinger . . .
> I. Hain, Ludwig Friedrich Theodor, 1781-1836. Repertorium bibliographicum.

or, instead of added entry make reference:

> **Hain, Ludwig Friedrich Theodor, 1781-1836.**
> Repertorium bibliographicum . . .
> *see also*
> **Copinger, Walter Arthur, 1847-1910.**
> Supplement to Hain's Repertorium bibliographicum . . .

> **Wheeler, Joseph Towne.**
> The Maryland press, 1777-1790, by Joseph Towne Wheeler; with an introduction by Lawrence C. Wroth.
> A continuation of Lawrence C. Wroth's History of printing in colonial Maryland. *cf.* Pref.
> I. Wroth, Lawrence Counselman, 1884-   A history of printing in colonial Maryland, 1686-1776.

or, instead of added entry make reference:

> **Wroth, Lawrence Counselman, 1884-**
> A history of printing in colonial Maryland
> For a continuation of this work
> *see*
> **Wheeler, Joseph Towne.**
> The Maryland press, 1777-1790.

B. Enter a continuation or supplement not independent of the work

47

to which it belongs (usually, but not necessarily, by the same author) with the original work.

> **Halévy, Élie, 1870–1937.**
> A history of the English people . . . by Élie Halévy. With an introduction by Graham Wallas; translated from the French by E. I. Watkin and D. A. Barker.
> ————Epilogue . . . translated from the French by E. I. Watkin.
> ɪ. Watkin, Edward Ingram, 1888–   tr. ɪɪ. Barker, Dalgairns Arundel, joint tr.

C. Enter a single monograph issued as a supplement to a periodical under the author, with added entry for the periodical, followed by the word Supplement.

> **Austin, Bryson Edward, 1851–1903.**
> . . . The story of a New England farm house. Boston, Ellis & Little, 1883.
> 106 p. 24$^{cm\cdot}$
> Supplement to Massachusetts magazine of historical research, v. 12, no. 3.
> ɪ. Massachusetts magazine of historical research. Supplement.

D. Enter a series of monographs forming a supplement to a periodical under the name of the periodical, unless the series has a distinctive title.

> **Zentralblatt für Bibliothekswesen.**
> Beihefte zum Zentralblatt für Bibliothekswesen . . . Leipzig, O. Harrassowitz, 1888–

26. Sequels.

Catalog a sequel as an independent work. If the sequel is by a different author, make an added entry under the author of the work which it continues, followed by a brief title thereof.

> **Aimard, Gustave, 1818–1883.**
> Trappers of Arkansas. A narrative. By Gustave Aimard . . .
> Sequel: The border rifles.

> **Aimard, Gustave, 1818–1883.**
> The border rifles. A narrative. By Gustave Aimard.
> Sequel to Trappers of Arkansas. Sequel: The freebooters.

> **Harris, Edwin.**
> John Jasper's gatehouse . . . A sequel to the unfinished novel, "The mystery of Edwin Drood," by Charles Dickens . . .
> ɪ. Dickens, Charles. The mystery of Edwin Drood.

27. Indexes.

A. Enter a separately published index to a single work of an author with the work, making added entry for the compiler.

B. Enter a separately published index to the collective works of an author under the compiler. Make subject entry for the author indexed with subheading Dɪᴄᴛɪᴏɴᴀʀɪᴇs, ɪɴᴅᴇxᴇs, ᴇᴛᴄ.

Saxton, Eugene Francis, 1884-1943, *comp.*
The Kipling index; being a guide to authorized American trade edition of Rudyard Kipling's works, compiled by Eugene F. Saxton, March, 1911.

1. Kipling, Rudyard, 1865-1936—Dictionaries, indexes, etc.

C. Enter cumulated indexes to periodicals and other serials with the serials to which they belong.

If a separate entry is necessary, give the title of the work indexed in the heading, followed by the word INDEXES in parentheses.

Société de linguistique de Paris. Mémoires. (*Indexes*)
Table analytique des dix premiers volumes des Mémoires de la Société de linguistique de Paris, par Émile Ernault . . . Paris, Imprimerie nationale, 1900.

I. Ernault, Émile Jean Marie, 1852-   comp.

The Classical journal. (*Indexes*)
. . . General index to volumes I-XXV [1905-1930] by Franklin H. Potter. Cedar Rapids, Iowa, The Torch Press [1930]

I. Potter, Franklin Hazen, 1869-   comp.

D. Enter a combined index to several publications of one society or institution under the name of the body, with added entry under the compiler, and under the several serials indexed, giving heading, brief title, and the word INDEXES in parentheses.

Society of Antiquaries of Newcastle-upon-Tyne.
General index to the Archaeologia Æliana (vols. I-IV. 4to; and I-XVI. 8vo.) and to the Proceedings (vol. I (o.s.); and I-V) of the Society of Antiquaries of Newcastle-upon-Tyne.

I. Archaeologia Æliana. (Indexes) II. Society of Antiquaries of Newcastle-upon-Tyne. Proceedings. (Indexes)

E. Enter a combined index to several publications of different origin under the compiler with added entry under the headings of the several publications. Use subject heading instead of added entry if the work indexed cannot be particularized.

Cole, George Watson, 1850-1939.
An index to bibliographical papers published by the Bibliographical Society and the Library Association, London, 1877-1932, by George Watson Cole . . .
Indexes also the Library, a quarterly review of bibliography.

1. Bibliography—Bibl. 2. Bibliographical Society, London—Bibl. 3. Library Association—Bibl. I. The Library; a quarterly review of bibliography. (Indexes)

F. Enter a general index, as a rule, under its compiler. However, enter under title indexes to periodical and miscellaneous literature if they are better known under their titles, especially such as are published periodically.

Griswold, William McCrillis, 1853-1899.
. . . An index to articles relating to history, biografy, literature, society, and travel contained in collections of essays (etc.) by W. M. Griswold . . . 2d ed., revised but not enlarged.

Poole's index to periodical literature, by William Frederick Poole . . . with the assistance as associate editor of William I. Fletcher . . . and the coöperation of the American Library Association and the Library Association of the United Kingdom . . . Rev. ed. Vol. i . . . 1802-1881.
> i. Poole, William Frederick, 1821-1894, ed. ii. Fletcher, William Isaac, 1844-1917, joint ed.

Essay and general literature index, 1900-1933; an index to about 40,000 essays and articles in 2144 volumes of collections of essays and miscellaneous works, edited by Minnie Earl Sears and Marian Shaw, preface by Isadore Gilbert Mudge . . .
> _____Supplement, July 1934-
> . . . Edited by Marian Shaw. New York, The H. W. Wilson Company, 1934-
> i. Sears, Minnie Earl, 1873-1933, ed. ii. Shaw, Marian, 1895- joint ed.

G. Enter indexes of laws which do not index a particular work under the name of the country or other jurisdiction, with form subdivision LAWS, STATUTES, ETC. (INDEXES). Make added entry for compiler.

Connecticut. *Laws, statutes, etc.* (*Indexes*)
Index to General statutes of Connecticut.

H. Enter an index to a particular code, but not to a particular edition of it, under the name of the jurisdiction with form subdivision LAWS, STATUTES, ETC., the name of the code, and form subdivision (INDEXES).

Mexico. *Laws, statutes, etc.* Código penal. (*Indexes*)

28. Concordances.

Enter a concordance under its compiler with subject entry under the heading appropriate to the work concordanced.

Cruden, Alexander, 1701-1770.
A complete concordance to the Holy Scriptures of the Old and New Testament . . . To which is added, A concordance to the books called Apocrypha . . .
> 1. Bible—Concordances, English.

Prendergast, Guy Lushington.
A complete concordance to the Iliad of Homer. By Guy Lushington Prendergast . . .
> 1. Homerus. Ilias—Concordances.

Broughton, Leslie Nathan, 1877-
A concordance to the poems of Robert Browning, by Leslie N. Broughton . . . and Benjamin F. Stelter.
> 1. Browning, Robert—Concordances. i. Stelter, Benjamin Franklin, joint author.

29. Commentaries and scholia.

A. Enter works containing both text and commentary (or scholia) under the author of the text with added entry for the commentator or scholiast.

Demosthenes.
Demosthenes, with an English commentary by the Rev. Robert Whiston . . .
   i. Whiston, Robert, 1808–1895, ed.

    B. Enter under commentator or scholiast commentaries (or scholia) with partial or fragmentary text, or with text obviously subordinated to the commentary either by its typographical disposition (e.g., in small type at the foot of the page, in parentheses to elucidate the commentary, or distributed through the commentary in such a way that it cannot be readily distinguished from it) or by the emphasis given by author or publisher. Make added entry under the heading appropriate to the text.[17]

Gill, William Hugh, 1841–1904.
The incarnate Word; being the Fourth Gospel elucidated by interpolation for popular use, by William Hugh Gill . . .
   1. Bible. N. T. John—Commentaries. i. Title.
   [*Text subordinate to commentary*]

Steuernagel, Carl, 1869–
Übersetzung und Erklärung der Bücher Deuteronium u. Joshua.
   (Handkommentar zum Alten Testament, i. Abth., 1.Bd.)
   1. Bible. O. T. Deuteronomy—Commentaries. 2. Bible. O. T. Joshua —Commentaries. i. Bible. O. T. Deuteronomy. German. ii. Bible. O. T. Joshua. German.
   [*Emphasis on the commentary*]

    C. Enter scholia without text and of unknown (probably diverse) authorship under the editor. Make form subject entry consisting of the name of the author upon whose works the scholia are based followed by the word Scholia. In the case of scholia limited to a particular work, include the title of the work in the form subject heading.

Mountford, James Frederick, 1897–   *ed.*
The scholia Bembina, edited with annotations by J. F. Mountford . . .
   1. Terentius Afer, Publius—Scholia. i. Title.

Wendel, Carl Theodor Eduard, 1874–   *ed.*
Scholia in Apollonium Rhodium vetera recensuit Carolus Wendel.
   1. Apollonius Rhodius—Scholia. i. Title.

White, John Williams, 1849–1917, *ed.*
The scholia on the Aves of Aristophanes, with an introduction on the origin, development, transmission, and extant sources of the old Greek commentary on his comedies; collected and edited by John Williams White . . .
   1. Aristophanes. Aves—Scholia. i. Title.

---

[17] Commentaries issued without text are entered, like criticism in general, under the author of the commentary, with *subject* entry for the work criticized.

Works of Doubtful or Unknown Authorship

30. Pseudonymous works.

Specification.—A pseudonymous work is one by an author who writes under a false name. (Cf. GLOSSARY.) The term is here extended to include those who conceal their identities (1) by assuming the name of another real person (allonym), e.g., "by Horacio Flaco"; (2) by rearranging the letters of the name (anagram), e.g., "by Olphar Hamst," i.e., Ralph Thomas; or by adopting an inverted spelling, e.g., "by Eidrah Trebor," i.e., Robert Hardie; (3) by using forename or forenames only, e.g., "by Aurelia," i.e., Aurelia Gay Mace; "by Anthony Berkeley," i.e., Anthony Berkeley Cox; (4) by rearranging the order of surname and Christian names, e.g., "by Leilani Jones Melville," i.e., Melville Leilani Jones; (5) by using as a name a specific word or phrase with or without a definite article, e.g., "by Acutus," "by Sigma," "by Cheiro," "by Ex-intelligence officer," "by Operator 1384," "by the Duchess," "by the Prig," etc. (Cf. also Anonymous works, 32.)

A. Enter works published under pseudonym under the author's real name when known, except as qualified below in (1)-(3) and B.

> [Mace, Aurelia Gay] 1835-1910.
> The alethia: spirit of truth. A series of letters in which the principles of the united society known as Shakers are set forth and illustrated. By Aurelia [pseud.]
> I. Title.
> *Refer from* Aurelia, *pseud.*

> [Clemens, Samuel Langhorne] 1835-1910.
> Following the equator; a journey around the world, by Mark Twain [pseud.]
> I. Title.
> *Refer from* Twain, Mark, *pseud.*

Exception is made in favor of entry under pseudonym followed by the abbreviation PSEUD.:

(1) When real name is unknown, or the author wishes it withheld.

> **Rockwood, Roy,** *pseud.*
> Bomba the jungle boy . . . by Roy Rockwood . . .
> I. Title.

> **Ex-convict no._____**[18]
> Dartmoor from within, by Ex-convict no. _____ ("Jock" of Parkhurst)
> I. Title.

(2) When the pseudonym has become fixed in literary history (including current criticism) and biography, and is therefore, the name

---

[18] The designation PSEUD. is not included in the heading when the pseudonym is obviously not a personal name.

looked for by the informed reader. If desirable for clarity, include real
name in heading or mention it in a note. Refer from real name.

> **Caballero, Fernán,** *pseud. of* **Cecilia Böhl de**
> **Faber,** 1796-1877.
> **Sand, George,** *pseud. of* **Mme. Dudevant,** 1804-1876.

This rule may be followed in cases where current popular authors
are better known by pseudonym than by real name, if they have never
published under the real name.

> **Winwar, Frances,** *pseud.*
> *Refer from*
> Grebanier, Frances (Vinciguerra) 1900-
> Webb, Frances (Vinciguerra) 1900-

In cases where the pseudonym and real name are used with about
equal frequency and are therefore equally well known, the real name
is likely to gain in ascendancy and should be favored.

(3) When two or more authors have written together under one
pseudonym, to avoid a cumbersome heading, give the real names in
a note,[19] and refer from them.

> **Queen, Ellery,** *pseud.*
> The Roman hat mystery . . . by Ellery Queen.
> Ellery Queen is the pseudonym of Frederic Dannay and Manfred
> Bennington Lee.

Make references:

> **Dannay, Frederic.**
> For works written in collaboration with Manfred Lee
> *see*
> **Queen, Ellery,** *pseud.*
> **Lee, Manfred Bennington.**
> For works written in collaboration with Frederic Dannay
> *see*
> **Queen, Ellery,** *pseud.*

But entry under one of the real names is to be preferred to entry
under initials.

> [**Young, Virginia C**]
> Philip; the story of a boy violinist, by T. W. O. [*pseud.*]
> T. W. O. is the pseudonym of Virginia C. Young and Mary C.
> Hungerford.
> ɪ. Hungerford, Mary C., joint author. ɪɪ. Title.
> *Refer from* T. W. O., *pseud.*

B. Other combinations of circumstances arise in which an individual case may require a special decision. For example, it is ordinarily better to enter under the real name authors who have written
under several pseudonyms, especially if they have ever published

---

[19] The Library of Congress gives this information in a note in the lower right-hand
corner of the card, e.g., Ellery Queen, *pseud. of* Frederic Dannay *and* Manfred Ben-
nington Lee.

under the real name; but exception might be made for a very well-known pseudonym.

When in doubt whether an assumed name is a pseudonym or a changed name (cf. 45) entry under the assumed name without the designation PSEUD. may be better.

> **Damase, Jean.**
> [*Name used by a novelist whose real name has been reported to be Jean Brun*]

31. Spurious works and works of doubtful authorship.

A. Enter under the name of an author (usually ancient, classic, or medieval) with form subdivision SPURIOUS AND DOUBTFUL WORKS, works that have been transmitted as his in manuscript and early printed editions without discrimination, but which have later been proved to be spurious or doubtful and excluded from the canon of his genuine works, though they are sometimes included in collected editions and are also issued as separate collections or individually. Restrict the use of this subdivision to the case of authors to whom several works (cf. B following) have been thus uncritically ascribed, the real authorship of which remains unknown or uncertain. It is to be used, however, for an edition of any one of these "spurious" works unless another heading is more suitable, (e.g., a uniform title heading) in which case make added entry, with this subdivision, under the name of the person to whom the work has been ascribed. Notable examples of authors with whose names this subdivision is appropriately used are Aristoteles, Cicero, Seneca, Thomas Aquinas, Dante, Shakespeare.

> **Aristoteles.** *Spurious and doubtful works.*
> Aristoteles qui ferebantur librorum fragmenta collegit Valentinus Rose.
>
> Collection of the fragments of Aristotle extant, all of which were considered by the editor to be spurious. Previously published with title: Valentini Rose Aristoteles pseudepigraphus. Lipsiae, 1863; also forms part of the edition of the Berlin Academy, vol. v (1870) p. [1463]-1589.
>
> I. Rose, Valentin, 1829-1916, ed.

> **Aristoteles.** *Spurious and doubtful works.*
> De spiritu [translated] by J. F. Dobson.
>
> Separate issue of part of vol. III of the Works of Aristotle translated into English under the editorship of J. A. Smith and W. D. Ross.
> "This treatise has been rejected as spurious by practically all editors."—Pref.
>
> I. Dobson, John Frederic, 1875-   tr. II. Title.

> **Yorkshire tragedy.**
> . . . A Yorkshire tragedy, 1608.
>
> Entered on the Stationers' register 2 May, 1608, as by "Wylliam Shakespeare," and published in the same year under his name. There is no sufficient reason for ascribing the play to him. *cf.* Camb. Eng. lit.
>
> I. Shakespeare, William. Spurious and doubtful works.

B. Enter under the name of an author followed by the designation SUPPOSED AUTHOR single works that have been generally attributed to him unless his authorship has been disproved. Make added entry under title.

> ₍Dennis, John₎ 1657-1734, *supposed author.*
> A true character of Mr. Pope. The 2d ed.
> Ascribed generally to John Dennis. *cf.* Dict. of nat. biog.; H. G. Paul's John Dennis, his life and criticism, p. 89-91.
> I. Title.

(1) But enter under title with added entry under the supposed author when there is good reason to doubt the ascribed authorship.

> The **law** scrutiny; or, Attornies' guide . . .
> A satire in verse, variously ascribed to Andrew Carmichael, William Norcott and others. *cf.* Dict. of nat. biog.; O'Donoghue's The poets of Ireland.
> I. Carmichael, Andrew Blair, ca. 1780-ca. 1854, supposed author.
> II. Norcott, William, 1770?-1820? supposed author.

The designation SUPPOSED AUTHOR is used with an added entry (or author and title reference) as well as in author heading.

(2) Enter single works that have been variously attributed to several authors, but with a strong probability in favor of one of them, under the most probable author with added entries or author and title references for the other supposed authors, and added entry under title.

> ₍Allestree, Richard₎ 1619-1681, *supposed author.*
> The whole duty of man . . .
> "Of the many persons to whom the authorship has been at various times ascribed, viz., Archbishop Sterne, Bishop Fell, Bishop Henchman, Bishop Chappell of Cork, Abraham Woodhead, Obadiah Walker, Archbishop Frewen, William Fulman, and Richard Allestree, besides one or two others, the preponderance of evidence seems to lie in favour of the last-named."—Dict. of nat. biog. v. 43, p. 87; for fuller discussion, *cf. also* C. E. Doble, in Academy, Nov. 1882, p. 348, 364, 382; Bibliographer, London, v. 2, p. 73, 94, 164; Notes and queries, ser. 5, 11, 12, etc.
> I. Sterne, Richard, Abp. of York, 1596?-1683, supposed author.
> II. Fell, John, Bp. of Oxford, 1625-1685, supposed author ₍and added entries III-VIII *for the other persons to whom authorship has been ascribed*₎ IX. Title.

or make references:

> Sterne, Richard, *Abp. of York,* 1596?-1683, *supposed author.*
> The whole duty of man
>   *see*
> **Allestree, Richard,** 1619-1681.
> ₍*etc., etc., for the various persons to whom authorship has been ascribed*₎

(3) If the actual authorship of a work which has been attributed to another author has been established, enter under the real author with added entry under title and added entry or author and title reference under the supposed author.

55

ₗ**Adams, Henry**ₗ 1838-1918.
  Democracy, an American novel.

  Variously attributed by different authorities to Henry Adams, John Hay and Clarence King. *cf.* W. R. Thayer, Life of John Hay, 1915, v. 2, p. 58-59. The authorship of Adams is affirmed by the publisher Henry Holt in the Unpartizan review, no. 29, Jan.-Mar. 1921, p. 156; and Literary review, Dec. 24, 1920.

  ɪ. Hay, John, 1838-1905, supposed author. ɪɪ. King, Clarence, 1842-1901, supposed author. ɪɪɪ. Title.

  ₗ*Author and title references may be used if preferred.* (*cf. example above: Allestree, Richard*)ₗ

C. Enter under the name of the person, real or invented, works which with no justification of authorship have become established in literature under that name. To distinguish such fictitious authors the term "pseudo" is prefixed to the name attributed to them, but in the author heading it is transposed.[20]

  Dionysius *Areopagita,* **Pseudo-**
    Refer from
  Pseudo-Dionysius *Areopagita.*

There was an historical Dionysius Areopagita, an Athenian, convert of Saint Paul. About the turn of the 6th century, a collection of Greek writings originated in Syria under the name of Dionysius Areopagita as author and became widely known and influential in patristic and scholastic literature, particularly after Joannes Scotus Erigena had made a Latin translation in the 9th century. The authorship of Severus, patriarch of Antiochia (d. 538) has been suggested, but not generally accepted.

  Callisthenes, Pseudo-
    Refer from
  Pseudo-Callisthenes.

Callisthenes, companion of Alexander the Great, was author of some historical works of which some fragments remain. Under his name has become transmitted a romantic history of Alexander, variously dated from the 2d century B.C. to the 3d century A.D. or later, and from which the later literature of Alexander romances is mainly derived.

  Turpin, Pseudo-
    Refer from
  Pseudo-Turpin.
  Turpin, *Abp. of Rheims.* (*see also*)

Similarly has become transmitted under the name of Turpin, Archbishop of Rheims (8th century) one of the paladins of Charlemagne, an unhistorical Chronicle or Historia Karoli Magni, the work of an unknown author of the 11th century.

In the "pseudo" type of literature is found occasionally a body of writings which, for many years wrongly attributed to an author, has come to be known under a conventional name usually derived from

---

[20] The Index to Maximilianus Manitius, *Geschichte der lateinischen Literatur des Mittelalters,* "Handbuch der Altertumswissenschaft" (München, Beck, 1911-31), 9. Bd., 2. Abt., 1.-3.Teil, gives an extensive list of "pseudo" authors of this kind; but Manitius is not to be followed necessarily, his list includes authors with whom the subdivision SPURIOUS AND DOUBTFUL WORKS is to be used.

the name of the author to whom it was attributed. For instance, the term Ambrosiaster has been applied to a series of commentaries on thirteen epistles of St. Paul, which until about 1600 were attributed to St. Ambrosius, and later to Hilarius, also to a Jew named Isaac. Entry should be made under AMBROSIASTER with appropriate references and added entries.

> **Ambrosiaster.**
> *Refer from*
> Ambrosius, Pseudo-
> Pseudo-Ambrosius
> Ambrosius, *Saint, Abp. of Milan. (see also)*
> *Make added entry or reference under*
> Isaac, *Jew, fl.* 372-378, *supposed author.*
> Hilarius, *praefectus urbis Romae, 408 A.D. Spurious and doubt-*
> *ful works.*

32. Anonymous works (General).

Specification.—A strictly anonymous work is one in which the author's name does not appear anywhere in the book. The term is here extended to include (*1*) works in which the author's name appears in the book only in a concealed manner, so that the authorship is not obvious;[21] (*2*) works whose authorship is indicated by a descriptive or generic word or phrase preceded by an article, e.g., "by a lover of justice," "by a physician," "by a bishop of the Church of England";[22] (*3*) works in which, instead of his name, the author gives the title of another of his books, e.g., "by the author of . . ."; (*4*) those in which the author uses initials, asterisks, or other symbols instead of his name.

Works in which an author uses *as a name* a specific word or phrase with or without a definite article are treated as pseudonymous. (Cf. 30.)

See also Anonymous classics (33-35).

General rule.

Enter works published anonymously under author when known. Make added entry under title and added entry or reference under any phrase used instead of the author's name.

> ₍Defoe, Daniel₎ 1661?-1731.
> The case of Protestant dissenters in Carolina . . .
> I. Title.

> ₍Cosgrove, Eugene Milne₎ 1886-
> The science of the initiates; a ready handbook on the age-
> less wisdom; questions and answers, by a server.
> I. A server. II. Title.

or if preferred, instead of the first added entry make reference:

---

[21] In case of doubt, consider the work anonymous.
[22] The author's use of a title instead of his name, e.g., "by the Bishop of York," "by the Secretary of State," does not constitute anonymity unless there is no evidence as to identity.

A server.
The science of the initiates
see
Cosgrove, Eugene Milne, 1886–

If the author is not known, enter under title, making added entry under the phrase expressing authorship.

Memoir of Bowman Hendry, M.D., late of Gloucester County, New Jersey. Compiled from the most reliable sources. By a physician.
i. A physician.

Medical observations and inquiries. By a society of physicians . . .
i. A society of physicians.

If the phrase expressing authorship is devoid of meaning when removed from the context of the title, no reference or added entry is necessary.

ₗMayhew, Experienceₗ 1673–1758.
A right to the Lord's Supper considered in a letter to a serious enquirer after truth. By a lover of the same.
i. Title.

ₗDigges, *Sir* Dudleyₗ 1583–1639.
The defence of trade. In a letter of Sir Thomas Smith, knight, gouernour of the East-India Companie, &c. from one of that societie.
i. Title.

A. Change of title in successive volumes of nonserial works. When the title pages of an anonymous work in several volumes vary, catalog from the title page of the first volume unless a majority of the volumes are issued under a later title and the work for this or some other reason is decidedly better known by this title. Refer from title not chosen as entry.

B. "By the author of . . ." When an anonymous work of undiscovered authorship bears on its title page such a phrase as "by the author of," enter it under its title with an added entry under the title quoted, followed by the words AUTHOR OF. If different titles are thus used by the author at various times, make the added entry under the title most frequently referred to, or, in case of doubt, under one of his best known or earlier works. Refer from the title of each work to the title thus chosen, using the following form: "For other works by the same author see . . ."

The **unveiled** heart; a simple story. By the author of Early impressions, etc., etc.
i. Early impressions, Author of.

Reference:
The **unveiled** heart.

For other works by the same author *see* Early impressions, Author of.

C. Initials, etc., identified. Enter under author's name books in which initials, asterisks, or other typographical devices, used in the place of the author's name have been identified. Make added entry under title and added entry, or reference if preferred, under initials (both first and last letters), asterisks, etc.

ₗGraefenberg, Rosie (Goldschmidt)ⱼ 1898-
 Prelude to the past; the autobiography of a woman, by R. G.
 ı. G., R. ıı. R. G. ııı. Title.

or make references:
 G., R.
 Prelude to the past
 see
Graefenberg, Rosie (Goldschmidt) 1898-

 R. G.
 Prelude to the past
 see
Graefenberg, Rosie (Goldschmidt) 1898-

ₗBordelon, Laurentⱼ 1653-1730.
 Les solitaires en belle humeur. Entretiens recueillis des papiers de feu M. le marquis de M***.
 ı. M***, marquis de. ıı. Title.

or make reference:
 M*, *marquis* de.**
 Les solitaires en belle humeur
 see
Bordelon, Laurent, 1653-1730.

ₗBrothers of the Christian Schoolsⱼ
 La Argentina; estudio físico, etnográfico, político y económico, por H. E. C.

Make references:
 H. E. C. ₗ*i.e.* **Hermanos de las Escuelas Cristianasⱼ**
 see
Brothers of the Christian Schools.

 Hermanos de las Escuelas Cristianas
 see
Brothers of the Christian Schools.

D. Initials, etc., not identified. Enter under title books in which initials, asterisks, or other typographical devices not identified are used in place of the author's name. Make added entry under the initials (both first and last letters), asterisks, etc.

Indiscretions of Dr. Carstairs, by A. De O.
 ı. De O., A. ıı. A. De O. ııı. O., A. De.

Relations d'un voiage de Pologne, fait dans les années 1688 et 1689.

Caption title: Relation d'un voiage de Pologne fait . . . par Monsr. l'abbé F. D. S.

ɪ. S., F. D. ɪɪ. F. D. S.

Voyages et aventures du chevalier de***. Contenant les voyages de l'auteur . . .

ɪ. ***, chevalier de.

. . . Un **aventurier** vous parle.

At head of title: ? ? ?

ɪ. ? ? ?

Initials, asterisks, etc., used in the place of name of editors, com‐ pilers, translators, etc., receive similar treatment.

ₗ**Ducray-Duminil, François Guillaume**₎ 1761–1819.
Celina, ou A filha do mysterio. Traduzida do francez por M. P. C. C. d'A. . . .

ɪ. A., M. P. C. C. d', tr. ɪɪ. M. P. C. C. d'A., tr. ɪɪɪ. Title. ɪᴠ. Title: A filha do mysterio.

Pollok, Robert, 1798–1827.
The course of time, a poem. By Robert Pollok, ᴀ. ᴍ. With a memoir of the author, an introductory notice, a copious index, and an analysis prefixed to each poem. 12th American ed.

Preface signed: N. W. F. ₗ*i.e.* Nathan Welby Fiske₎

ɪ. Fiske, Nathan Welby, 1798–1847, ed.

Make references:

F., N. W.
see
Fiske, Nathan Welby, 1798–1847.

N. W. F.
see
Fiske, Nathan Welby, 1798–1847.

Thompson, George.
Der Zar, Rasputin und die Juden. Meine Erlebnisse und Errinnerungen aus der Zeit vor und während des Krieges, vor und während der Revolution, von George Thompson. Nach dem in englischer Sprache verfassten Manuskript wiedergegeben von *ₓ* . . .

ɪ. *ₓ*, tr.

E. Different spelling.[23] If the first word of a title entry or refer‐ ence may be spelled in more than one way, follow the spelling of the title page and refer from other forms.

---

[23] (British) Library Association rule (1908): When the first word of the title of an anonymous work is spelled in more than one way, choose one form of spelling and refer from the others.

    Inquiry, An enquiry into the nature and origin of literary property.
    Enquiry *see* **Inquiry**
Where different spellings have been used in successive editions, enter under the earliest form and refer from the others. In the case of obsolete or archaic forms of spelling, enter under the modern form and refer from variants.

Where different spellings have been used in successive editions, follow the title page in each case and make added entry under the original form.

> An **enquiry** into the causes of the miscarriage of the Scots colony at Darien. Or An answer to a libel entituled A defence of the Scots abdicating Darien. Submitted to the consideration of the good people of England . . .

> An **inquiry** into the causes of the miscarriage of the Scots colony at Darien . . .
> First published Glasgow, 1700, as "An enquiry into the causes of the miscarriage of the Scots colony at Darien."
> I. An enquiry into the causes of the miscarriage of the Scots colony at Darien . . .

> An **inquiry** into the revenue, credit, and commerce of France. In a letter to a member of this present Parliament. The 2d ed.

> A **letter** to the author of An enquiry into the revenue, credit, and commerce of France. Wherein the former and present state of the power and commerce of that kingdom are fully consider'd and deduced from authentic accounts. By a member of Parliament . . .
> 1. An inquiry into the revenue, credit, and commerce of France. 1742. I. A member of Parliament.

Make reference:

> An **enquiry** into the revenue, credit, and commerce of France
> *see*
> An **inquiry** into the revenue . . .

F. Related works. When the title of an anonymous work begins with a word indicating numerical sequence, or defining its relation to another work, make added entry or reference under the title of the principal work, thus collecting related material under that title.'

> A **letter** to a late noble commander of the British forces in Germany. The 3d ed., revised and corrected by the author, to which is added a postscript.
> "The writer . . . supposed to be Owen Ruffhead."—European magazine, v. 14, p. 168.
> "A late noble commander" *i.e.* Lord Sackville.
> 1. Sackville, George Sackville Germain, 1st viscount, 1716-1785. I. Ruffhead, Owen, 1723-1769, supposed author.

> A **second** letter to a late noble commander of the British forces in Germany. In which the noble commander's Address to the public, his Letter to Colonel Fitzroy, together with the Colonel's Answer, and Captain Smith's Declaration, are candidly and impartially considered. By the author of the first letter.
> "The writer . . . supposed to be Owen Ruffhead."—European magazine, v. 14, p. 168.
> "A late noble commander" *i.e.* Lord Sackville.
> 1. Sackville, George Sackville Germain, 1st viscount, 1716-1785. I. Ruffhead, Owen, 1723-1769, supposed author. II. A letter to a late noble commander of the British forces.

An **answer** to A letter to a late noble commander of the British forces. In which the candor is proved to be affected, the facts untrue, the arguments delusive, and the design iniquitous . . .

Authorship ascribed to John Shebbeare, *cf.* European magazine, v. 14, p. 168; Douglas, John, The conduct of a late noble commander, p. 8.
"A late noble commander" *i.e.* Lord Sackville.

1. Sackville, George Sackville Germain, 1st viscount, 1716-1785. 2. A letter to a late noble commander of the British forces. I. Shebbeare, John, 1709-1788, supposed author.

G. Translations.[24] Enter a translation of an anonymous work under the translated title as it appears on the title page and make added entry under the original title.

Histoire géographique de la Nouvelle Écosse, contenant le détail de sa situation, de son étendue & de ses limites; ainsi que des différens démêlés entre l'Angleterre & la France, au sujet de la possession de cette province . . .

Translated by E. de Lafargue from "A geographical history of Nova Scotia," London, 1749.

I. Lafargue, Étienne de, 1728-1795, tr. II. A geographical history of Nova Scotia.

As they are; French political portraits, by ***; translated from the French by Winifred Katzin.

I. ***. II. Katzin, Winifred, tr. III. Ceux qui nous mènent.

33. Anonymous classics.[25]

Definition.—An anonymous classic is a work of unknown or doubtful authorship, commonly designated by title, which may have appeared in the course of time in many editions, versions, and/or translations.

Specification.—The term includes (*1*) single anonymous texts, e.g., poems, epics, romances, tales, plays, chronicles, etc.; (*2*) composite anonymous texts collectively known by a specific title, e.g., early Greek and Latin literary collections, medieval collections of stories or laws, series of poems, romances, etc., sacred literature, collections of early English plays, collections of legends, etc. Some of these composite texts form organized literary units; others are simply unorganized collections.

Texts may be considered from three aspects depending upon their interrelationship: (*1*) those which are entirely independent with a single text of fixed content; (*2*) those represented in different languages by a more or less close translation of an original text of fairly fixed content, the original text being in some cases available and in

---

[24] (British) Library Association rule (1908): Enter a translation of an anonymous work under the heading adopted for the original work and make added entry under the first word of the translated title.

[25] These definitions, specifications, and rules can only be considered as tentative. A series of studies applying the rules to special literary groups is essential before basic principles of entry can be considered standardized and necessary exceptions can be formulated. A list of established headings is a desirable adjunct.

others lost; (3) those centering around one character or group of characters or events which are closely related but which have grown up in one or various literatures independently of each other, and which together are commonly designated as cycles.[26]

A. General rule. Enter editions of anonymous classics and their translations under a uniform heading consisting of the traditional or conventional title[27] of the work in the language of the original version when known. For parts of composite classics and cycles[28] see 33B and C.

Chanson de Roland.	**Nibelungenlied.**
Völsunga saga.	**Edda Sæmundar.**
Stabat Mater.	**Mahābhārata.**
Everyman.	**Digby plays.**

However, prefer entry under the English form, if the classic is known equally well in many languages.

Arabian nights.
Bible.[29]
Seven sages.

Refer from forms not chosen for entry.

Chanson de Roland.
 Refer from
Roland.
Song of Roland.

Seven sages.
 Refer from
Historia septem sapientum.
Le roman des sept sages.
Seven wise masters.
Die sieben weisen Meistern.

---

[26] A cycle is a series of poems or prose romances, collected around or relating to a central event or epoch of mythic history and forming a continuous narrative. (New English dictionary) The term cycle as used in these rules is limited to a series of texts, which originally appeared independently, relating to a central hero, event or epoch, and forming a fairly continuous narrative.

[27] Initial articles and unimportant introductory phrases as "The comedy of," "Here begins the tale of," etc., are ordinarily omitted, and a running title is preferred to an inverted form, e.g., Book of Hierotheus, *not* Hierotheus, Book of.

[28] Popular and school libraries may prefer to enter all texts under the uniform heading for the most inclusive title, using the best-known English form unless the vernacular form is decidedly better known.

  Roland.
   Refer from
  Song of Roland.
  Chanson de Roland.

  Reynard the Fox.
   Refer from
  Le roman de Renart.

but

  Nibelungenlied.
   Refer from
  Nibelungs, Lay of.
  Lay of the Nibelungs.
  Song of the Nibelungs.

[29] For special rules for the Bible and other sacred literature see 34-35.

Make added entries under names of editors, translators, and any authors to whom the classic may have been attributed; and under title when sufficiently distinctive and not used popularly enough to justify a reference, or when the title covers only a part of the classic.

> **Chanson de Roland.**
> La chanson de Roland. Texte critique, traduction et commentaire par Léon Gautier . . . 5. éd.
> I. Gautier, Léon, 1832-1897, ed.

> **Chanson de Roland.**
> The song of Roland; translated into English verse by Arthur S. Way . . .
> I. Way, Arthur Sanders, 1847-1930, tr.

> **Chanson de Roland.**
> . . . A chevalier of old France, the Song of Roland; translated and adapted from old French texts by John Harrington Cox . . .
> I. Cox, John Harrington, 1863-   tr. II. Title.

(1) To avoid confusion with entries of similar phraseology, and to aid in identification, where necessary or helpful, a term denoting literary type may be added after the uniform heading.[30]

> **Genesis** (*Anglo-Saxon poem*)
> **Genesis** (*Middle High German poem*)
> **Genesis** (*Old Saxon poem*)
> **Antioche** (*Chanson de geste*)

The advantage of such a practice is especially obvious when the uniform heading resembles a personal name, whether real or fictitious.

> **Beatrix** (*Chanson de geste*)
> **Guillaume d'Orange** (*Chansons de geste*)
> [*A composite anonymous work made up of several individual anonymous texts*]
> **Guy of Warwick** (*Romance*)
> **Arthur, King** (*Romances, etc.*)
> [*A compilation of independent texts*]
> **Richard II** (*Drama*)
> **Jack Juggler** (*Interlude*)

For anonymous classics based on the lives of saints, other holy personages, or holy things, add the term LEGEND to the heading. It is used for the entry of a single text, for entry of different texts, or in added entries under which different texts are assembled. When the

---

[30] Appropriate terms are:

Ballad	Interlude	Prose romance
Block book	Liturgical play	Romance
Chanson	Masque	Romances, etc.
Chanson de geste	Miracle play	Saga (for headings not including the term Saga or tháttr)
Comedy	Morality play	
Drama	Mystery play	
Fabliau	Pantomime	Tale
	Poem	Tragedy

legend concerns an individual, the heading follows the rules for personal names.[31]

Alexius, *Saint.* **Legend.**
[*One text*]
Francesco *d'Assisi, Saint.* **Legend.**
[*A compilation of texts*]
Grail. Legend.
[*Used only as assembling added entry*]
Gregorius I, *the Great, Saint, Pope.* **Legend.**
Cyprianus, *of Antioch.* **Legend.** *Martyrium Cypriani et Justae.*
The martyrdom of Cyprian and Justa . . .
Refer from
Martyrdom of Cyprian and Justa.[32]
Martyrdom of Justa.
Cyprian, Martyrdom of.
Justa, Martyrdom of.

(2) When the classic appears in many languages either as direct translations or as versions, add to the uniform heading the name of the language[33] of the text of the translation or version.

Floire and Blancheflor. *French.*
Floire and Blancheflor. *Spanish.*
Floire and Blancheflor. *Swedish.*
Seven sages. *Catalan.*
Seven sages. *English.*
Seven sages. *English* (*Middle English*)
Seven sages. *French.*
Upanishads. *English.*
Upanishads. *German.*

(3) For anonymous classics which appear as variants in differing manuscripts add the name of the manuscript in parentheses.

Second shepherds' play (*Towneley ms.*)
Abraham and Isaac (*Brome ms.*)

(4) When the titles of anonymous classics involve personal names, either real or fictitious, the uniform heading may be limited to the

---

[31] Because of the prominence of individuals concerning whom a body of literature has grown up, dates of birth and death are usually unnecessary when the literary type is used after a personal name, but should be used if needed to distinguish those of the same name.

[32] For a limited number of *historical* documents on martyrdoms (cf. Otto Bardenhewer, *Geschichte der altkirchlichen Literatur* (2. umbearb. Aufl.; Freiburg im Breisgau, Herder, 1914), v. 2, p. 664.) the Library of Congress enters or makes added entry under a uniform heading beginning Martyrdom, of e.g., MARTYRDOM OF CARPUS, PAPYLUS AND AGATHONICE.

[33] Use the name of the language as given in U. S. Library of Congress, Catalog Division, *Literature subject headings* . . . *and Language subject headings* (5th ed.; Washington, Govt. Print. Off., 1926).

If the text is given in two or more languages in the same work, make an added entry for each language, e.g., main entry: **Seven sages.** *Catalan;* added entries: SEVEN SAGES. English; SEVEN SAGES. French.

name involved, retaining titles of honor and address. Make subject entry if the individual is real.

> **Captain Thomas Stukeley.**
> The famous history of the life and death of Captain Thomas Stukeley . . .
> 1. Stucley, Thomas, 1525?-1578—Drama.

> **Richard Cœur de Lion** (*Romance*)
> Der mittelenglische Versroman über Richard Löwenherz . . .
> 1. Richard I, King of England, 1157-1199—Poetry.

> **Godly Queene Hester.**
> A new enterlude of Godly Queene Hester.
> 1. Esther, Queen of Persia—Drama.

(5) If the titles of anonymous classics involve place names, enter usually under the name of the place without designation of country, followed by literary type in parentheses. However, use a phrase which includes the place name if it is more distinctive.

> **Antioche** (*Chanson de geste*)
> La chanson d'Antioche . . .

> **Aspremont** (*Chanson de geste*)
> La chanson d'Aspremont . . .

but

> **Siège d'Orléans** (*Mystery play*)
> Saint Joan of Orléans; scenes from the fifteenth century Mystère du siège d'Orléans.

(6) Enter fragments and extracts as if they were complete.

> **Partonopeus de Blois.**
> Ouddietsche fragmenten van den Partonopeus van Bloys . . .

For treatment of manuscripts and manuscript reproductions see 9A. For treatment of commentaries and criticisms see 29.

B. Parts of composite classics.[34]

(1) Enter parts of a composite anonymous classic which forms an organized literary unit, so that the parts when issued separately are remembered in relation to the whole title, under the uniform heading for the classic as a whole, followed by a uniform title for the part. Refer from the various names of the part.

> **Corpus juris civilis.** *Codex.*
>   *Refer from*
> Codex Justinianus.

> **Corpus juris civilis.** *Digesta.*
>   *Refer from*
> Digesta Justiniani.
> Pandectae Justinianeae.
> Corpus juris civilis. *Pandectae.*

> **Edda Sæmundar.** *Völuspá.*
>   *Refer from*
> Völuspá.

---

[34] See footnote 28, p. 63.

> Patrick, *Saint.* Legend. *Purgatorium.*
>   *Refer from*
> Purgatory of St. Patrick.
> Purgatorium S. Patricii.

Cf., 34-35.

(2) Enter parts of a composite anonymous classic which is merely a collection, so that the parts when issued separately are remembered as independent titles, under their own uniform headings. Make *see also* or explanatory reference cards[35] from the title of the composite classic to the headings for the parts, and from the individual part to the whole.

Collection:

> Towneley plays.
>   The Towneley mysteries.

Individual part:

> Second shepherds' play (*Towneley ms.*)
>   The adoration of the shepherds.

A collection which is also a cycle:

> Guillaume d'Orange (*Chansons de geste*)
>   Guillaume d'Orange, le marquis au court nez.

Individual parts:[36]

> Aliscans.
> Charroi de Nîmes.
> Couronnement de Louis.
> Chevalerie Vivien.

C. Cycles.

(1) Enter combined editions according to the general rule (33A) since cycles represent a collection of texts. However, combined editions are rare, since these texts have usually grown up in various literatures.

> Guillaume d'Orange (*Chansons de geste*)
> Arthur, King (*Romances, etc.*)

(2) Enter parts of cycles, since they are independent single anonymous classics, under their own individual uniform headings.[37]

> Ecbasis captivi.
>   [*Early Latin version*]
> Reinaert de Vos.
>   [*Flemish version*]
> Reinhart Fuchs.
>   [*High German version*]

---

[35] Cf. 33C (2).

[36] All these headings might be followed by the designation CHANSON DE GESTE in parentheses (Cf. 33A (1).)

[37] See footnote 28, p. 63.

> **Reinke de Vos.**
> [*Low German version*]
> **Renart le contrefait.**
> [*French sequel to the original French version*]
> **Roman de Renart.**
> [*French version*]

Make *see also* references to and from the uniform heading for the cycle.

> **Reynard the Fox**
> *see also*
> **Ecbasis captivi.**
> **Isengrimus.**
> [*etc., etc.; list all available versions*]

or better an explanatory reference card:

> **Reynard the Fox.**
> The story of Reynard the Fox appears in many versions in varying languages. Versions will be found in this catalog under their own titles. Here are entered critical discussions of the cycle, and miscellaneous editions, adapted or abridged, chapbooks, juveniles, etc., etc., of which the immediate source or relation to other versions is not known or is uncertain.
> For the varying versions see entries under:
> Ecbasis captivi.
> Isengrimus.
> Reinaert de Vos.
> [*etc.*]

Translations of parts of cycles are entered under the uniform heading for the part.[38]

> **Reinke de Vos.**
> Reynard the Fox, a renowned apologue of the middle age, reproduced in rhyme . . .
> "The Low-German edition . . . is that from which I have worked: 'hovering . . . between translation and paraphrase'."—Pref. signed: S. Naylor.

> **Reinke de Vos.**
> Die Historie von Reineke dem Fuchs nach dem niederdeutschen Epos von 1498 neuerzählt . . .

> **Perlesvaus.**
> The high history of the Holy Graal. Translated from the Old French . . .

(3) Added entries and references. In large collections where it is desirable to assemble in one place all the entries for a cycle, *see also* or explanatory reference cards indicated in (2) above, may be omitted and an added entry for each work, including editions, translations and adaptations, may be made under a uniform heading for the cycle

---

[38] If desired the language *of the text* may be specified in the heading, e.g., **Reinke de Vos.** *English.*

followed by the language of *the text*. Such added entries may also be used to assemble texts influenced by or based upon cycle versions.

If necessary to conserve space, only one edition of a given text need be represented under a specific assembling added entry. The note "For other editions see cards under ₁heading₁" on one card, or an explanatory reference card, may stand for many available books.

Assembling added entries are not to be made for (*1*) mere title allusions to cycle stories, (*2*) minor incidents or references to a hero or event, (*3*) musical scores unaccompanied by words. Form subject subdivisions may be used to gather together these and other types of related materials where the size of the collection and needs of scholars warrant such treatment.

> **Libro de Alixandre.**
> . . . El libro de Alixandre . . .
> ɪ. Alexander the Great (Romances, etc.) Spanish.

> **Prise de Defur.**
> La prise de Defur et Le voyage d'Alexandre au paradis terrestre . . .
> ɪ. Voyage d'Alexandre au paradis terrestre. ɪɪ. Alexander the Great (Romances, etc.) French.

> **Wars of Alexander.**
> The wars of Alexander; an alliterative romance . . .
> ɪ. Alexander the Great (Romances, etc.) English.

Version entry	*Cycle entry*
₁No original version₁	**Reynard the Fox.** *English.*
Renart-le-Nouvel.	**Reynard the Fox.** *French.*
Roman de Renart.	**Reynard the Fox.** *French.*
Goethe, Johann Wolfgang von.	
Reineke Fuchs [*an adaptation*][39]	**Reynard the Fox.** *German.*
Reinhart Fuchs [*an edition in the original language*]	**Reynard the Fox.** *German.*
Reinke de Vos	
Reinhart Fuchs [*a translation in German, from the low German*]	**Reynard the Fox.** *German.*
Reinke de Vos.	**Reynard the Fox.** *Low German.*

Version entries with added entries for cycles.

> **Chrestien** *de Troyes, 12th cent.*
> Perceval le Gallois; ou, Le conte du Graal . . .
> "Earliest known account of the Grail."
> ɪ. Perceval (Romances, etc.)[40] ɪɪ. Grail. Legend.[41] French.

---

[39] See 33D.

[40] Here and in the examples following, this heading might also be **divided** by language.

[41] For a discussion of the use of **Legend** in this heading, see Clarice **Krieg,** "The cataloging of Grail literature. Abstract," *Catalogers' and classifiers' yearbook,* no. 5, (1936), p. 91-92.

Lovelich, Herry, *fl.* 1450.
. . . The history of the Holy Grail, English . . .
I. Grail. Legend. English. II. Estoire del Saint Graal.
[*Based on the Estoire del Saint Graal*]

Perceval of Galles.
. . . Sir Perceval of Gales . . .
I. Perceval (Romances, etc.)
[*The one Perceval story which does not mention the Grail*]

Perlesvaus.
Le haut livre du Graal; Perlesvaus . . .
I. Grail. Legend. French. II. Perceval (Romances, etc.)
[*Original French*]

Perlesvaus.
The high history of the Holy Graal . . .
I. Perceval (Romances, etc.) II. Grail. Legend. English.
[*A translation in English*]

La queste del Saint Graal.
The quest of the Holy Grail . . .
I. Grail. Legend. English.
[*A translation in English*]

La queste del Saint Graal.
. . . La queste del Saint Graal . . .
I. Grail. Legend. French.
[*Original French*]

La queste del Saint Graal.
. . . La versione catalana della Enchiesta del San Graal . . .
I. Grail. Legend. Catalan.
[*Translation in Catalan*]

Y Seint Greal.
Y Seint Greal . . .
I. Grail. Legend. Welsh. II. Grail. Legend. English. III. Perceval
(Romances, etc.) IV. Galahad (Romances, etc.)
[*Welsh text with English translation*]

Wagner, Richard, 1813-1883.
Parsifal, von Richard Wagner. Vocal score with pianoforte
accompaniment by R. Kleinmichel. With original German text
and English translation.
I. Perceval (Romances, etc.) II. Grail. Legend. English. III. Grail.
Legend. German.

Wolfram *von Eschenbach, 12th cent.*
. . . Parzival . . .
I. Perceval (Romances, etc.) II. Grail. Legend. German.
[*Original German*]

Wolfram *von Eschenbach, 12th cent.*
Parzival, a knightly epic . . .   '
I. Grail. Legend. English. II. Perceval (Romances, etc.)
[*English translation*]

D. Adaptations. (Cf. 22B.)

(1) Enter an adaptation[42] which is more or less a free translation of the original text under the uniform heading of the original text with an added entry under the adapter or translator.

>**Lancelot.**
>. . . Les amours de Lancelot du Lac . . .
>Modern French version by Jacques Boulenger, adapted and abridged from the Vulgate romance, Le livre de Lancelot del Lac.
> i. Boulenger, Jacques Romain, 1879-

(2) Enter adaptations or paraphrases which have become literary works in their own right, or which have been freely made from many texts, as in the case of many adaptations for the use of juvenile readers, under the author of the adaptation. Make added entry under the uniform heading for the anonymous classic.

>**Lovelich, Herry,** *fl.* 1450.
>Merlin, a Middle-English metrical version of a French romance . . .
> i. Merlin.

>**Gray, Terence.**
>Cuchulainn, an epic drama of the Gael . . .
> 1. Cuchulain. i. Cuchulain.
> [*Long discussion of the legend justifies the subject.*]

>**Colum, Padraic,** 1881-
>The island of the mighty.
> i. Mabinogion. ii. Title.

(a) The versions of the King Arthur stories which bear Malory's name on the title page are always entered under Malory even though they are not always editions nor confined to adaptations of Malory's version of the tales of the cycle.

>**Malory,** *Sir* **Thomas,** *15th cent.*
>The boy's King Arthur; Sir Thomas Malory's history of King Arthur and his knights of the Round Table; edited for boys by Sidney Lanier . . .
> i. Arthur, King (Romances, etc.) ii. Lanier, Sidney, 1842-1881, ed.
> [*Follows the wording of Malory*]

>**Malory,** *Sir* **Thomas,** *15th cent.*
>The story of Sir Galahad, retold from the Le morte d'Arthur of Sir Thomas Malory and the original stories, by Mary Blackwell Sterling . . .
> i. Sterling, Mary Blackwell. ii. Galahad (Romances, etc.)

but

>**Westwood, Thomas,** 1814?-1888.
>The sword of kingship. A legend of the "Mort d'Arthure" . . .
>"The framework of the following legend will be found in . . . the

---

[42] The term adaptation as used on title pages of anonymous classics may denote either a free translation of a given version, or a rewritten work possibly based on many versions. The term translation is sometimes used when adaptation would be more exact. When loosely used on title pages, the terms should be properly interpreted in notes.

first book of 'La mort d'Arthure' as compiled by Sir Thomas Malory."
—Prefatory note.

I. Arthur, King (Romances, etc.) II. Malory, Sir Thomas, 15th cent.
Le morte d'Arthur. III. Title.

Pyle, Howard, 1853-1911.
The story of the Grail and the passing of Arthur . . .
I. Arthur, King (Romances, etc.) II. Grail. Legend. III. Title.

(b) For adaptations of parts of cycles, make added entry for the
uniform heading[43] for the part of the cycle involved, as well as that
for the whole classic. The language, if specified in the heading, is the
language of the text in hand.

Goethe, Johann Wolfgang von, 1749-1832.
Reineke Fuchs . . .
Based upon Gottsched's prose version of the Low German poem
Reineke de Vos.
I. Reinke de Vos. German. II. Reynard the Fox. German. III. Title.

Goethe, Johann Wolfgang von, 1749-1832.
Reynard the Fox, after the German version of Goethe, by
Thomas James Arnold, esq. . . .
A translation of Goethe's Reineke Fuchs.
I. Reinke de Vos. English. II. Reynard the Fox. English.

Johnson, Clifton, 1865-1940.
Reynard the Fox, by Clifton Johnson; adapted from Goethe's
Reineke Fuchs . . .
I. Goethe, Johann Wolfgang von, 1749-1832. Reineke Fuchs. II.
Reinke de Vos. English. III. Reynard the Fox. English.

(3) Enter any anonymous adaptation under the uniform heading
for the anonymous classic.

Reynard the Fox. *English.*
The history of Reynard the Fox, and Reynardine his son . . .

E. Annals, chronicles, and similar records (chiefly medieval).[44]
Enter annals and anonymous chronicles clearly known to have orig-

---

[43] Popular and school libraries may prefer a subject entry, if a hero, event or place
is involved.

Wolfram *von Eschenbach, 12th cent.*
The story of Parzival, the Templar . . .
1. Percival. I. Title.

[44] Chronicles differ from annals in that the former are usually in narrative form
and fuller in content than the latter, which merely record individual occurrences
under the successive years or other dates. According to H. F. Delaborde (École des
chartes) the term chronicle applies to accounts of a universal character while annals
relate to a locality or religious community. Medieval scribes, however, apparently
made no clear distinction between the two, often using the terms indiscriminately.
Both had their origin for the most part in abbeys and monasteries as marginal or
interlinear notes of current events made by various hands in the church calendar
and were, of course, without titles; these were assigned later by editors, the title
varying with the editor. As these chronicles developed, they were loaned by one
institution to another where they were copied in whole or in part, often without indication of source, so that in many cases the place of origin is difficult to determine.
Cf. R. L. Poole, *Chronicles and annals* (Oxford, Clarendon Press, 1926); T. F. Tout,
The study of mediæval chronicles (Manchester, University Press, 1922); *Encyclopaedia Britannica; New International encyclopaedia.*

inated in an institution under the institution with added entries for editors, translators, titles, variant titles, attributed authors, and other individuals whose names have for some reason become closely associated with the work.

If not of institutional origin, or if the institution of origin is doubtful, enter under a uniform heading for the title by which the work is best known. Make added entries for the institution with which the work is associated, editors, translators, etc., and references from variant titles. Added entries need not be made for earlier titles used as sources even though known.

Warneton, *Belgium* (*Augustinian abbey*)
Chronicon abbatiæ Warnestoniensis, ordinis canonicorum regularium S. Augustini, ex actis quibusdam monasterii et ex auctoribus collectum, cura et studio duorum Dioec. Brug. sacerdotum ₁C. L. Carton et F. van de Putte₁

ɪ. Carton, Charles Louis, 1802-1863, ed. ɪɪ. Putte, Ferdinand van de, 1807-1882, ed. ɪɪɪ. Title.

Annals of the Four masters.
. . . Annals of the kingdom of Ireland, by the Four masters, from the earliest period to the year 1616. Edited from the mss. in the library of the Royal Irish Academy and of Trinity College, Dublin, with a translation and copious notes, by John O'Donovan . . .

English title preceded by title in Irish; Irish and English on opposite pages.

"The Four masters . . . were Michael, Conary, and Cucogry O'Clery, together with Ferfeasa O'Mulconry."—Introductory remarks, v. 1, p. xix.

The Catalogue of Irish manuscripts in the British Museum, v. 1, p. 20, gives Peregrine (Cucogry) O'Duigenan in place of Conary O'Clery, which agrees with Colgan's statement in his Acta sanctorum Hiberniæ, 1645.

Known also as the Annals of Donegal.

ɪ. O'Clery, Michael, 1575-1648. ɪɪ. O'Clery, Cucogry, d. 1664. ɪɪɪ. O'Mulconry, Ferfeasa, fl. 1636. ɪv. O'Duigenan, Cucogry, fl. 1636. v. O'Clery, Conary, fl. 1636. vɪ. O'Donovan, John, 1809-1861, ed. and tr. vɪɪ. Title.

Refer from
  Four masters
  Annals of Donegal
  Donegal, Annals of
  Annales Dungallensis
  Annales quatuor magistrorum

Sächsische Weltchronik.
Das Zeitbuch des Eike von Repgow in ursprünglich niederdeutscher Sprache und in früher lateinischer Übersetzung herausgegeben von H. F. Massmann.

The first German chronicle in prose, formerly ascribed to Eike von Repgow, who possibly wrote the prologue in rime, in which his name appears. The Latin translation formerly held to be the original has title: Historia imperatorum.

ɪ. Massmann, Hans Ferdinand, 1797-1874, ed. ɪɪ. Title.

Refer from
  Chronica imperatorum Saxonica
  Chronica Romanorum

Chronicon imperatorum et pontificum
Chronicon Lüneburgicum Saxonica lingua conscriptum
Chronicon Repegovii
Chronicon Heren Eiken von Repgow
Historia Romanensis
Historia imperatorum
Repgauische Chronik
Sachsenchronik
Sassenkroneke

34. Bible.

Enter the Bible or any part of it[45] (including the Apocrypha) under
the word BIBLE. Include as subheading, O. T. (Old Testament), N. T.
(New Testament), the name of the book or group of books, as the
case requires, the language of the text, the date of publication, and
when known, the version.

> **Bible.** *English. 1611. Authorized.*
> **Bible.** *O. T. German. 1876.*
> **Bible.** *O. T. Genesis. English. 1851.*
> **Bible.** *N. T. John. English. 1900.*
> **Bible.** *O. T. Pentateuch. English. 1904.*
> **Bible.** *N. T. Gospels. Greek. 1896.*
> **Bible.** *O. T. Kings. English. 1900.*
>   *[includes 1-2 Kings]*
> **Bible.** *O. T. 1 Kings. English. 1900.*
> **Bible.** *O. T. Apocrypha. English. 1938. Goodspeed.*
> **Bible.** *O. T. Apocryphal books. 1 Enoch. Ethiopic. 1851.*

For the form and spelling of the names of Biblical books, follow the
Authorized version of the English Bible. Refer from variant forms
and spellings.

> **Bible.** *Paralipomena see* **Bible.** *O. T. Chronicles.*
> **Bible.** *Canticles see* **Bible.** *O. T. Song of Solomon.*

Refer also from the names of individual books to the heading under
which they appear in the catalog.

> **Song of Solomon** *see* **Bible.** *O. T. Song of Solomon.*
> **Isaiah** *(Book of the Old Testament) see* **Bible.** *O. T. Isaiah.*

A. Polyglot texts. Enter Bibles containing the identical Biblical
text in three or more languages under the heading BIBLE. POLYGLOT,
the word polyglot bearing the same relation to the heading as the
name of a language.

> **Bible.** *Polyglot. 1629.*
> **Bible.** *O. T. Psalms. Polyglot. 1900.*

B. Diglot texts.

(1) Enter a Bible containing the identical Biblical text in two
languages under the original language, if one is the original.

(2) If the two languages are of equal importance, and there is but
one title page, enter under the one mentioned first in the title, or if

---

[45] The Library of Congress, by exception, uses Lord's prayer as author entry.

neither is mentioned in the title, under the one whose text precedes.

(3) If the two languages are of equal importance and there are two title pages facing each other preceded by a half title that names both languages, enter under the one named first on the half title page.

(4) If one of the two languages is clearly of more importance or interest because the purpose is to edit the text in that language and the other is printed for convenience, enter under the more important language.

In each case make added entry for the language not adopted for the main entry.

C. Name of language in the heading.

(1) The language of the text is specified in the heading in the form adopted in the Library of Congress list of literature and language subject headings:

> **Bible.** *English (Middle English) 1878.*
> **Bible.** *Anglo-Saxon. 1857.*
> **Bible.** *French (Old French) 1890.*
> **Bible.** *Basque (Labourdin) 1903.*
> **Bible.** *N. T. English (Scotland) 1867.*
> *but*
> **Bible.** *Latin. 1647. Old Latin.*

because Old Latin is the name of a version (as distinguished from the Vulgate) not an older form of language.

(2) The language specified in the heading for a translation of a version is the language into which the translation is made. If the translation is intended to show the peculiarities of that version as far as it is possible by means of a translation, make a subject entry for the version.

> **Bible.** *N. T. English. 1855. Murdock.*
> . . . The New Testament; or, The books of the Holy Gospel of Our Lord and Our God, Jesus the Messiah. A literal translation from the Syriac Peshito version, by James Murdock.
> 1. Bible. Syriac—Translations into English.

(3) For Bibles in which the Old Testament is in Hebrew and the New Testament in Greek, the whole published as one work, give both languages in the heading. Make added entry for each Testament showing the languages involved.

> **Bible.** *Hebrew-Greek. 1900.*

with added entries:

> Bible. O. T. Hebrew. 1900.
> Bible. N. T. Greek. 1900.

This is the only instance in which two languages appear in a heading.

(4) For the Aramaic translations (targumim) of the Old Testament, add the name of the targum after the date if there is more than one targum to the same Biblical text.[46]

> **Bible.** *O. T. Ezekiel. Aramaic. 1902.*
> **Bible.** *O. T. Esther. Aramaic. 1920. Targum sheni.*
> **Bible.** *O. T. Pentateuch. Aramaic. 1900. Targum Onkelos.*

Refer from TARGUM to BIBLE. O. T. [PART] ARAMAIC., e.g., **Bible.** *O. T. Ezekiel. Aramaic.*

Since there are no targumim extant for Ezra and Daniel for large portions of which the original text is in Aramaic, there is no possibility of conflict with the headings

> **Bible.** *O. T. Ezra. Aramaic.*
> **Bible.** *O. T. Daniel. Aramaic.*

which headings, as occasion arises, will be used for the original text of these books if published separately. For works containing all originally Aramaic portions[47] of the Old Testament the heading is

> **Bible.** *O. T. Aramaic. Selections.*

D. Date in heading.

(1) If an edition is issued in one binding, but special title page for the New Testament or for the Apocrypha has a date earlier than the general title page, use the date of the general title page in the heading.

> **Bible.** *Tonga (Tonga Islands) 1862.*
> Koe Tohi Tabu katoa . . . 1862.
> 2 v. in 1.
> Vol. 2 with ti le "Koe Tohi oe Fuakava Foou" has special title-page only, dated 1860.

(2) If an edition is issued in more than one binding, give the date of the earliest volume in the heading.

> **Bible.** *Malay. 1820.*
> Biblia malaica . . . [1820]-24.
> 3 v.
> Vols. 1-2 (1824) paged continuously.
> Vol. 3 has title: Novum Testamentum malaice . . . 1820.

(3) Undated Bibles have the same date in the heading as has been supplied in the imprint, but without brackets.

> **Bible.** *English. 18--*
> [*avoid such an incomplete date if possible*]
> **Bible.** *English. 180-?*
> **Bible.** *English. 1800?*
> **Bible.** *English. ca. 1800.*
> [*approximation, not so close as 1800?*]
> **Bible.** *English. 1800.*

---

[46] This will apply for all practical purposes only to the Pentateuch for which three targumim exist: Targum Onkelos, Targum Pseudo-Jonathan, Targum Yerushalmi, and the book of Esther for which there are also three, known as Rishon (first), Sheni (second), and Shelishi (third).

[47] These are: Genesis XXXI, 47 (one word); Ezra IV, 8-VI, 18; VII, 11-26; Daniel II, 46-VII, 28; Jeremiah X, 11.

(4) For modern facsimile reprints of old editions give the original date in parentheses followed by actual date of reprint.

Make added entry with date of actual imprint.

> **Bible.** *O. T. Psalms. English (1535) 1838. Coverdale.*

with added entry:

> Bible. O. T. Psalms. English. 1838.

(5) For ordinary reprints give the date of the reprint only, with added entry for the date of the Bible reprinted in exceptional cases.

> **Bible.** *German. 1904.*
> Die erste deutsche Bibel . . . 1904.

with added entry:

> Bible. German. ca. 1466.

E. Version in heading.

(1) In order to distinguish readily one version from another, add (if ascertainable) after the date in the heading, in English, the name of the version or the translator; or the name of the printer; or the name of the place and printer.

> **Bible.** *Dutch. 1690. States-general version.*
> **Bible.** *English. 1560. Geneva version.*
> **Bible.** *English. 1611. Authorized.*
> **Bible.** *English. 1901. American revised.*
> **Bible.** *N. T. English. 1923. Goodspeed.*
> **Bible.** *German. 1534. Luther.*
> **Bible.** *Latin. 1450-1455. Mainz. Gutenberg.*

(2) If the translator is not the same as the commentator, use the name of the translator in the heading for the main entry and make an added entry giving the commentator's name.

The name of the paraphraser or of the paraphrase may be added to the heading for all metrical versions of the Psalms.

> **Bible.** *O. T. Psalms. French. Paraphrases. 1904. Marot.*

F. Form divisions in heading. The form divisions when required in a Bible heading follow immediately after the language specification. These form divisions are For the blind; Harmonies; Lessons, Liturgical; Manuscripts;[48] Paraphrases; Selections; Shorthand.

> **Bible.** *O. T. Psalms. English. For the blind. 1924.*
> **Bible.** *O. T. Psalms. English. Selections. 1824.*
> **Bible.** *N. T. Gospels. English. Harmonies. 1937. Moffatt.*

If two of these should be applicable in a given instance, use only one in the heading, making the choice on the basis of the following

---

[48] Reference only in this position. For exceptional treatment of Bible manuscripts see 9A (1).

priority[49] table (1) For the blind, (2) Shorthand, (3) Paraphrases, (4) Harmonies, (5) Lessons, Liturgical, (6) Selections.

Make added entry using the form not adopted in the heading.

> **Bible.** *O. T. Psalms. English. Paraphrases. 1858.*
> A paraphrase of selected Psalms . . .
> I. Bible. O. T. Psalms. English. Selections. 1858.

35. Sacred literature (other than the Bible).

A. Jewish sacred literature.

(1) Talmud. Enter editions of the Talmud under the uniform heading TALMUD (for the Babylonian Talmud) or TALMUD YERUSHALMI (for the Palestinian or Jerusalem Talmud). Include the language in the heading for texts other than Hebrew. Distinguish selections from complete works by means of the form subheading SELECTIONS. Make added entries for editors, translators, etc.

> **Talmud.**
> New edition of the Babylonian Talmud, English translation. Original text edited, formulated, and punctuated by Michael Rodkinson.
> I. Talmud. English. II. Rodkinson, Michael Levy, ed.

> **Talmud.** *English. Selections.*
> . . . The wisdom of Israel; being extracts from the Babylonian Talmud and Midrash Rabboth, translated by Edwin Collins . . .
> I. Collins, Edwin, tr.

> **Talmud Yerushalmi.**
> . . . Yerushalmi fragments from the Genizah. Text with various readings from the editio princeps, edited by Louis Ginzberg.
> I. Ginzberg, Louis, ed.

(a) Enter the various orders (sedarim) as subheadings under the uniform heading TALMUD or TALMUD YERUSHALMI, as the case may be.

> **Talmud.** *Nashim. English.*
> The Babylonian Talmud; seder Nashim translated into English with notes, glossary, and indices under the editorship of Rabbi Dr. I. Epstein.
> I. Epstein, Isidore, ed. ⌈With further added entries for translators mentioned in contents.⌉

For the form of the names of the orders and tractates follow the usage of the Jewish encyclopedia. For necessary references see (4) below.

(b) Enter separate tractates (masektot) of the Talmud (including minor treatises) under the uniform heading TALMUD, or TALMUD YERUSHALMI, as the case may be, with the name of the tractate as subheading, disregarding the name of the order.

---

[49] This order is established on the principle that the more unusual a form is, the more necessary it is to specify it.

Talmud. *Hagigah. English.*
. . . Translation of the treatise Chagigah from the Babylonian
Talmud, with introduction . . . by A. W. Streane . . .
    I. Streane, Annesley William, ed.

Talmud Yerushalmi. *Ta'anith.*
. . . A translation of the treatise Taanith . . . from the Palestinian Talmud.

(2) Mishnah. Enter texts of the Mishnah under the uniform heading MISHNAH. In other respects the entries are analogous to those
under Talmud.

Mishnah.
Die Mischna. Text, Übersetzung und ausführliche Erklärung
. . . Herausgegeben von G. Beer . . . und O. Holtzmann . . .
    I. Mishnah. German. II. Beer, Georg, ed. III. Holtzmann, O., joint ed.

Mishnah. *'Abodah zarah. English.*
The Mishna of idolatry, 'Aboda zara, ed. by W. A. L. Elms-
lie . . .
    I. Elmslie, William Alexander Leslie, ed. and tr.

(3) Tosefta. Enter collections of the Tosefta (additions to the
Mishnah) under the uniform heading TOSEFTA. Subheadings correspond to those of the Mishnah.

Tosefta. *Baba kamma.*
Die Tosefta des Traktates Nesikin Baba kamma geordnet und
kommentiert . . . von Adolf Schwarz.
    I. Schwarz, Adolf, ed.

(4) References. Because of the various forms under which an
entry may be made for a given tractate, a complete system of references is necessary to indicate the possible entries under which it
may be found—the details in the second element of the reference
to be added as material appears in the library.

Baba kamma.
    see
Talmud. *Baba kamma.*
Talmud Yerushalmi. *Baba kamma.*
Mishnah. *Baba kamma.*
Tosefta. *Baba kamma.*

Similarly, reference is made from the name of the orders (sedarim)
to the Talmud.

Nezikin.
    see
Talmud. *Nezikin.*
Talmud Yerushalmi. *Nezikin.*
Mishnah. *Nezikin.*
Tosefta. *Nezikin.*

Also a general reference from the order (seder) to the tractate.

Talmud. *Nezikin.*
For separate tractates belonging to this order see under

> **Talmud.** ₍name of tractate₎ *e.g.*
> **Talmud.** *Baba ḳamma.*

(5) Baraita (Tannaitic traditions not incorporated in the Mishnah but surviving in the two Talmuds, in the Tannaitic Midrashim, and in the Tosefta). To be used as subject heading only. Enter collections under editor.

(6) Midrash. Enter early anonymous midrashic material under the uniform heading MIDRASH with the name of the particular midrash as a subheading. For form of name follow the usage of the Jewish encyclopedia. For midrashim on a special book of the Bible, make subject heading appropriate to that book with subheading COMMENTARIES.

> **Midrash.** *Mekilta.*
> . . . Ein tannaitischer Midrasch zu Exodus. Erstmalig ins Deutsche übersetzt und erläutert von Jakob Winter und Aug. Wünsche . . .
> 1. Bible. O. T. Exodus—Commentaries. I. Winter, Jakob, ed. II. Wünsche, August, joint ed.

> **Midrash.** *Tanḥuma.*
> Midrasch Tanchuma, ein agadischer Commentar zum Pentateuch von Rabbi Tanchuma ben Rabbi Abba. Kritisch bearbeitet . . . von Salomon Buber.
> 1. Bible. O. T. Pentateuch—Commentaries. I. Buber, Salomon, ed.

For the sake of uniformity prefer the use of the period in the heading even in cases where the word Midrash is an integral part of the name of the particular midrash, e.g.,

> **Midrash.** *Ḳohelet.*
> *not* Midrash Ḳohelet.
> *nor* Midrash. *Midrash Ḳohelet.*
> *but by exception*
> **Midrash ha-gadol.**

Where midrashim with identical names deal with different books of the Bible, add the name of the book in parentheses.

> **Midrash.** *Sifre* (*Numbers*)
> **Midrash.** *Sifre* (*Deuteronomy*)

B. Buddhist scriptures. Enter the collected Buddhist scriptures under the heading TRIPIṬAKA; the three divisions, Vinayapiṭaka, Suttapiṭaka, and Abhidhamma under those names; and each individual treatise under its own name. Correlate the whole by means of *see also* references from the subject heading BUDDHA AND BUDDHISM—SACRED BOOKS. Specify in the heading, if desirable, versions, and language of text. Distinguish selections from complete works by means of the form subheading SELECTIONS.

> **Tripiṭaka.**
> **Tripiṭaka.** *German. Selections.*
> **Vinayapiṭaka.**
> **Suttapiṭaka.**

Abhidhamma.
Dhammapada. *Chinese version (Fa chü pi yü) English.*
Jātakas.

C. Hindu scriptures.

(1) Enter general collections of Vedic texts under the uniform heading VEDAS using language specification and the form subheading SELECTIONS when such delimitation is desirable.

Vedas. *German. Selections.*

(2) Enter the four separate collections of hymns and prayers known respectively as Rigveda, Samaveda, Yajurveda, and Atharvaveda under the uniform heading VEDAS. Subdivide by the name of the collection and refer from it. Further subdivision by version and by language may be made.

Vedas. *Atharvaveda.*
   Refer from
  Atharvaveda.
Vedas. *Rigveda. English. Selections.*
Vedas. *Samaveda.*
Vedas. *Yajurveda.*
Vedas. *Yajurveda. Vājasaneyīsaṃhitā. English. Selections.*

(3) Enter the various collections of commentaries and treatises known respectively as Brahmanas, Aranyakas, Upanishads, under the uniform headings BRAHMANAS, ARANYAKAS, UPANISHADS. Subdivide in each case by the name of individual treatises, and refer from the latter.[50]

Brahmanas. *Adbhutabrahmana.*
   Refer from
  Adbhutabrahmana.
Aranyakas. *Aitareyaranyaka.*
Upanishads. *Chandogya-upanishad.*

D. Koran. Enter texts of the Koran under the word KORAN. Refer from variant transliterated forms. Include the language in the heading for translations and distinguish selections from complete texts by the use of the form subdivision SELECTIONS.

Koran.
Koran. *French.*
Koran. *Selections.*
Koran. *English. Selections.*
   Refer from
  Alcoran.
  Alkoran.
  Coran.
  Qu'ran.

---

[50] Library of Congress enters Vedas and Upanishads as above, but enters each separate Brahmana and Aranyaka under its own name.
British Museum usage is as recommended above.

II. Personal Authors
(Form of Entry)

36. General rule.

In the heading give the author's name in full and in the vernacular form with certain specified exceptions. (See 40, 44, 47-49, 51, 53-56.) If an author is known in literature, history or common parlance by more than one name, prefer (1) the most authentic, (2) the best known when the most authentic has been but little used and another form has been in use predominantly both by the person concerned and in records and literature.

The form adopted for a given person is used without variation whenever it occurs as a heading, whether as author, added entry, or subject.[1] Refer from forms not adopted.

37. Modern authors.

Enter persons of modern times under the family name followed by the forenames and the dates of birth and death when available. Variations from this practice are noted in succeeding rules.

> East, Edward Murray, 1879-1938.
> Joad, Cyril Edwin Mitchinson, 1891-
> Chase, Mary Ellen, 1887-
> Powers, Margaret.
> Brennan, Paul C

38. Compound surnames.[2]

In general enter compound surnames under the first part of the name and refer from the other parts. (See also 46F.)

---

[1] By exception, the Library of Congress has shortened the author form Dante Alighieri to Dante when the heading is used with a subject subdivision (e.g., DANTE-BIBL.) (Cf. footnote 6 rule 42 for use of dates.)

[2] Not to be confused with compound names are:

(1) names apparently compound but actually the names of two distinct persons, e.g., Erckmann-Chatrian, i.e., Émile Erckmann and Alexandre Chatrian

(2) hyphenated names (especially in French) in which the first part of the compound is a forename, e.g., Lassar-Cohn, i.e., Cohn, Lassar

(3) hyphenated names (especially in German) in which the second part of the compound is the place of residence, e.g., Pelka-Berlin

(4) English names in which the middle name is a family name but not a part of the surname, e.g., John Stuart Mill

(5) Hungarian names in which the first part of an apparently compound name is actually a title, e.g., Kőrösi Csoma Sándor, i.e., Csoma, Sándor, kőrösi. (Cf. 57B, note.)

    Watts-Dunton, Theodore, 1832-1914.
    Cotarelo y Mori, Emilio, 1857-1936.
    Schulze-Delitzsch, Hermann, 1808-1883.
    Vivien de Saint Martin, Louis, 1802-1897.
    Bijll Nachenius, Henri Joachim de, 1842-1910.

Exception is made, however, in favor of entry under some other part of the name when it is found that the author's own usage or the custom of his country as indicated in national biographical dictionaries, bibliographies, etc., distinctly favors entry under that part of the name rather than the first part.

    Salomons, *Sir* **David Lionel Goldsmid-Stern,** *bart.,* 1851-1925.
    Fénelon, François de Salignac de La Mothe-, *Abp.,* 1651-1715.

This exception rarely applies to Spanish names since the compound usually consists of the father's surname followed by the mother's surname.[3]

Portuguese and Brazilian names are treated with more variation since the mother's name is generally the first part of the compound and the father's normally the last. Enter usually under the last of the surnames which the author regularly uses in full in his writings or by which he is known (rather than under the last of the names found by research). Do not, however, separate parts which form a phrase, e.g., Espirito Santo, São Tiago, Castelo Branco. Entry may be under a surname other than the last when a compound form is hyphenated, or, rarely, when an author is very well known by the compound form. (Cf. 42, footnote 7, 46F(2).)

    Siqueira, José de Lima.
        Refer from
        Lima Siqueira, José de.

    Espirito Santo, Vicente Antonio de.
        Refer from
        Santo, Vicente Antonio Espirito de.
but
    Roquette-Pinto, Edgardo, 1884-
        Refer from
        Pinto, Edgardo Roquette-.

    Machado de Assis, Joaquim Maria, 1834-1908.
        Refer from
        Assis, Joaquim Maria Machado de.

39. Surnames with prefixes.
    A. Attributive prefixes. Enter under the prefix in all languages surnames with attributive prefixes such as A', Ap, Fitz, M', Mac, Mc, O', Saint, San, etc.

    A'Beckett, Gilbert Abbott, 1811-1856.
    Fitz Gibbon, Abraham Coates, 1823-1887.

---

[3] For a treatise on Spanish personal names see C. F. Gosnell, *Spanish personal names; principles governing their formation and use* (New York, Wilson, 1938).

> MacDonald, William, 1863–
> O'Casey, Sean, 1884–
> Saint Jean, Robert de.
> San Cristóval, Evaristo, 1894–
> Santa Cruz, Alonso de, *d.* 1567.

B. Prepositions and articles as prefixes. Names beginning with a preposition, an article, a preposition and an article, or a contraction of the two are entered under the prefix, or the part of the name following the prefix, variously in different languages.

When the bearer of a name with a prefix has changed his citizenship, enter according to the rules for the language of the country adopted.

Exception is to be made in any case where established usage or the known preference of the bearer of the name is contrary to the prescribed rule.

(1) Enter under the prefix and refer from the part following the prefix.

(a) English names.

> Le Gallienne.
> De Morgan.
> Van Buren.
> De La Rue.
> Du Maurier.

(b) French names when the prefix consists of an article or the contraction of a preposition and an article.

> Le Sage.
> Des Essarts.
> Du Moulin.

(c) Italian names when the prefix consists simply of an article.

> La Farina.
> Li Gotti.
> Lo Savio.

(d) Scandinavian names of romance origin (*1*) all Swedish names, and (*2*) Danish and Norwegian names when the prefix consists of or contains an article.

> De la Gardie, Magnus Gabriel, *grefve,* 1622–1686.
> La Cour, Jens Lassen, 1876–

(e) In all languages when the prefix and name are written as one word.

> Delacroix.
> Lafuente.
> Dallolio.
> Zurlauben.

Since such names occur sometimes as separate words, make reference from the component parts, e.g.,

Delacroix *with references from* Croix,—de la; La Croix,—de.
Zurlauben *with reference from* Lauben,—zur.

(2) Enter under the part of the name following the prefix in all cases not specified above and refer from name beginning with the prefix.

(a) French names when the prefix consists of a preposition.

Alembert, Jean Lerond d', 1717-1783.
Faye, Eugène de, 1860-1929.

In French names containing a preposition and an article (not a contraction of the two) the article precedes and the preposition follows the name.

La Fontaine, Jean de, 1621-1695.
La Borderie, Arthur de, 1827-1901.

(b) Italian names when the prefix consists of or contains a preposition.

Ancona, Alessandro d', 1835-1914.
Alberti, Antonio degli, *fl. 15th cent.*

(c) Dutch and Flemish names.

Brink, Jan ten, 1834-1901.
Laer, Willem van.
Vondel, Joost van den, 1587-1679.
Hoff, Jacobus Hendricus van't, 1852-1911.

In Dutch names the prefix *de* has the same significance as *van* and follows the forename as do also articles and prepositions in names of French origin.

Helm, Cornelis de.
Faille, Jacob Baart de la, 1795-1867.

(d) German names.

Hagen, Maximilian von, 1886-
Mühll, Peter von der.
Ende, Erich vom, 1890-
Linde, Otto zur, 1873-1938.
Busch, Josef Paul zum.
Weerth, Ernst aus'm, 1829-1909.
Rhyn, August am, 1880-

(e) Scandinavian names when the prefix consists of the preposition *av* (*af*) or the German equivalent *von*.

Hällström, Gunnar Johannes af, 1908-
Linné, Carl von, 1707-1778.

(f) Spanish and Portuguese names. With very rare exceptions, Spanish and Portuguese names are entered under the part of the name following the prefix.

Ripa, Domingo la, 1622-1696.
Rio, Antonio del.

Casas, Bartolomé de las, *Bp. of Chiapa,* 1474-1566.
Cunha, Xavier da, 1840-1920.
Santos, João Adolpho dos, 1859-

40. Forenames (form when used with surname).
    A. Language. Give forenames in the form most common in the author's native or adopted language; or in doubtful cases, in the form proper to the language in which he has written most of his work, e.g., Masaryk, Tomáš Garrigue *not* Thomas Garrigue. (Cf. 45B.)

In German and Swedish forenames, when the author's usage is in doubt, prefer *f* to *ph* and *k* to *c*, e.g., Adolf rather than Adolph, Karl rather than Carl. In names of classical origin prefer *ae* to *e*, Aegidius *not* Egidius.

B. Unused forenames. Unused forenames, middle as well as first names, are as a rule to be omitted in author headings, especially in the case of living authors. When a shortened form is used, refer from full name if the first forename has been omitted.[4]

> Humboldt, Alexander, *Freiherr* von, 1769-1859.
>   *Refer from*
>   Humboldt, Friedrich Wilhelm Heinrich Alexander, *Freiherr*
>   von.
> Tarkington, Booth, 1869-1946.
>   *Refer from*
>   Tarkington, Newton Booth.
> Windisch-Graetz, Lajos, *herceg,* 1882-

C. Forenames with variants. Give forenames which have a distinct variant in the form of the variant whenever the author uses it regularly. Refer from the original form when necessary.

> Droysen, Hans.
>   *Refer from*
>   Droysen, Johannes.
> Reuter, Fritz.
>   *Refer from*
>   Reuter, Friedrich.
> Whitman, Walt, 1819-1892.
> Carleton, Will, 1845-1912.
>   *Refer from*
>   Carleton, William McKendrie.

D. Compound forenames.
    (1) Do not separate into their component parts forenames that appear combined in one word unless it is known that the separate

---

[4] On entries where a shortened form is used in the heading and the full form does not appear in the title, the Library of Congress prints the full name in a note in the lower right-hand corner of the card in the following form: *Full name:* Friedrich Wilhelm Heinrich Alexander *Freiherr* von Humboldt.
    In the case of Hungarian authors, the full name note is given in inverted form according to Hungarian custom, e.g., *Full name:* Windisch-Graetz Lajos Alfréd Viktorin Aurél Márk Feliczián *herceg.*
    In the case of Russian and Hebrew authors, the full name note is given in roman transliteration.

form represents the author's own usage. If, however, the author sometimes uses the full and sometimes the contracted form, prefer the full form.

> **Martini, Giambattista** *not* Giovanni Battista.
> *but*
> **Bodoni, Giovanni Battista** *not* Giambattista.
> **Ortes, Giovanni Maria** *not* Giammaria.

(2) Do not use hyphens between forenames, even though it is the practice of the country, e.g., **Roy, Pierre Georges** *not* Pierre-Georges. The use of hyphens in Chinese given names (cf. 67) is an exception.

> **Wang, An-shih,** 1021–1086.

41. Titles of nobility, office, etc.

A. Included in heading. Add in the heading titles which indicate nobility and the higher offices or ranks when they are commonly used in referring to a person.

(1) Titles of nobility are given in the vernacular when surname is the entry word. (See 43 and 55–56 for language when forename is entry word.)

> **Lichnowsky, Karl Max,** *Fürst* von, 1860–1928.
> **Ferrero, Augusto,** *barone,* 1866–
> **Du Cange, Charles Du Fresne,** *sieur,* 1610–1688.

(2) Titles indicating office are given in English whenever possible, whether entry is under forename or surname, and follow titles of nobility when both are included in the heading.

> **Andreas,** *margrave of Burgau, Cardinal,* 1558–1600.
> **Du Perron, Jacques Davy,** *Cardinal,* 1556?–1618.
> **Plunket, William Conyngham Plunket,** *baron, Abp. of Dublin,* 1828–1897.
> **Calleja, Félix María,** *conde de Calderón, Viceroy of Mexico, b.* 1750.
> **Masaryk, Tomáš Garrigue,** *Pres. Czechoslovak Republic,* 1850–1937.

B. Omitted in heading. Omit from the heading titles of address (Miss, Mr., Mrs., Frau, Mme., etc.); minor ecclesiastical titles (abbé, archdeacon, dean, rabbi, reverend, etc.); governmental titles below the highest rank (vice-president, senator, governor, etc.); military and naval titles; academic and professional titles.

Make exceptions in cases where the inclusion of the title is necessary to distinguish between two or more persons having the same name and whose dates are unknown, or when needed as an aid in identification. (Cf. 42.)

> **Mendell,** *Miss* **Clyde.**
> **Tourte,** *Mme.* **Jo Roger.**
> **Castagnier,** *Mme.* **H.**
> **Erskine,** *Mrs.* **Payne.**

Deidier,   *abbé.*
Brown, George, *captain.* (dates unknown)
Brown, *Rev.* **George.** (dates unknown)

42. Dates and designations.

For medieval and modern names add dates of birth and death in the heading when they can be discovered with a reasonable amount of search.[5] They are not, as a rule, to be given for classical names, and may also be omitted in the case of well-known persons when the name is followed by a subheading.[6]

Shakespeare, William, 1564-1616.
Shakespeare, William—*Characters.*
Shakespeare, William. *Spurious and doubtful works.*

Distinguish persons of the same name whose dates are not known, by descriptive designations denoting profession, occupation, residence, etc., in English if possible.

Smith, John, 1536-1616.
Smith, John, 1580-1631.
Smith, John, Mar. 8, 1882-
Smith, John, Aug. 5, 1882-

---

[5] Dates are important not only for distinguishing persons of the same name, but also for placing more or less obscure personalities, even when only approximate dates can be given. The following practice is observed by Library of Congress:

    Smith, John, 1837-1896. (Both dates established with certainty)
    Smith, John, 1836 *or* 7-1896. (Date of birth deduced from age at date of death)
    Smith, John, 1837?-1896. (Authorities differ as to date of birth; 1837 probable)
    Smith, John, 1837 (*ca.*)-1896. (Date of birth uncertain by several years)
    Smith, John, 1837-*ca.* 1896. (Date of death approximate only)
    Smith, John, *ca.* 1837-*ca.* 1896. (Both dates approximate only)
    Smith, John, *b.* 1825. (Date of death unknown with little likelihood of discovery)
    Smith, John, *d.* 1859. (Date of birth unknown with little likelihood of discovery)
    Joannes *Diaconus, fl.* 1210 (*fl.* 1226-1240; *fl.* 1260-1280; *fl.* 1290; *fl.* 1287-1313, as the case may be; prefer longest ascertainable interval)
    Joannes *Diaconus, 12th cent.* (When not possible to identify within a more limited period)

[6] Following is a list of names after which dates are omitted on Library of Congress cards when subheadings occur in the heading.

Ariosto, Lodovico
Bach, Johann Sebastian
Bacon, Francis, *viscount St. Albans*
Balzac, Honoré de
Beethoven, Ludwig van
Boccaccio, Giovanni
Browning, Robert
Bunyan, John
Burns, Robert
Byron, George Gordon Noël Byron, 6th baron
Carlyle, Thomas
Cervantes Saavedra, Miguel de
Chaucer, Geoffrey
Colombo, Cristoforo
Corneille, Pierre
Cromwell, Oliver
Dante Alighieri (see note 1, p. 82)
Dickens, Charles
Eliot, George, *pseud., i.e.,* **Marian Evans,** *afterwards* **Cross**
Goethe, Johann Wolfgang von
Goldsmith, Oliver
Hawthorne, Nathaniel
Heine, Heinrich
Hugo, Victor Marie, *comte*
Ibsen, Henrik
Irving, Washington
Lessing, Gotthold Ephraim
Lincoln, Abraham, *Pres. U. S.*
Longfellow, Henry Wadsworth
Luther, Martin
Marie Antoinette
Milton, John
Molière, Jean Baptiste Poquelin
Mozart, Johann Chrysostom Wolfgang Amadeus
Napoléon I
Petrarca, Francesco
Pushkin, Aleksandr Sergeevich
Racine, Jean Baptiste
Rousseau, Jean Jacques
Ruskin, John
Schiller, Johann Christoph Friedrich von
Scott, *Sir* **Walter,** *bart.*
Shakespeare, William
Spenser, Edmund
Tasso, Torquato
Tennyson, Alfred Tennyson, *baron*
Thackeray, William Makepeace
Tolstoi, Lev Nikolaevich, *graf*
Voltaire, François Marie Arouet de
Wagner, Richard
Washington, George, *Pres. U. S.*

88

> Smith, John, *clockmaker.*
> Smith, John, *of Malton, Eng.*
> Smith, John, *rector of Baldock.*
> Smith, John, *surgeon and trading captain.*
> Evans, Montgomery, ii. (author's usage, dates unknown)
> Small, Frank, Jr.[7] (author's usage, dates unknown)
> Brown, George, F. I. P. S. (dates unknown)
> Stuart, John, *writer on aviation.* (dates unknown)

43. Forename as entry word.

Sovereigns, ruling princes, saints and other persons known by their forenames only, are entered under forename. (Cf. 47-49, 51, 53-56, 61.)

Add titles of nobility in English. (Cf. 41A.)

Add any epithet, byname or adjective of origin, nationality, etc., by which the person is usually known. If such word or phrase may be considered as part of the name, give it in the same language as the forename. If a descriptive word or phrase is added for the sake of identification but is not considered part of the name, give it preferably in English. (Cf. 47, 54, 55, 61.)

Add dates in accordance with rule 42.

> Karl, *Archduke of Austria,* 1771-1847.
> Amalie, *Princess of Saxony,* 1794-1870.
> Kazimierz III, *Wielki, King of Poland,* 1310-1370.
> Joannes *Eleemosynarius, Saint, Patriarch of Alexandria, d.* 616?
> Guilelmus *Arvernus, Bp. of Paris, d.* 1249.
> Joannes *Braidensis, fl.* 1419.
> Augustine, *Saint, Abp. of Canterbury, d.* 604.
> Elijah, *the prophet.*

44. Writers known under sobriquets, nicknames, etc.

In a few cases, chiefly names of artists, a universally used sobriquet or nickname is to be selected as entry word, provided it is not one of the forenames of the person in question. Refer from real name.

> Tintoretto, Jacopo Robusti, *known as,* 1512-1594.
>> *Refer from*
>> Robusti, Jacopo.
> Correggio, Antonio Allegri, *known as,* 1494-1534.
>> *Refer from*
>> Allegri, Antonio.
> Ucello, Paolo di Dono, *known as,* 1396 *or* 7-1475.
>> *Refer from*
>> Dono, Paolo di.
>> Paolo *di Dono.*

---

[7] The word Junior (Jr.) or a foreign equivalent when used with the author's name on the title page is disregarded in establishing the heading unless needed to distinguish between authors of the same name. In Portuguese, refer from the name proper compounded with the word Junior (or Filho). Treat in a similar manner the words Netto, Neto (grandson) and Sobrinho (nephew) when they are known to express relationship only, not to form legally part of the name.

> **Marques Junior, Henrique**
>> *see*
> **Marques, Henrique.**

If the real name is chosen as entry word, the sobriquet or nickname is added in the heading and reference is made from it to the real name.

> **Grazzini, Antonio Francesco,** *called* **Il Lasca,** 1503-1584.
> *Refer from*
> Il Lasca.

> **Theotocopuli, Dominico,** *called* **El Greco,** *d.* 1614.
> *Refer from*
> El Greco.

> **Fiorella, Tiberio,** *called* **Scaramouche,** 1604-1694.
> *Refer from*
> Scaramouche.

45. Changed names.

A. Enter under the adopted name a person who in civil life has changed his name unless the original one is decidedly better known. (Cf. 30B, 53, 65B(2), 69B.) This includes legal changes of name, assumed names such as pseudonyms and professional names that have been adopted for general use, and also cases in which merely the spelling of the name has been altered. Refer from the form not chosen as heading.[8]

> **Burn, Bruno,** 1891-
> *Refer from*
> Birnbaum, Bruno.

> **France, Anatole,** 1844-1924.
> *Refer from*
> Thibault, Anatole.

> **Angell,** *Sir* **Norman,** 1874-
> *Refer from*
> Angell, *Sir* Ralph Norman.
> Lane, *Sir* Ralph Norman Angell.

> **Sadleir, Michael,** 1888-
> *Refer from*
> Sadler, Michael Thomas Harvey.

> **Farrère, Claude,** 1876-
> *Refer from*
> Bargone, Charles.
> Bargone, Frédéric Charles Pierre Édouard.

> **Stalin, Iosif,** 1879-
> *Refer from*
> Dzhugashvili, Iosif Vissarinovich.

> **Barrymore, Maurice,** 1847-1905.
> *Refer from*
> Blythe, Herbert.

> **Douglas, Melvyn,** 1901-
> *Refer from*
> Hesselberg, Melvyn.

---

[8] On Library of Congress printed cards the original name is usually given in a note in the lower right-hand corner of the card, e.g., *Name originally:* Bruno Birnbaum.

B. When a person regularly uses a foreign form of his name, enter under this form.

> **Mirkine-Guetzévitch, Boris** *not*
>   Mirkin-Getsevich, Boris Sergeevich.
> **Tschermak, Gustav von,** *not* Čermak.

This practice applies to authors whose works have originally appeared in a foreign or adopted tongue, and whose names may therefore be given in the form adopted by them.

Follow this practice also in the case of transliterated names, if the author has himself consistently used a particular form when among foreigners, or is always known by a transliteration differing from the one provided for in these rules.

> **Rachmaninoff, Sergei,** *not* Rakhmaninov, Sergeĭ Vasil'evich.
> **Rangabë,** *not* Rankabes.
> **Vlachos,** *not* Blachos.

46. Married women.

Enter a married woman under her latest name unless, as specified below, she has consistently written under another name.

The heading is to consist of (*1*) husband's surname,[9] (*2*) her own forenames, and (*3*) her maiden name, when known, in parentheses. (For the use of the title *Mrs.*, or its equivalent, see 41B.)

> **Stowe, Emily Howard (Jennings)**
> **Curie, Marie (Skłodowska) 1867-1934.**
> **Bonin, Anna (von Zanthier) von, 1856-1933.**
> **Hamsun, Marie (Andersen) 1881-**
> **Viterbi, Bona (Benvenisti)**

A. When a woman uses her husband's forenames or initials in place of her own on the title page of her books, enter under her own name and refer from her husband's name.

---

[9] (*1*) German women of the 16th to 18th centuries who added the suffix *in* to their surname or family name (e.g., Welserin, Gottschedin, Karschin) are entered under the name without the suffix. Refer from name with suffix.

> **Karsch, Anna Luise (Dürbach) 1722-1791.**
>   *Refer from*
>   Karschin, Anna Luise (Dürbach)

(*2*) The enclitic *né* added by Hungarian married women is omitted in the heading, e.g.,

> **Magyary, Margit (Techert)**
>   Refer from the form with the enclitic added to the surname: Magyaryné, Margit (Techert)
>   Refer also from the form with the enclitic added to the husband's forename if the woman has used this form or is known by it.
>   Magyary, Zoltanné.
>   Use this last form as the entry if the woman's forenames are not known.

(*3*) Women's names, both married and single, in Polish, Russian, and Czech retain the feminine ending with exception in favor of the masculine form when it is the prevalent usage.

> **Elizarova, Anna Il'inichna (Ul'ianova)**
> **Votočková-Lauermannová, O.**

> **Ward, Mary Augusta (Arnold)** 1851-1920.
>   *Refer from*
> Ward, *Mrs.* Humphry.
> **Bussy, Dorothy (Strachey)**
>   *Refer from*
> Bussy, *Mme.* Simon.

B. Omit the name of an earlier husband in the heading unless it continues to appear in the form of name which the author customarily uses.

> **Eddy, Mary (Baker)** 1821-1910, *not* Eddy, Mary (Baker) Glover.
> *but*
> **Jackson, Helen Hunt,** 1831-1885.
>   *Refer from*
> Hunt, Helen Maria (Fiske)
> Jackson, Helen Maria (Fiske) Hunt.

C. Enter a married woman who continues to write under her maiden name under the maiden name. Refer from married name.

> **Brontë, Charlotte,** 1816-1855.
>   *Refer from*
> Nicholls, Charlotte (Brontë)
> **Earhart, Amelia,** 1898-1937.
>   *Refer from*
> Putnam, Amelia (Earhart)
> **Millay, Edna St. Vincent,** 1892-
>   *Refer from*
> Boissevain, Edna St. Vincent (Millay)
> **Sawyer, Ruth,** 1880-
>   *Refer from*
> Durand, Ruth (Sawyer)

D. Enter a woman who remarries but continues to write or is best known under the name of a former husband under the name of the former husband. Refer from later married name.

> **Wiggin, Kate Douglas (Smith)** 1856-1923.
>   *Refer from*
> Riggs, Kate Douglas (Smith) Wiggin.
> **Wylie, Elinor (Hoyt)** 1885-1928.
>   *Refer from*
> Benét, Elinor (Hoyt) Wylie.
> **Forbes, Rosita (Torr)**
>   *Refer from*
> Forbes, Joan Rosita (Torr)
> McGrath, Rosita (Torr) Forbes.

E. When a divorced woman resumes her maiden name, enter under the maiden name. If she has written under her married name, refer from it.

F. Compound names consisting of a combination of the surnames of husband and wife are frequently found on the title pages of books by married women. As a rule these are not treated as compound names, but are entered according to the general rule for married women. (46) However, exceptions are sometimes made, especially in the case of foreign names if custom favors entry under the compound form.

In any language when the maiden name appears in the heading as a part of a compound name, it is not enclosed in parentheses; and in all cases references are made from parts of the surname not chosen as entry word.

(1) Spanish names.[10] In Spanish names the customary usage is for a woman to add to her own surname the surname of her husband, connecting the two by the preposition *de*. Ordinarily the part of each surname which represents the mother's name is dropped, but it is sometimes retained if the mother's name is a particularly distinguished one, or, as a means of identification if the father's name is a very common one.

Enter according to the general rule for compound names, the entry word in this case being the woman's maiden name.

> **Molina y Vedia de Bastianini, Delfina.**
> [*Father's name: Octavio T. Molina.*
> *Mother's name: Manuela Vedia de Molina.*
> *Maiden name: Delfina Molina y Vedia.*
> *Husband's name: René Bastianini*]
>   *Refer from*
> Bastianini, Delfina Molina y Vedia de.
> Vedia de Bastianini, Delfina Molina y.

(2) **Portuguese names.** The usage in Portuguese and Brazilian names is less consistent than in Spanish, but in general names are formed in the same way. At present, however, the tendency is toward use of the last surname, the husband's, rather than the full compound form. Enter under the last surname, with reference from any other surnames which form part of the name.

> **Vasconcellos, Carolina (Michaëlis) de,** 1851-1925.
> [*Father's name: Gustavo Michaëlis.*
> *Husband's name: Joaquim de Vasconcellos*]
>   *Refer from*
> Michaëlis de Vasconcellos, Carolina.

(3) **Dutch names.** The Dutch custom is to use a hyphenated compound in which the husband's name is followed by the wife's maiden name. Treat as any compound name.

> **Ammers-Küller, Jo van,** 1884-
>   *Refer from*
> Ammers, Johanna (Küller) van.
> Küller, Jo van Ammers-

---

[10] Cf. C. F. Gosnell, *Spanish personal names; principles governing their formation and use.* (New York, Wilson, 1938).

(4) Italian names. In Italian names the compound form is frequently found, the wife's name sometimes preceding and sometimes following the husband's name. In general enter under the maiden name or the married name according to the rules for the names of married women, using the compound form only when it is the author's consistent usage, or when it is impossible to distinguish between maiden name and married name.

> **Fusinato, Erminia (Fuà)** 1834-1876.
> *Refer from*
> Fuà-Fusinato, Erminia.
>
> **Negri, Ada,** 1870-1945.
> *Refer from*
> Negri-Garlanda, Ada.
> Garlanda, Ada (Negri)
>
> **Pierantoni-Mancini, Grazia,** 1843-1915.
> *Refer from*
> Pierantoni, Grazia (Mancini)
> Mancini, Grazia Pierantoni-

(5) German, Swiss, Scandinavian, and Russian married women who use a compound form of name on the title pages of their books are entered according to the general rules for married women unless the compound form is known to be the preferred usage.

47. Saints.

A. Enter saints of the early and medieval church like other writers of the same period under the forename, using the Latin form, followed by the designation SAINT in English.

Since the same name is frequently borne by several saints, descriptive or definitive epithets or appellatives are necessary for the purpose of differentiation. The designation SAINT follows epithets or appellatives qualifying the name of the saint and titles of nobility (cf. D) but precedes titles of office.

> **Benedictus,** *Saint, Abbot of Monte Cassino.*
> **Theodorus** *Studita, Saint,* 759?-826.
> **Joannes** *Eleemosynarius, Saint, Patriarch of Alexandria, d.* 616?

Refer from English or other forms of name, using when possible a general reference, e.g.,

> **Benedict**
> For saints and popes bearing this name *see*
> **Benedictus.**

Exception from the Latin form is made for (*1*) Biblical saints who are entered under the English form of name (cf. 54), and (*2*) national saints or saints of predominantly local interest who are entered under the vernacular form of name.

> **James,** *Saint, apostle.*
> **Augustine,** *Saint, Abp. of Canterbury, d.* 604.

> **Geneviève,** *of Paris, Saint, 5th cent.*
> **Patrick,** *Saint, 373?-463?*
> **Ansgar,** *Saint, Abp. of Hamburg and Bremen, 801-865.*
> **Ciaran,** *Saint, Abbot of Clonmacnois.*

Because saints are officially listed under the forename in Latin, reference should always be made from that form when any other form of entry is adopted.

> **Augustinus,** *Saint, Abp. of Canterbury*
> *see*
> **Augustine,** *Saint, Abp. of Canterbury, d. 604.*
> **Genovefa,** *of Paris, Saint*
> *see*
> **Geneviève,** *of Paris, Saint, 5th cent.*

B. Enter modern saints preferably under the forename in the vernacular. Refer from Latin form of name and from surname or secular name and any variant names by which the saint is known.

> **Filippo Neri,** *Saint, 1515-1595.*
> *Refer from*
> Philippus Nerius, *Saint.*
> Neri, Filippo, *Saint.*
> **Luigi Gonzaga,** *Saint, 1568-1591.*
> *Refer from*
> Aloysius, *Saint.*
> Gonzaga, Luigi, *Saint.*
> **Konrad** *von Parzham, Saint, 1818-1894.*
> *Refer from*
> Conradus *a Parzham, Saint.*
> Birndorfer, Johannes Evangelist.
> **Thérèse,** *Saint, 1873-1897.*
> *Refer from*
> Teresia *a Jesu Infanta, Saint.*
> Thérèse de l'Enfant Jésus, *Saint.*
> Martin, Marie Françoise Thérèse.

Exception is made in favor of entry under surname for saints canonized long after death and known in history and literature by their surnames. Refer from name with forename as entry word in both Latin and vernacular forms.

> **Fisher, John,** *Saint, Bp. of Rochester, 1469?-1535.*
> *Refer from*
> John Fisher, *Saint.*
> Joannes Fisher, *Saint.*
> **Loyola, Ignacio de,** *Saint, 1491-1556.*
> *Refer from*
> Ignatius Loyola, *Saint*
> Ignacio de Loyola, *Saint.*
> **Hofbauer, Klemens Maria,** *Saint, 1751-1820.*
> *Refer from*
> Clemens Maria Hofbauer, *Saint.*
> Klemens Maria Hofbauer, *Saint.*

C. Enter popes, kings, etc., who have achieved sainthood under the rules for popes, kings, etc.

> **Pius V,** *Saint, Pope,* 1504-1572.
> **Gregorius I,** *the Great, Saint, Pope,* 540 *(ca.)*-604.
> **Olav II,** *Saint, King of Norway,* 995-1030.

D. Enter noblemen who have achieved sainthood under the rule for noblemen. Make references as prescribed for names of noblemen and, in addition, from the forename in both Latin and vernacular forms.

> **Chantal, Jeanne Françoise (Frémiot) de Rabutin,** *baronne* **de,**
> *Saint,* 1572-1641.
> *Refer from*
> Joanna Francisca Frémiot de Chantal, *Saint.*
> Jeanne Françoise de Chantal, *Saint.*
> Jane Frances de Chantal, *Saint.*
> Chantal, *Saint.*
> Frémiot, Jeanne Françoise, *baronne de Chantal.*
> Fremyot, Jeanne Françoise, *baronne de Chantal.*
> Rabutin-Chantal, Jeanne Françoise (Frémiot) *baronne* de.
> **More,** *Sir* **Thomas,** *Saint,* 1478-1535.
> *Refer from*
> Thomas More, *Saint.*
> Thomas Morus, *Saint.*

48. Popes.

Enter a pope under his Latin pontifical name, followed by the title POPE. Popes having the same name are distinguished by a numeral. Refer from the vernacular form and from his family name.

> **Pius XI,** *Pope,* 1857-1939.
> *Refer from*
> Pio (Make a general reference. Cf. 47A.)
> Ratti, Achille.

An antipope is entered under his Latin pontifical name with the numeral by which he is usually known, followed by the title ANTIPOPE.

> **Clemens VII,** *antipope,* 1342-1394.
> *Refer from*
> Robert *de Genève.*

Works emanating from a pope in his capacity as head of the church are entered under CATHOLIC CHURCH. (See 118A.) Correlate the two types of entry by references.

> **Pius IX,** *Pope,* 1792-1878.
> *See also*
> **Catholic Church.** *Pope, 1846-1878 (Pius IX)*

49. Patriarchs.

Enter a patriarch under the name by which he is known in his own country, usually a name assumed in religion, sometimes in Latin and sometimes in the vernacular. Include in the heading the title PATRIARCH and the name of the patriarchate. Refer from secular name if known.[11]

> **Cyrillus,** *Saint, Patriarch of Alexandria,* 376 (ca.)-444.
> **Dositheos,** *Patriarch of Jerusalem,* 1641-1707.
> **Tikhon,** *Patriarch of Russia,* 1865-1925.
> > *Refer from*
> > Belavin, Vasiliĭ.

50. Cardinals.[12]

Enter a cardinal according to the rule of entry appropriate to his station at the time of his elevation. Earlier ecclesiastical titles, except those of ecclesiastical princes, give way to the title CARDINAL, but titles of nobility are retained in the heading.

> **Gibbons, James,** *Cardinal,* 1834-1921.
> **Richelieu, Armand Jean du Plessis,** *duc de, Cardinal,* 1585-1642.
> **Albrecht** *von Brandenburg, Cardinal, Abp. and elector of Mainz,*
> > 1490-1545.
> **Andreas,** *margrave of Burgau, Cardinal,* 1558-1600.

51. Ecclesiastical princes.

Enter under forename in the vernacular an archbishop or bishop who, in addition to his see, rules a territory as a temporal prince. Include in the heading, in English, the title PRINCE-ARCHBISHOP, ABP. AND ELECTOR, or PRINCE-BISHOP, as the case may be, and the name of the see. (Cf. 52, 55.)

> **Neithard,** *Prince-Bishop of Bamberg,* 1545?-1598.

This rule applies to German and Austrian prince-bishops before secularization of 1803, those after 1803 being entered according to the rule for bishops and archbishops. (52)

52. Bishops and archbishops.

Enter bishops and archbishops under the surname with the designation BP. or ABP. Retain titles of nobility in the heading.

> **Shahan, Thomas Joseph,** *Bp.,* 1857-1932.
> **Söderblom, Nathan,** *Abp.,* 1866-1931.
> **Waitz, Siegmund,** *Prince-Archbishop of Salzburg,* 1864-

The titles *vicar apostolic, prefect apostolic, administrator apostolic,* and *vicar-general* are not included in the heading, even though these officials exercise episcopal jurisdiction. If such officers are consecrated titular bishops, then the title BP. or ABP. is used.

Exceptions to entry under surname are made in cases where the rules require another form of entry, e.g., an early or medieval bishop under forename, a nobleman under title.

---

[11] When it can be ascertained the Library of Congress gives the secular name in a note in the lower right-hand corner of the catalog card in the following form *Secular name:* Vasiliĭ Belavin.

[12] The term *cardinal* includes *cardinal archbishop, cardinal bishop, cardinal priest, cardinal deacon.*

Further variations and specifications.

A. Include the name of the see in the heading:

(1) For bishops and archbishops of the Church of England in Great Britain and Ireland, and of the pre-Reformation Catholic Church in Great Britain (but not for Catholic bishops after the reconstitution of the hierarchy in 1850, nor for the vicars apostolic with the title of bishop in charge after the extinction of the old hierarchy).

(2) For the ecclesiastical princes of the Holy Roman Empire. (Cf. 51.)

(3) For bishops and archbishops of the Orthodox Eastern Church who bear the title *Metropolitan.* (Cf. E. below.)

(4) For any bishop when desirable for the purpose of identification or distinction, especially early Christian and medieval bishops.

Fleetwood, William, *Bp. of Ely,* 1656-1723.
Edmund Rich, *Saint, Abp. of Canterbury, d.* 1240.
Colenso, John William, *Bp. of Natal,* 1814-1883.
Grégoire, Henri, *Constitutional Bp. of Blois,* 1750-1831.
Gregorius, *Saint, Bp. of Tours,* 538-594.
Gregorius, *Abp. of Corinth, fl. ca.* 1200.
Hilarianus, Quintus Julius, *Bp. in proconsular Africa, 4th cent.*
Paulus, *Nestorian Bp. of Nisibis, d.* 571.

Do not include the name of the see in the heading for suffragan, auxiliary, coadjutor, titular, and assistant bishops, and chorepiscopi.

B. When there have been several bishops of the same name in one see, especially in the early period, include the number in the heading if they have been so distinguished.

Ruricius I, *Bp. of Limoges, d. ca.* 507.

C. In the case of translation from one see to another, include the latest see only in the heading.[13]

Andrewes, Lancelot, *Bp. of Winchester,* 1555-1626.
(not successively Bp. of Chichester, Ely, and Winchester)
Lang, Cosmo Gordon Lang, *baron, Abp. of Canterbury,* 1864-
(not successively Bp. of Stepney and Abp. of York and Canterbury)

Refer from see, or successive sees, held by a bishop.

Markham, William, *Abp. of York,* 1719-1807.
Refer from
Chester, William Markham, *Bp. of.*
York, William Markham, *Abp. of.*

---

[13] Exception may be made in favor of the earlier see if a bishop has died shortly after his translation without becoming known or having published as bishop of the later see. However, the later see is invariably to be used if (1) a suffragan bishop has been made a diocesan bishop, (2) a bishop has been made an archbishop, (3) an archbishop of York has been translated to the see of Canterbury.

When a bishop of the Church of England uses as signature his forename followed by the abbreviated Latin name of the diocese (e.g., Cantuar, Dunelm, Winston) refer also from this form.

> **Lang, Cosmo Gordon Lang,** *baron, Abp. of Canterbury,* 1864-
> > *Refer from*
> > Cantuar, Cosmo Gordon.

If a Catholic bishop is translated to a titular archdiocese do not change the title unless he has ruled an archdiocese or published as an archbishop.

> **Canevin, Regis,** *Bp.,* 1852-1927.
> > [*Bishop of Pittsburgh; resigned 1921; titular archbishop of Pelusium 1921*]
>
> **Basin, Thomas,** *Abp.,* 1412-1491.
> > [*Bishop of Lisieux, 1447-1474; resigned and was made archbishop of Caesarea; continued to publish*]

D. In case of deposition, especially if accompanied by change of denomination and no elevation to the episcopate in the new denomination, the title of bishop is omitted.

> **Ives, Levi Silliman,** 1797-1867.
> > [*Consecrated Protestant Episcopal bishop of North Carolina, 1831; resigned the see, Dec. 22, 1852; became a Catholic Dec. 25, 1852; deposed Oct. 14, 1853; active as layman in the Catholic Church because as a married man he could not enter the priesthood*]

E. Enter a bishop or an archbishop of the Orthodox Eastern Church who bears the title "Metropolitan" under the name by which he is known in religion followed by the title METROPOLITAN and the name of the see. Refer from secular name if known.[14]

> **Platon,** *Metropolitan of Moscow,* 1737-1812.
> > *Refer from*
> > Levshin, Petr Georgievich.
>
> **Dimitriĭ,** *Saint, Metropolitan of Rostov,* 1651-1709.
> > *Refer from*
> > Tuptalo, Daniil Savvich.

F. Enter the official acts and records of a bishop under the diocese, subheading BISHOP, YEARS OF INCUMBENCY and, in parentheses, the NAME OF THE BISHOP. Correlate the two types of entry by means of references.[15]

---

[14] Cf. footnote 11, rule 49.

[15] To make these references intelligible, an explanatory card should be filed at the head of the entry for each diocese with the subheading BISHOP.

> **Winchester,** *Eng. (Diocese) Bishop.*
> > Only official acts or records are entered under this heading, subdivided when necessary by date of incumbency and name of incumbent. Works of bishops as personal authors are entered under their family name (in the case of noblemen under their title). For a list of the bishops of Winchester consult Crockford's clerical directory.

Footnote continued on next page.

> **Winchester,** *Eng.* (*Diocese*) *Bishop, 1367-1404* (*William of Wykeham*)
> *with references to and from*
> Wykeham, William of, *Bp. of Winchester, 1323?-1404.*

Pastoral letters and charges, not being considered official, are entered under the bishop as personal author.

53. Religious orders, Changed names of persons in.

Enter writers who have adopted a religious name upon entering orders, modifying or relinquishing the original secular name, under the modified secular or religious name as further specified under A, B and exception C. Add, in English, the designation FATHER for priests, BROTHER for those not priests; MOTHER for heads of religious houses or those called Mother by the order, and SISTER for those not designated Mother.[16] (Cf. 47-49.)

A. Enter under surname writers known to the lay public under the surname combined with the name in religion. Refer from the name in religion and from full secular name.[17]

> **Bransiet, Philippe,** *Brother, 1792-1874.*
> *Refer from*
> Philippe, *Brother.*
> Bransiet, Matthieu.

> **Miley, Mary Hilda,** *Sister, 1881-*
> *Refer from*

Footnote continued from preceding page.

An explanatory card should also be filed under the name of the see city followed by the words BISHOP OF.

> **Winchester, Bishop of.**
> Official acts are entered under the heading Winchester, *Eng.* (*Diocese*). Other works are under the family name of the bishop (in the case of noblemen, under his title). For a list of the bishops of Winchester consult Crockford's clerical directory.

The reference to the authoritative list of bishops is altered according to the denomination of which the diocese is a unit.

Lists of bishops:
> Catholic bishops: Gams. *Series episcoporum, 1873.*
> Catholic bishops in Great Britain: *Catholic directory.*
> Catholic bishops in the U. S.: *Official Catholic directory.*
> Anglican bishops: *Crockford's clerical directory.*
> Protestant Episcopal bishops: *Living church annual.*

[16] The name of the order should be included in the heading *only* when necessary to distinguish between two or more persons having the same religious name. This duplication of names occurs frequently when entry is under forename and in references from forename to full name entry.

> **Mary Barbara,** *Sister, 1866-*
> (Of the Congregation of the Daughters of Charity of St. Vincent de Paul in St. Louis)
> *see*
> **Regan, Mary Barbara,** *Sister, 1866-*
> **Mary Barbara,** *Sister, 1886-*
> (Of the Congregation of the Sisters of St. Joseph in Michigan)
> *see*
> **McCarthy, Mary Barbara,** *Sister, 1886-*

[17] The Library of Congress gives the name in religion (or the secular name as the case may be) in a note in the lower right-hand corner of the catalog card in the following form:

> *Name in religion:* Jacqueline de Sainte Euphémie, *Sister.*
> or *Secular name:* Lawrence Anthony Hess.

Mary Hilda, *Sister.*
Hilda, *Sister.*
Miley, Gertrude Ann.

B. Enter under religious name writers who have published all or most of their works under that name. Refer from secular name if ascertainable.[18]

Cuthbert, *Father,* 1866-1939.
   Refer from
Hess, Lawrence Anthony.
Clotilde Angela, *Sister,* 1895-
   Refer from
McBride, Regina Margaret.

When the name Mary is abbreviated to M. by the author, indicating that the name following the initial is the distinctive part of the name, it is omitted in both purely religious names and in combinations of secular family name and religious given name except in cases where the distinctive part of the religious name is a masculine name adopted by a nun.

Eleanore, *Sister,* 1890-
   Refer from
Mary Eleanore, *Sister.*
Brosnahan, Katharine Mary.
Hayden, Bridget, *Mother,* 1814-1890.
   Refer from
Hayden, Mary Bridget, *Mother.*
Mary Bridget, *Mother.*
Bridget, *Mother.*
Hayden, Margaret.
but
Mary Bartholomew, *Sister.*
   Refer from
Bartholomew, *Sister.*
Frederick, Elizabeth Eva.

The word SAINT is spelled out when it is the entry word of a religious name, either as main entry or reference.

Saint Catharine, *Sister,* 1878-
LeClair, St. Ida, *Sister,* 1891-
   Refer from
Saint Ida, *Sister.*
but
Mary of St. Peter, *Mother,* 1838-1924.
   Refer from
Garnier, Marie Adèle.

The prepositional phrase indicating place of birth is italicized when it is made a part of the religious name.

---

[18] See footnote 17, p. 100.

Francis *da Offeio, Father.*
Egidio *da Caraglio, Father.*
José *de Sigüenza, Father,* 1544 (*ca.*)-1606.

C. Enter under the secular name[19] writers who have published works under the original name and are not known, or not so well known, under their religious names. Refer from name in religion.[20]

Pascal, Jacqueline, 1575-1661.
    Refer from
    Jacqueline de Sainte Euphémie, *Sister.*
Lathrop, Rose (Hawthorne) 1851-1926.
    Refer from
    Mary Alphonsa, *Mother.*
    Lathrop, Mary Alphonsa, *Mother.*

54. Bible characters.

Give names of Bible characters in English in the form in which they appear in the Authorized version, followed by any necessary distinguishing epithet. Refer from variant forms as used in other versions, as for example the Douay version.

James, *Saint, apostle.*
Elijah, *the prophet.*
    Refer from
    Elias, *the prophet.*
Gideon, *judge of Israel.*
    Refer from
    Gedeon, *judge of Israel.*
Absalom, *son of David.*
Judith (*Jewish heroine*)
Rahab (*Biblical character*)

55. Sovereigns and rulers.

Enter sovereigns and ruling princes under their forenames in the vernacular,[21] followed by title in English. Refer from the English form of name if it differs from the vernacular.

James I, *King of Great Britain,* 1566-1625.
    [*Kings prior to James I have title: King of England*]
Franz Joseph I, *Emperor of Austria,* 1830-1916.
Friedrich I, *Barbarossa, Emperor of Germany,* 1121-1190.
Wilhelm II, *German Emperor,* 1859-1941.
    [*form of title after 1870*]
Henri IV, *King of France,* 1553-1610.
Napoléon III, *Emperor of the French,* 1808-1873.
Umberto I, *King of Italy,* 1844-1900.

---

[19] It is to be noted that the designations *Father, Brother, Mother, Sister* are not used in the heading with secular names. This applies as well to those orders in which the secular name is retained without change. The designation *father, brother,* etc., on the title page does not necessarily presuppose a religious name.

[20] See footnote 17, p. 100.

[21] Use the English form of name for sovereigns of European nations not using alphabets in roman or gothic characters, e.g., Paul not Pavel. This does not apply to other members of the royal family (consort, grand dukes, etc.).

Paul I, *Emperor of Russia*, 1754-1801.
Hirohito, *Emperor of Japan*, 1901–
Wilhelmina, *Queen of the Netherlands*, 1880–
Margaretha, *of Parma, Regent of the Netherlands*, 1522-1586.
Albert I, *Prince of Monaco*, 1848-1922.
Franz Egon, *Prince-Bishop of Hildesheim and Paderborn*, 1737-1825.

Enter the consorts of sovereigns under forename in the form used in the country of the sovereign, with the titles in English and the name of the sovereign in English form.

Albert, *consort of Victoria, Queen of Great Britain*, 1819-1861.
Marie Antoinette, *consort of Louis XVI, King of France*, 1755-1793.
Mariĩa Feodorovna, *consort of Alexander III, Emperor of Russia*, 1847-1928.
Maria de la Paz, *consort of Louis Ferdinand, Prince of Bavaria*, 1862–
Isabel de Valois, *consort of Philip II, King of Spain*, 1545-1568.
 Refer from
Élisabeth *de France.*
Elizabeth *of Valois.*

A. Enter Roman emperors of the West according to the rule for classical Latin authors (60), i.e., under the name by which they are most generally known in history. Follow the practice of standard classical dictionaries.
Thus we have under praenomen:

Tiberius, *Emperor of Rome*, 42 B.C.-37 A.D.
Titus, *Emperor of Rome*, 40-81.

Under nomen:

Aurelius Antoninus, Marcus, *Emperor of Rome*, 121-180.

Under cognomen:

Aurelianus, Lucius Domitius, *Emperor of Rome*, d. 275.
Severus, Lucius Septimius, *Emperor of Rome*, 146-211.
Trajanus, *Emperor of Rome*, 53-117.

Under nickname:

Caligula, *Emperor of Rome*, 12-41.
Caracalla, *Emperor of Rome*, 186-217.

Refer from parts of name not used as entry word.
B. Enter Roman emperors of the East under forename in the Latin form followed by name of family or dynasty, or (before family names came into use) by any epithet or descriptive appellative by which the emperor is known. (Cf. 59.) Refer from family name.
Emperors having the same forename are distinguished by a numeral

which immediately follows the forename and precedes the family name or epithet as the case may be.

> **Constantinus III,** *Emperor of the East, d. 641.*
> **Leo III,** *the Isaurian, Emperor of the East, ca. 680-ca. 740.*
> **Leo VI,** *the Wise, Emperor of the East, 865-911.*
> **Joannes I Zimiskes,** *Emperor of the East, d. 976.*
>> *Refer from*
>> Zimiskes, Joannes.
>
> **Joannes II Comnenus,** *Emperor of the East, 1088-1143.*
>> *Refer from*
>> Comnenus, Joannes.
>
> **Joannes VI Cantacuzenus,** *Emperor of the East, d. 1383.*
>> *Refer from*
>> Cantacuzenus, Joannes.

C. Enter Mohammedan sovereigns under their given names only, transliterated from the original.

> **Hārūn al-Rashīd,** *Caliph, 763 (ca.)-809.*
> **'Abd al-Majīd,** *Sultan of the Turks, 1823-1861.*
> **'Abbās I,** *the Great, Shah of Persia, 1571-1629.*
> **Sulaimān I,** *the Magnificent, Sultan of the Turks, 1494-1566.*

When necessary for identification, add the sovereign's patronymic compounded with the word "ibn," i.e., "son of."

> **'Alī ibn Abī Ṭālib,** *Caliph, 600 (ca.)-661.*
> **'Uthmān ibn Affān,** *Caliph.*

Prefer the European form of name for Mohammedan sovereigns who have become widely known in European literature under a form of name differing from the native form.

> **Saladin,** *Sultan of Egypt and Syria, 1137-1193.*
>> *Refer from*
>> Salāh al-Dīn Yūsuf ibn Aiyūb, *Sultan of Egypt and Syria.*
>
> **Selim I,** *Sultan of the Turks, ca. 1465-1520.*
>> *Refer from*
>> Salīm I, *Sultan of the Turks.*

D. Enter Chinese emperors, with the exception of those of the Ming and Ch'ing dynasties, under the name of the dynasty followed by the temple-name (commonly known as dynastic title), which was given posthumously. In all cases refer from reign-titles and personal names of the emperors. The name of the dynasty is not to be separated from the temple-name, or the reign-title, by a comma. The two words which form, in each case, the temple-name and the reign-title are to be hyphenated and the first only is to be capitalized.

> **T'ang Hsüan-tsung,** *Emperor of China, 685-762.*
>> *Refer from*
>> T'ang K'ai-yüan. ⟦*name of dynasty and reign-title*⟧
>> T'ang T'ien-pao. ⟦*name of dynasty and reign-title*⟧
>> Li, Lung-chi. ⟦*personal name*⟧

104

Hsüan-tsung.	[temple-name]
Ming-huang.	[alternate temple-name]
K'ai-yüan.	[reign-title]
T'ien-pao.	[reign-title]

Enter Ming and Ch'ing emperors, who are better known by their reign-titles, under reign-titles only, not preceded by name of the dynasty. Refer from their temple-names as well as from their personal names.

Hung-wu, *Emperor of China*, 1328-1398.
  Refer from

Ming T'ai-tsu.	[name of dynasty and temple-name]
Ming Hung-wu.	[name of dynasty and reign-title]
Chu, Yüan-chang.	[personal name]
T'ai-tsu.	[temple-name]

K'ang-hsi, *Emperor of China*, 1654-1723.
  Refer from

Ch'ing Shêng-tsu.	[name of dynasty and temple-name]
Ch'ing K'ang-hsi.	[name of dynasty and reign-title]
Hsüan-yeh.	[personal name]
Shêng-tsu.	[temple-name]

E. Enter presidents or other chief executives officially known by their surnames under the surname, and add the designation of their office.

Jefferson, Thomas, *Pres. U. S.,* 1743-1826.
Masaryk, Tomáš Garrigue, *Pres. Czechoslovak Republic,* 1850-1937.
Fonseca, Hermes Rodrigues da, *Pres. Brazil,* 1855-1923.

Edicts, proclamations, etc., emanating from a ruler in the exercise of his official duties are considered government publications and are entered under the country. (Cf. 73.) Correlate the two types of entry by references.

Charles II, *King of Great Britain,* 1630-1685.
  with references to and from
Gt. Brit. *Sovereigns, etc., 1660-1685 (Charles II)*

Laws and edicts and ordinances having the force of laws are to be entered under country with the subheading LAWS, STATUTES, ETC. (Cf. 84.)

56. Princes of the blood.

In general, enter members of the immediate families of sovereigns under forename (for members of Russian royal families, include patronymic) and refer from title; but enter under title those who are decidedly better known by that designation. (Cf. 41A (1), 43.)

Eulalia, *Infanta of Spain,* 1864-
Carlos, *Prince of Asturias,* 1545-1568.
  Refer from
Asturias, Carlos, *Principe* de.

Philippe, *count of Flanders,* 1837-1905.
> *Refer from*
> Flandre, Philippe, *comte* de.

George, *duke of Kent,* 1902-1942.
> *Refer from*
> Kent, George, *duke* of.

Kirill Vladimirovich, *grand duke of Russia,* 1876-1938.
> *Refer from*
> Cyril, *grand duke of Russia.*

Yasuhito, *Prince Chichibu,* 1902–
> *Refer from*
> Chichibu-no-miya.

but

Orléans, Philippe I, *duc* **d'**, 1640-1701.
> *with reference from*
> Philippe ɪ, *duke of Orleans.*

Members of mediatized families are entered under the family name (title).

Wied-Neuwied, Maximilian Alexander Philipp, *Prinz* **von,** 1782-1867.

57. Noblemen.

Enter a nobleman under his latest title unless he is decidedly better known by an earlier title or by the family name.[22] In either case refer from the name not adopted as entry word.

A. The form of entry for English nobility is shown in the following examples:

Duke: **Wellington, Arthur Wellesley,** *1st duke of,* 1769-1852.
> *Refer from*
> Wellesley, Arthur, *1st duke of Wellington.*

Marquis: **Queensberry, John Sholto Douglas,** *8th marquis of,* 1844-1900.
> *Refer from*
> Douglas, John Sholto, *8th marquis of Queensberry.*

Earl: **Chesterfield, Philip Dormer Stanhope,** *4th earl of,* 1694-1793.
> *Refer from*
> Stanhope, Philip Dormer, *4th earl of Chesterfield.*

Viscount: **Grey of Falloden, Edward Grey,** *1st viscount,* 1862-1933.
> *Refer from*
> Grey, Edward, *1st viscount Grey of Falloden.*

Baron: **Lytton, Edward George Earle Lytton Bulwer-Lytton,** *baron,* 1803-1873.
> *Refer from*
> Bulwer-Lytton, Edward George Earle Lytton, *baron Lytton.*

Baronet: **Scott,** *Sir* **Walter,** *bart.,* 1771-1832.

---

[22] Exceptions in favor of entry under better-known family name:
Bacon, Francis, *viscount St. Albans,* 1561-1626.
Walpole, Horace, *4th earl of Orford,* 1717-1797.
Sousa Coutinho, Rodrigo de, *conde de Linhares,* 1745-1812.

Knight: **Landseer,** *Sir* **Edwin Henry,** 1802-1873.
Dame: **Campbell,** *Dame* **Janet Mary.**
Lord:
   [*Courtesy title of younger son of a duke or marquis*]
Gordon, *Lord* **George,** 1751-1783.
Lady:
   [*Courtesy title of the daughter of a duke, marquis or earl*]
Stanhope, *Lady* **Hester Lucy,** 1776-1839.
Honorable:
   [*Courtesy title of younger sons of an earl and sons and daughters*
   of a viscount or baron; the title honorable is also given to a maid
   of honor to a queen]
Keppel, *Hon.* **Arnold Joost William,** 1884-
Russell, *Hon.* **Harriet.**
Right honorable:
   [*This title which belongs of right to all peers is never used by them*
   except on bills or legal official documents. It is the prerogative
   of members of the Privy Council and is borne by those of them
   who are not peers, and by cabinet ministers. It is not used in the
   heading of a catalog entry]
   (cf. Brit. Mus. Rules. 1936. 14; Cutter, 214; Eclectic card catalog
   rules, 446-452; Enc. Brit. 14th ed.)

(1) The titles of address *Lord* and *Lady* are commonly applied to all members of the English peerage except dukes and duchesses. In the heading the appropriate title is substituted, e.g., Lord Macaulay becomes:

Macaulay, Thomas Babington Macaulay, *baron,* 1800-1859.

(2) Enter judges of the Court of Sessions of Scotland who bear the title *Lord,* followed by a family or territorial name, under the title with the designation Lord following instead of preceding the forename as in the case of the courtesy title *Lord.* Refer from family name when it differs from the title.

If a judge bears a nobility title as well as a law title, prefer entry under the nobility title, especially if it is hereditary, unless he is generally known by the law title.

Kames, Henry Home, *Lord,* 1696-1782.
   Refer from
  Home, Henry, *Lord Kames.*
Guthrie, Charles John Guthrie, *Lord,* 1849-1920.
Grant, *Sir* **Francis,** *bart.,* 1658-1726.
   Refer from
  Cullen, Francis Grant, *Lord.*

(3) The wife of a peer takes the title corresponding to that of her husband, i.e., *duchess, marchioness, countess, viscountess, baroness.*

Devonshire, Georgiana (Spencer) Cavendish, *duchess of,* 1757-1806.

(4) The wife of a baronet or knight has the title *Lady.* Whether this title precedes or follows her forename in the heading depends upon whether she is entitled to it in virtue of her father's rank or whether she acquired it through marriage.

Montagu, *Lady* **Mary (Pierrepont) Wortley,** 1689-1762.
[*Daughter of a duke*]
Duff-Gordon, Lucie (Austin) *Lady,* 1821-1869.
[*Title by marriage*]

(5) The daughter of a viscount or baron married to a baronet or knight keeps her own title and adds the title *Lady.*

Acland, *Hon.* **Anna Emily,** *Lady.*

If her husband has no title, she retains the title *Hon.*

Douglas-Hamilton, *Hon.* **Agnes Rosamund (Bateman-Hanbury)**

(6) The wife of a younger son of a duke or marquis without title in her own right becomes, e.g.,

Campbell, Elizabeth (McNeil) *Lady John Campbell.*

(7) The wife of the younger son of an earl, or of the son of a viscount or baron without title in her own right becomes *Hon. Mrs.,* e.g.,

Montague, Margaret (Wilson) *Hon. Mrs. Charles Montague.*

(8) A maid of honor retains her title after her service has ceased or after marriage unless merged in a higher title.

Grant, *Hon.* **Margaret (Dawnay)**

Do not use the numeral in the entry for a baronet, nor usually for a baron, unless it has some special importance.

B. Titled persons of other countries are treated in the same way as far as possible. In many instances, as in England below the peerage, the title is simply an epithet indicating varying degrees of rank. In such cases entry is of course under the family name. (Cf. 41A.)

Cavour, Camillo Benso, *conte di,* 1810-1861.
Alba, Fernando Alvarez de Toledo, *duque de,* 1508-1582.
Egloffstein, Hermann, *Freiherr von und zu,* 1861-
Mises, Ludwig, *Edler von,* 1881-
Tolstoĭ, Lev Nikolaevich, *graf,* 1828-1910.
Åkerhielm, Anna Vilhelmina Elisabeth (Quiding) *friherinna,* 1869-
Hatvany, Lajos, *báró,* 1880-
Csoma, Sándor, *kőrösi,* 1784-1842.[23]
Tokugawa, Yoshitoshi, *baron,* 1884-
Tokugawa, Ieyasu, *shogun,* 1542-1616.

---

[23] In the lower ranks of Hungarian nobility a title consisting of an adjectival term derived from place of origin, family estate, or, sometimes a fictitious geographical location, often precedes the family name, the combination having the appearance of a compound name and being so treated in some reference books. In such cases enter under the family name with reference from title followed by family name. Cf. *Instruktionen für die alphabetischen Kataloge der preuszischen Bibliotheken* (2d ed.; Berlin, Behrend, 1915 [Manuldruck 1934]) ¶119.

    Csoma, Sándor, *kőrösi,* 1784-1842.
      Refer from
      Kőrösi Csoma, Sándor.
    Nagy, Pál, *felső-büki,* 1777-1857.
      Refer from
      Felső-büki Nagy, Pál.

C. Use a papal title as entry word only if the title coincides with the family name, e.g., **Loubat, Joseph Florimond,** *duc* **de.** However, add the title in the heading if helpful to distinguish the individual, e.g., **Morone, Girolamo,** *duc di Bovino.*

Ancient and Medieval Writers

58. Ancient Greek writers.

Enter ancient Greek authors under the Latin form of their names and refer from the English and Greek forms. In selecting the proper entry word follow the practice of the classical dictionaries.[24]

Homerus.
  Refer from
  Homer.

Aeschylus.
  Refer from
  Aischylos.
  Eschylus.

Aristides, Aelius.
  Refer from
  Aelius Aristides.

Cassius Dio Cocceianus.
  Refer from
  Dio Cocceianus.
  Dion Cassius Cocceianus.

59. Byzantine writers.

Enter Byzantine authors under personal name or byname, depending upon which has become prevalent in literary and historical usage. Absolute uniformity in treatment is not practicable. For doubtful entries follow Krumbacher,[25] using the Latin form for names prior to 1450. Later names, especially where entry is under family name with forenames added, are best given in the Greek transliterated form. Refer from part of name not chosen as entry word and from variant forms of name.

Acropolita, Georgius.
  Refer from
  Georgius Acropolita.

Comnena, Anna, b. 1083.
  Refer from
  Anna Comnena.
  Komnena, Anna.

Georgius Syncellus, *fl.* 800.
  Refer from
  Syncellus, Georgius.

Georgius Trapezuntius, *d.* 1484.
  Refer from
  George, *of Trebizond.*
  Trebizond, George of.
  Trapezuntius, Georgius.

For Roman emperors of the East see 55B.

---

[24] For a guide to the form of entry for ancient Greek authors, see U. S. Library of Congress, Classification Division, *Classification. Class P. P-PA* (Washington, Govt. Print. Off., 1928), PA 3818—PA 4500: Greek literature. Individual authors to 700 A.D.; *also* List of authorities, *ibid.*, p. 426-427.

[25] Karl Krumbacher, "Register der Personen und Sachen," in his *Geschichte der byzantinischen Litteratur* (2d ed.) "Handbuch der klassischen Altertumswissenschaft," 9. Bd., 1. Abt. (München, Beck, 1897), p. 1153-1193.

60. Classical Latin writers.[26]

Enter Latin authors under the original Latin form of the name. Refer from variant Latin spellings and from the English form if it differs from the original.

Enter under the name by which the author is best known and most frequently cited in standard classical dictionaries.[27]

Under nomen:

> **Lucretius Carus, Titus.**
> **Terentius Afer, Publius.**

Under cognomen:

> **Cicero, Marcus Tullius.**
> **Varro, Marcus Terentius.**
> **Scipio Africanus major, Publius Cornelius.**
> **Scipio Aemilianus Africanus minor, Publius Cornelius.**

Under agnomen:

> **Columella, Lucius Junius Moderatus.**

Under praenomen:

> **Tiberius,** *Emperor of Rome,* 42 B.C.–37 A.D.

When it is doubtful which of two names has been preferred as entry word by the best authorities, enter under the first and refer from the second.

> **Martianus Capella.**
> *Refer from*
> Capella, Martianus.
> **Vergilius Maro, Publius.**
> *Refer from*
> Virgilius Maro, Publius.
> Virgil.

For Roman emperors of the West see 55A.

61. Medieval writers.

Enter medieval authors under the given name, favoring the Latin form in case of doubt for names prior to 1400.[28] Include in the head-

---

[26] Every freeborn Roman citizen had three names, *praenomen, nomen,* and *cognomen.* To these was sometimes added an *agnomen,* occasionally more than one. The second name (nomen) distinguished one gens from another; the third name (cognomen) distinguished one family from another; the first name (praenomen) distinguished members of the same family from each other; the additional name (agnomen) was given ordinarily in allusion to some achievement but might have various significations, e.g., adoption from one gens into another, some moral or physical characteristic, etc., and the individual may be known in literature and history by any one of these names or by all of them.

[27] For a guide to the best form of heading for Latin authors, see U. S. Library of Congress, Classification Division, *Classification. Class P. P-PA.* (Washington, Govt. Print. Off., 1928), PA 6202—PA 6971: Latin literature to *ca.* 700 A.D. Individual authors; *also* List of authorities, *ibid.,* p. 426–427.

[28] E.g., where both Joannes and Johannes are found in reference works, prefer Joannes; similarly prefer Guilelmus to Gulielmus, Guliermus, etc.

ing any epithet or byname denoting place of origin, domicile, occupation, or distinguishing characteristic by which the individual is known. Refer from byname, variant forms of personal name, and any other names by which the author is known in literature and history.

Epithets or bynames when given as part of the name should be in the same language as the forename. A descriptive word or phrase added for the sake of identification is given preferably in English. (Cf. 43.)

> **Giovanni** *da Ravenna,* 1343-1408.
> *Refer from*
> Ravenna, Giovanni da, 1343-1408.
> Johannes *de Ravenna,* 1343-1408.
> John *of Ravenna,* 1343-1408.
> Giovanni *di Conversino.*
> **Conversino, Giovanni di.**
>
> **Guilelmus** *Arvernus, Bp. of Paris, d.* 1249.
> *Refer from*
> Arvernus, Guilelmus.
> Alvernus, Guilelmus.
> Auvergne, Guillaume d'.
> Gulielmus *Arvernus.*
> Guillaume *d'Auvergne.*
> Guillaume *de Paris.*
>
> **Joannes** *Braidensis, fl.* 1419.
> *Refer from*
> Braidensis, Joannes.
> Joannes *de Brera.*
> Brera, Joannes de.
>
> **Joannes** *de Garlandia, fl.* 1204-1229.
> *Refer from*
> Garlandia, Joannes de.
> Garland, John.
> John *of Garland.*
> Joannes *Grammaticus.*
>
> **Johannes** *von Holleschau,* 1366 (*ca.*)-1436.
> *Refer from*
> Holleschau, Johannes von.
>
> **John** *of Hexham, fl.* 1180.
> *Refer from*
> Hexham, John of.
> Joannes, *prior of Hexham.*
> Joannes *Hagustaldensis.*
> Hagustaldensis, Joannes.
>
> **Paulus** *Diaconus,* 720 (*ca.*)-797.
> *Refer from*
> Paulus *Casinensis.*
> Paulus *Levita.*
> Warnefrid, Paul, *son of.*
> Paulus *Warnefridus.*
> Warnefridus, Paulus, *diaconus.*
> Paul the *deacon.*
> Paulo *Diacono.*
>
> **Johannes,** *notary, fl.* 1334.

111

> **Burchardus,** *provost of Ursperg, d.* 1250.
> *Refer from*
> Burchardus *Urspergensis.*
>
> **Jan,** *of Nepomuk, Saint, 14th cent.*
> *Refer from*
> Nepomuk, Jan of, *Saint.*
> Nepomucky, Jan, *Saint.*
> Jan Nepomucky.
> Pomuk, John, *Saint.*
> John *of Nepomuk, Saint.*
> John *of Pomuk, Saint.*
>
> **Johannes,** *of Winterthur, fl.* 1348.
> *Refer from*
> Winterthur, Johannes von.
> Vitoduranus, Johannes.
> Duranus, Johannes Vito.
> Johannes *Vitoduranus.*

Exception is made in favor of entry under the byname if it is better known than the personal name, or has come to have the character of a modern surname.

> **Abailard, Pierre,** 1079-1142.
> *Refer from*
> Petrus *Abaelardus.*
> Abélard, Pierre.
> Abaelardus, Petrus.
>
> **Wolkenstein, Oswald von,** 1367-1445.
> *Refer from*
> Oswald *von Wolkenstein.*

62. Medieval, Renaissance and Reformation writers with classicized names.

Enter under the adopted form of name authors of the Middle Ages and the Renaissance and Reformation periods who have translated their names into one of the classic languages, or who, with or without reference to the original, have adopted a name Greek or Latin in form.

> **Agricola, Rudolf,** 1443-1485.
> *Refer from*
> Huisman, Roelof.
> Huysmann, Roelof.
>
> **Melanchthon, Philipp,** 1497-1560.
> *Refer from*
> Schwarzerd, Philipp.
> Schwartzerd, Philipp.
>
> **Naogeorgius, Thomas,** 1511-1563.
> *Refer from*
> Kirchmaier [*also* Kirchmair, Kirchmeyer] Thomas.
> Kirchbauer, Thomas.
> Neubauer, Thomas.
>
> **Œcolampadius, Joannes,** 1482-1531.
> *Refer from*
> Hausschein [*also* Heusgen, Husschin, Hussgen] Johann.
> Œkolampadius, Joannes.

> **Xylander, Wilhelm,** 1532-1576.
> *Refer from*
> Holtzmann, Wilhelm.

A. But enter under the original name when it has become so firmly established, through the author's own usage or otherwise, that he is known by that rather than by the adopted name.

> **Birck, Sixt,** 1500-1554.
> *Refer from*
> Betulius, Xystus.
> Bircken, Sixtus von.
> **Reuchlin, Johann,** 1455-1522.
> *Refer from*
> Capnion, Johannes.
> Kapnion, Johannes.

In either case refer from the form of name not chosen as entry word.

B. Medieval family names translated into Latin in the genitive form retain the genitive form when it indicates father's surname or occupation from which the surname is derived.[29]

> **Fabri, Felix,** 1441?-1502.
> [*Father's name, or occupation, Schmid*]
> **Institoris, Henricus,** d. 1508.
> [*Father's name, or occupation, Krämer*]
> **Molitoris, Johannes,** fl. 1480.
> [*Father's name, or occupation, Müller*]

63. Post-Reformation and modern writers with classicized names.

Enter post-Reformation and modern writers whose names are found both in a Latin form and in the vernacular under the Latin form whenever this is decidedly better known. Refer from the vernacular.

> **Grotius, Hugo,** 1583-1645.
> *Refer from*
> Groot, Hugo de.
>
> *but*
>
> **Ritschl, Friedrich Wilhelm,** 1806-1876.
> *Refer from*
> Ritschelius, Fridericus.

Oriental Names

64. Arabic names.

Enter Arabic, Persian, and Turkish writers, up to about the year 1900, living in Mohammedan countries and writing only, or predominantly, in their native tongues, under the given name compounded with the patronymic (the latter preceded by the word "ibn," i.e., "son of"; in rare cases "akhū," i.e., "brother of") as well as with the surname

---

[29] Cf. *Basler Chroniken,* I (Leipzig, 1872), p. 241, note 2.

and nickname, usually derived from place of birth or residence (*nisbah*), occupation, physical peculiarities, etc.

> **Muḥammad ibn Yūsuf, Abū ʿUmar,** *al-Kindī,* 897-961.
> *Refer from*
> Abū ʿUmar Muḥammad ibn Yūsuf, *al-Kindī.*
> al-Kindī, Abū ʿUmar Muḥammad ibn Yūsuf.
>
> **Muḥammad ibn Walīd,** *al-Ṭurṭūshī, called* **Ibn al-Rundaḳah,** *ca.* 1059-*ca.* 1126.
> *Refer from*
> al-Ṭurṭūshī, Muḥammad ibn Walīd, *called* Ibn al-Rundaḳah.
> Abū Bakr Muḥammad ibn Walīd, *al-Ṭurṭūshī.*
> Abū Bakr *al-Ṭurṭūshī.*
> Abubéquer *de Tortosa.*
> Ibn al-Rundaḳah, Muḥammad ibn Walīd, *al-Ṭurṭūshī.*
> Ibn Abī Randaqa.
> Abenadirandaca.

A. Distinguish with care cases where "ibn" and "abū" indicate patronymics and honorifics, from other cases where these words are merely integral parts of given names and nicknames.

> **Abū Bakr ibn al-Ṭufail, Abū Jaʿfar,** *al-Ishbīlī, d.* 1185.
> [*In this case "abū" in Abū Bakr is an integral part of a given name*]
> **Abū al-Fidāʾ,** 1273-1345.
> [*In this case "abū" is an integral part of a nickname*]
> **Ibn al-Athīr,** 1160-1234.
> [*In this case "ibn" is an integral part of a surname*]

B. Exception is made in favor of entry under another part of the name when an author of great prominence has become generally known under his honorific name, surname, nickname, etc.

> **al-Ghazzālī,** 1058-1111.
> *Refer from*
> Muḥammad ibn Muḥammad, *al-Ghazzālī.*
> Algazel.
> Algazzali.
> al-Gazzālī.
>
> **Abū al-ʿAlaʾ.**
> *Refer from*
> Aḥmad ibn ʿAbd Allāh, Abū al-ʿAlāʾ, *al-Maʿarrī.*
> al-Maʿarrī, Abū al-ʿAlāʾ Aḥmad ibn ʿAbd Allāh.

C. Enter writers of the Middle Ages, whose works have been translated into Latin and were widely read in Western Europe, under the Latin form of their name.

> **Avicenna,** 980?-1037.
> *Refer from*
> al-Ḥusain ibn ʿAbd Allāh, Abū ʿAlī, *called* Ibn Sīnā.
> Abū ʿAlī al-Ḥusain ibn ʿAbd Allāh, *called* Ibn Sīnā.
> Ibn Sīnā, Abū ʿAlī al-Ḥusain ibn ʿAbd Allāh.
>
> **Averroës,** 1126-1198.
> *Refer from*
> Muḥammad ibn Aḥmad, Abū al-Walīd, *called* Ibn Rushd.

Abū al-Walīd Muḥammad ibn Aḥmad, *called* Ibn Rushd.
Ibn Rushd, Abū al-Walīd Muḥammad ibn Aḥmad, *called*.

D. Enter modern (after 1900)[30] Mohammedan writers under such shortened forms of name as they habitually use, surname, followed by forename, providing, of course, that the second element of the name is really a family name and not merely an additional name.

Naṣr, Yūsuf.
Khūri, Shukrī.

E. Enter modern Turkish writers under the family name,[31] when known, and refer from the other names.

Baltacioğlu, İsmail Hakkı.
Refer from
İsmail Hakkı Baltacioğlu.
Hakkı Baltacioğlu, İsmail.

Prior to the adoption of family names, Turkish names ordinarily consisted either of a personal name or a personal name in combination with a distinguishing name (epithet, nickname, name denoting locality of author's birth or residence, etc.). When it is impossible to learn the family name, enter under the distinguishing name whenever one is used, otherwise under personal name. Refer from the personal name if it is not the entry.

Kamil, Mehmet.
Refer from
Mehmet Kamil.

F. Enter Arabic names of modern writers who write both in their native tongue and in a European language, under the European form or name if it differs considerably, for filing purposes, from the oriental form.

Gibran, Kahlil, 1883-1931.
Refer from
Jibrān, Kahlīl.

G. The Arabic article "al"[32] (used also in Persian, Turkish, and other names) is not capitalized, even when it stands at the beginning of an entry. The article "al" should always be written out in full, notwithstanding that in actual pronunciation the "a" is elided under

---

[30] "In modern Syria and Egypt, among both Christians and Moslems, a *family* name now exists. This may originally have been the given name of a prominent ancestor, or it arose out of the trade or profession of an ancestor, e.g., Haddād (=Smith), hence *nisbahs* often become family names in which case the article is frequently dropped." —A. A. Brux, "The treatment of Arabic proper names," *American journal of Semitic languages and literatures,* v. 47 (1930), no. 1, pt. 2, p. 199 note.
Since 1921, family names have been required in Iran.
[31] A Turkish ordinance of Dec. 14, 1934, decreed that the head of every family, between the dates of Jan. 2, 1935, and July 2, 1936, was to select a name and register it as a surname of the family. Cf. *Resmi gazete,* par. 2891, Dec. 27, 1934, p. 4589-4591.
[32] In some transliterations written "el" or "ul."

the influence of a preceding vowel, and the "l" is assimilated with certain following consonants. In filing, disregard the article when it occurs initially.

> **Abū al-'Alā'** *not* Abū'l-'Alā'.
> **Abū al-Fidā'** *not* Abū'l-Fidā'.
> **Muḥammad ibn Zakarīyā, Abū Bakr,** *al-Rāzī,* not *ar-Rāzī.*
> **al-Ghazzālī** *not* Al-Ghazzālī.

H. Give Arabic given names of Biblical origin in their native form, e.g., Yūsuf, not Joseph; Mūsā, not Moses; Ibrāhīm, not Abraham. The same rule applies to Arabic names borrowed from the Greek, Latin, etc., e.g., Jirjīs, not Georgius; Buṭrūs, not Petrus.

65. Hebrew names.

A. Enter Hebrew and Yiddish writers, up to about the year 1800, under the given name compounded with the patronymic, the latter preceded by the word "ben," i.e., "son of." This may be followed by any other designation referring to place of birth, residence, rank, etc.

> **Abraham ben Joseph,** *ha-Levi, of Cracow.*
> **Judah ben Jehiel,** *called* **Messer Leon,** *fl.* 1470.
> > *Refer from*
> > Leon, *Messer.*
> > Messer Leon.
> > Jehuda ben Jechiel, *called* Messer Leon.

Exceptions are to be made where writers are best known under their surname.

> **Abravanel, Isaac,** 1437-1508.
> > *Refer from*
> > Isaac ben Judah Abravanel.
> **Zacuto, Abraham ben Samuel,** *b. ca.* 1450.
> > *Refer from*
> > Zacuth, Abraham ben Samuel.
> > Abraham ben Samuel Zacuto.

(1) If a writer is known by an initialism, i.e., a combination of the initials of his personal names and appellatives, refer from this initialism. It is to be written in capitals with the auxiliary letters in lower case.[33]

> **Isaac ben Sheshet,** 1326-1408.
> > *Refer from*
> > Barfat, Isaac ben Sheshet.
> > Perfet, Isaac ben Sheshet.
> > RIBaSH.

If the initialism is as well known as the name, it may be added to the heading with the word CALLED.

---

[33] This is the practice of the Jewish encyclopedia, not always followed by other works of reference.

> **Solomon ben Isaac,** *called* **RaSHI,** 1040-1105.
> *Refer from*
> RaSHI.

(2) The Hebrew article should always be written "ha-" or "he-," and should never be capitalized. It is to be disregarded in filing when it occurs initially.

> **Judah,** *ha-Levi, fl. 12th cent.*
> *Refer from*
> ha-Levi, Judah.

(3) Hebrew authors writing both in Hebrew and Arabic or Persian should be entered under the Hebrew form of name, if known.

> **Japheth ben Eli,** *the Karaite.*
> *Refer from*
> Yāfith ibn Alī, *the Karaite.*
> Abū Alī Jephet.
> Jephet ibn Alī.
>
> **Moses ben Maimon,** 1135-1204.
> *Refer from*
> Maimonides.
> Mūsā ibn Maimūn, Abū Imrān.
> RaMBaM.

(4) In the case of Arabic surnames and nicknames, the rules given for Mohammedan names should be observed, and the Arabic article "al-" should be so written and not capitalized.

> **al-Ḥarīzī, Judah ben Solomon,** *d.* 1235.
> *Refer from*
> Alharizi, Judah ben Solomon.
> Judah ben Solomon al-Ḥarīzī.
> Juda Alcharisi ben Salomo.
> Charisi, Jehuda ben Salomo.
> Jehuda ben Salomon ben Charizi.
> Judah ben Solomon Charizi.

(5) Exceptions, however, may be made where a surname, though originally Arabic, has been spelled generally in the Hebrew manner.

> **Alshech, Moses.**
> *Refer from*
> al-Shaikh, Moses.
> Moses Alshech.

(6) For Hebrew writers before 1800, given names of Biblical origin are to be spelled in the form in which they are given in the Authorized version. Other Hebrew names are to be faithfully transliterated from the original, e.g., Yom-Tob, Hayyim.

B. Enter Hebrew writers after 1800 under the surname. If the given name is of Biblical origin, but the bearer consistently uses a Hebrew or Yiddish form, his usage is to be preferred to the form in the Authorized version.

Shunami, Shlomo *not* Solomon.
Nadir, Isaac Moishe *not* Moses.

(1) Enter writers who use a Jewish given name for their Hebrew or Yiddish works, and a non-Jewish name for their writings in other languages, under the given name by which they are best known, preferring the Jewish form in case of doubt. Refer from the name not used.

> **Berliner, Abraham,** 1833-1915.
> *Refer from*
> Berliner, Adolf.
> **Rogoff, Hillel,** 1882-
> *Refer from*
> Rogoff, Harry.
> **Jellinek, Adolf,** 1821-1893.
> *Refer from*
> Jellinek, Aaron.

(2) For Jews who have settled in Palestine and have adopted Hebrew names there, use the adopted form, and refer from the original name.

> **Ibn-Sahav, Ari,** 1899-
> *Refer from*
> Goldstein, Leo.

But enter an author under his original name if most of his works have appeared under that name and he is so known in literature and history.

66. Japanese names.

Enter Japanese writers under the family name followed by the given name as in the case of western writers.[34]

> **Miyoshi, Kiyotsura,** 847-918.
> **Noguchi, Hideyo,** 1876-1928.

Exception is made in favor of entry under pseudonym, nickname, or other assumed name when such name has become more firmly established in literature and history than the real name.

> **Jippensha Ikku,** 1775?-1831.
> [*Here the "literary name," a phrase, is the one by which this artist and writer is best known*]
> *Refer from*

---

[34] The application of the rule to modern Japanese names is comparatively simple since, by a law promulgated in 1870, each person is required to have a surname and a forename. Before that time, however, family names were borne only by court nobles, the military class, and specially privileged members of the lower classes. Others were restricted to personal names, or personal names combined with place or trade names. Names were frequently changed and pseudonyms were freely used by writers, actors, artists, etc. These pseudonyms were often passed on to a favorite pupil and a new pseudonym adopted. Noguchi Yonejiro in his book, *Katsushika Hokusai,* lists 53 pseudonyms used by the artist best known to the western world as Hokusai. These earlier names must in many cases, be established each on its own merits, with the aid of the best authorities available.

Shigeta, Teiichi.
[his legal name]
Chikamatsu, Yoshichi.
[the name he assumed as a playwright]
Hokusai, 1760-1849.
Refer from
Katsushika, Iitsu.
[his legal name]
Katsushika, Hokusai.
Katsukawa, Shunro.
Hishikawa, Sori.
[These are the better-known forms of name by which Hokusai was known. Reference may be made from other names if desired]

67. Chinese names.

Enter a Chinese writer under the family name, separated from the given names by a comma. The given names are hyphenated and the first only is capitalized.

Chinese surnames date from approximately 3000 B.C. As among other peoples with whom surnames were a later development, they were derived from place of origin, or domicile, occupation, hereditary title, etc.

Every Chinese rightfully has three names, a family name and two given names. Of these given names, the first, as a rule, indicates the generation and is common to all members of a family belonging to the same generation. The second is the personal name. Each individual may have also one or more courtesy names selected by himself or given to him by another. He may, in addition, have one or more pseudonyms and in some cases a posthumous appellative.[35]

Wang, An-shih, 1021-1086.
Li, Shao-kêng, 1897-

The courtesy name is not used officially and does not appear in the heading except occasionally in the case of distinguished personages who have come to be generally known by that name rather than by their real name, in which case it takes the place of the given names, and reference is made from any other names, real or assumed, by which the person is known. For entry of Chinese emperors see 55D.

Sun, Yat-sen, 1866-1925.
Refer from
Sun, Wên.
Sun, Chung-shan.
Sun, I-hsien.
[Yat-sen (or, I-hsien) the name by which he is best known, assumed by him while in college; Wên, a name, also assumed later in life, which he used for official purposes; Chung-shan, the Chinese equivalent of Nayakami, a name he assumed while living in disguise in Japan, and which became his posthumous appellative. His given names, variously cited as Tai Chu, Tai Cheong, Tai Tseung, were not used by him after his boyhood]

[35] Cf. Kiang Kang-hu, *On Chinese studies* (Shanghai, Commercial Press, 1934); *Encyclopaedia sinica* (Shanghai, Kelly & Walsh, 1917); British Museum. Dept. of Oriental Printed Books, *Catalogue of Chinese printed books* (London, Longmans, 1877). As authority for Chinese surnames, cf. H. A. Giles, "A list of Chinese surnames," in his *A Chinese-English dictionary* (2d ed.; Shanghai, Kelly & Walsh, 1912), v. 1, tables, p. 1-8.

Kiang, Kang-hu, 1883–
   Refer from
Kiang, Shao-ch'üan.
Chiang, K'ang-hu.
   [*Kang-hu, courtesy name selected by himself and used on the
     title-pages of his later works; Shao, generation name; Ch'üan,
     personal name*]

The names should, as far as possible, be given in the standard romanization, including indication of aspiration ('), of the Wade system (used by Giles in his Chinese-English dictionary) with reference from any variant forms (including non-Chinese names).

Chang, Chung-lin.
   Refer from
Tchang, Tchung-lin.
Lin, Ch'i-hung, 1889–
   Refer from
Lynn, Jermyn Chi-hung.

A. On the title pages of western publications, Chinese names sometimes occur in the normal Chinese order, i.e., family name followed by given names, and sometimes in the western order. If there is any doubt as to which part of the name is the family name, refer from the part not used as entry word.

Ma, Hêng, 1880–
   The fifteen different classes of measures as given in the Lü li
   chih of the Sui dynasty, by Ma Hêng . . .
      Refer from
   Hêng, Ma.
Fêng, Han-chi, 1902–
   The Chinese kinship system . . . [by] Han Yi Fêng . . .
      Refer from
   Fêng, Han-yi.
   Han Yi Fêng.

B. Chinese names for which particular forms have become firmly established in western literature are to be entered under these forms with reference from the original.

Confucius.
   Refer from
Kong-Kew.
Kung Fu-tze.
K'ung, Ch'iu.

68. Annamese names.[36]
   Enter Annamese writers under their names, in full, without inversion, in the normal Annamese order. Connect the three names by hyphens and lower case the middle word, or name. Refer from the

---

[36] For an explanation of Annamese names, the following works may be consulted: Tran-van-Trai, *La famille patriarcale annamite* (Paris, 1942), p. [276]-281; *Variétés tonkinoises* (Hanoi, 1903), p. 122-123.

third name. Enter under the first name and refer from the second when the name consists of only two words.

Usually Annamese names consist of three characters, or words, with the family, or clan, name given first. The second name is an intercalary word indicating sex, place in family (i.e., third son, second daughter); rank (i.e., duke (*cong*), baron (*ba*)), etc. The third word is the given name.

Among the most common family names are Nguyen, Tran, Le, Ly, Pham, Phan, Lam, and Luong. Of the intercalary words the two denoting sex are the most commonly used (i.e., *van* for the males and *thi* for the females). Of the given names those most frequently used are Vang, Ngoc, Nga, Cuc, and Huong.

> **Tran-van-Trai.**
> *Refer from*
> Trai, Tran-van-
>
> **Nguyen-xuan-Nguyen.**
> *Refer from*
> Nguyen, Nguyen-xuan-
>
> **Do-Than.**
> *Refer from*
> Than, Do-

69. Burmese and Karen names.

A. Enter **Burmese** writers under their names in full, without inversion, in the normal Burmese order, followed by the term of address.

Burmese do not have family names. Their names consist of one, two, or in some rare cases, three words, preceded by a term of address or a title. The term of address is inseparable from the name and must be retained. For Burmese men the terms of address are *Maung* (abbr. *Mg.* or *M.*), *Ko* or *U*—the latter being used to designate men of prominence, high social position, professional standing, or age. For the women the terms of address are *Ma* or *Daw*—the latter corresponding in meaning to *U*. In some cases the term of address may be a word which is identical with one of the words constituting the name. Reference should always be made from parts of name not used as the entry word.

> **On Kin,** *U.*
> *Refer from*
> Kin, U On.
> Kin, On.
> U On Kin.
>
> **Ba U,** *U.*
> *Refer from*
> U, U Ba.
> U Ba U.
>
> **U Shan Maung,** *Maung.*
> *Refer from*
> Maung, Maung U Shan.
> Maung U Shan Maung.

> **Mya Sein,** *Daw.*
> *Refer from*
> Sein, Daw Mya.
> Daw Mya Sein.

B. Enter under the latest form of name, with reference from the other names, a Burmese who has changed his name, either completely, or by adding parts to a former name. This change of name, permissible in Burma, seldom occurs after a writer has become well known. The new name is *not* a pseudonym, it becomes the real name of the writer.

> **Pe Maung,** *Maung.*   ₍*name used to about 1911*₎
> **Tin,** *Maung.*   ₍*name used between 1911 and 1921*₎
> **Pe Maung Tin,** *U.*   ₍*name used since about 1921*₎

C. Enter under the name, or names, in full, without inversion, in the normal Burmese order, followed by the title, those Burmese in the professional groups or those holding high government positions, who have titles added to their names. In some cases the title is substituted for the term of address; in others both are retained. Refer from the parts not used as entry word. The most common of these titles include: *saya* (a man skilled in any art or science), *sayadaw* (a Buddhist monk of rank), *bhikkhu* (a Buddhist mendicant) and *thakin* (a member of the Thakin political party).

> **Silacara,** *bhikkhu.*
> *Refer from*
> Bhikkhu Silacara.
> **Sakkapala,** *sayadaw U.*
> *Refer from*
> U Sakkapala, *sayadaw.*
> Sayadaw U Sakkapala.
> **Po E,** *saya U.*
> *Refer from*
> U Po E, *saya.*
> Saya U Po E.
> E, Saya U Po.
> E, Po.

D. Enter **Karen** names in the same manner as Burmese, since they follow the same general pattern as Burmese names, and refer from parts not used as entry word. Karen names differ, however, from Burmese in that there is only one term of address for the men (i.e., *Saw*) and one for the women (i.e., *Naw*). Care should be exercised not to confuse *Saw*, the Karen term of address (corresponding to Burmese *U*) with the *Saw* used as part of a Burmese name.

> **Pwa Sein,** *Naw.*
> *Refer from*
> Sein, Naw Pwa.
> Naw Pwa Sein.
> Sein, Pwa.
> **Chit Maung,** *Saw.* ₍*Karen name*₎
> *Refer from*

Maung, Saw Chit.
Saw Chit Maung.
Maung, Chit.

Saw, U. [*Burmese name*]
Refer from
U Saw.

Enter under the names, in full, without inversion, in the normal Karen order, with references from parts not used as entry word, those Karens who have incorporated western names as part of their names.

Moses Dwe, *Saw.*
San Crombie Po, *Sir.*
Joseph Maung Gyi, *Sir.*
Katie Kaing, *Naw.*

Among the Karens the most common title is *thra* (corresponding to the Burmese *saya*, i.e., a man skilled in any art or science).

San Baw, *thra.*

70. Indic names.

A. Enter Indic writers prior to the middle of the nineteenth century under the personal name (usually the first) and refer from the family name or surname (usually the third). When there are only two names refer from the second.[37]

Rāmamohana Rāya, *Raja,* 1774?-1833.
Refer from
Rāya, Rāmamohana.
Ram Mohun Roy.
Roy, Ram Mohun.
Rammohun Roy.
Roy, Rammohun.

Īśvara Kaula, 1833-1893.
Refer from
Īśvarakaula.
Kaula, Īśvara.
Īçvara-kaula.

B. Where family names have been adopted according to western usage, enter under the family name, preferring the transliterated form adopted by the author when he has consistently used a form differing from the generally accepted transliteration.[38] Refer from variant forms and from parts of name not chosen as entry word.

Indic names present many difficulties to the cataloger, due in part to different usage in the various linguistic areas of India, in part to the widely varying transliterated forms in which the name may appear, and also to the great freedom exercised by the individual in

---

[37] This is the general practice of the British Museum in its various catalogs of Indic literature.
[38] This system of transliteration appears in the Journal of the Bombay Branch of the Royal Asiatic Society. Since April, 1944, the Library of Congress has used this transliteration with the exception of the *anusvāra* and *anunāsika*, both of which are transliterated by ṃ, and the use of ṛi for the RAS's ṛ.

his treatment of his own name. Hence whatever form of the name is selected as heading, the importance of adequate references cannot be overemphasized.

> **Bose, Chunilal,** *rai bahadur,* 1861-
> *Refer from*
> Chunilal Bose.
> Chunīlāl Vasu.
> Vasu, Chunīlāl.
> Basu, Chuni Lal.
> Chuni Lal Bose.

> **Mookerji, Radha Kumud,** 1884-
> *Refer from*
> Radha Kumud Mookerji.
> Rādhākumuda Mukhopādhyāya.
> Mukhopādhyāya, Rādhākumuda.
> Mukerjee, Radha Kumud.
> Mukharji, Radha Kumud.

> **Mukerjee, Radhakamal,** 1889-
> ₁*brother of the preceding*₁
> *Refer from*
> Radha Kamal Mukerjee.
> Rādhākamala Mukhopādhyāya.
> Mukhopādhyāya, Rādhākamala.
> Mookerji, Radha Kamal.

The following rule (1212) from S. R. Ranganathan, *Classified catalogue code* (Madras, Madras Library Association, 1934), together with some of the discussion which accompanies it, is quoted here as an aid to the understanding and treatment of Indic names:

> In the case of modern Hindu names, the last substantive word in the name is to be written first and all the earlier words and initials are to be added thereafter; except that, in the case of South Indian names if the last substantive word merely indicates caste or community and the penultimate word is given in full on the title page; the two last substantive words are both to be written first in their natural order.
> The substantive words in a modern Hindu name may represent one or more of the following:
>> (1) the personal name of the person;
>> (2) the personal name of the father of the person;
>> (3) the name of a place, usually of birth or of ancestral residence; and
>> (4) the patronymic name denoting the caste or the profession, or any religious, academic, military or other distinction or place of residence or birth, of an ancestor.
>
> These words do not occur in the same order in all cases.
> About the middle of the nineteenth century a tendency appeared among the Hindus of North India and West India to assimilate their names to the English forms of Christian name and surname, by adopting the patronymic name as the surname and making the other words in the name answer to Christian names.
> In Western India, the patronymic name is usually preceded by two names. The first name is the personal name and the second name is the personal name of the father—*e.g.* in Mohandas Karamchand Gandhi, Mohandas is the personal name of *Mahatma* Gandhi, Karamchand is his father's personal name and Gandhi is his patronymic name. Till about the middle of the nineteenth century, it was not the practice to give prominence to the third name. The second name also was

124

not much used, except for purposes of distinguishing two or more persons having the same personal name. But now the fashion is to give prominence to the third name and to relegate the first two names to the status of initials.

In Bengal, the caste-name is usually preceded by a personal name originally treated as a single word. This single word is now, in most cases, split up into two words to be used as if they are two distinct Christian names, *e.g.* Ramamohan Roy has come to be written as Ram Mohan Roy; Rameshacandra Dutt, as Romesh Cunder Dutt; Cittaranjan Das, as C. R. Das. It has also to be stated that certain caste-names occur as double words, *e.g.* Rai Mahassi, Roy Choudhuri.

. . . ₁In₁ South India . . . except in a few very recent, cases, the word denoting caste or having some patronymic significance is subordinated to the personal name, though it is either written after it in full as a separate word or compounded with the personal name so as to form a single word, but it is never contracted to initials. Some also omit it altogether. In the case in which it is omitted or assimilated with the personal name, the last word in the name is the personal name; otherwise, the penultimate word is the personal name. The word representing the personal name is usually preceded by one or two words. What the words represent would depend upon the part of South India to which the person belongs.

For titular or descriptive words in Indian names see S. R. Ranganathan, "A list of the more common South Indian words indicating caste or community," *op. cit.*, p. 68-70; and K. A. Linderfelt, "List of Oriental titles and occupations with their significance," in his *Eclectic card catalog rules* (Boston, Cutter, 1890), p. 76-97.

Roy Chowdhury, Brajendra Kishore.
   ₁*caste name*₁
   Refer from
Chowdhury, Brajendra Kishore Roy.
Brajendra Kishore Roy Chowdhury.
Vrajendra-kiṣora Rāya-chaudhurī.

Gopalaswami Ayyangar, *Sir* **Narasimha,** *diwan bahadur,* 1882-
   ₁*patronymic and caste names*₁
   Refer from
Ayyangar, *Sir* Narasimha Gopalaswami.
Narasimha Gopalaswami Ayyangar, *Sir, diwan bahadur.*
Aiyangar, *Sir* Narasimha Gopalaswami.
Iyengar, *Sir* Narasimha Gopalaswami.
Gopalaswami Iyengar, *Sir* Narasimha.
Gopalswamy Iyengar, *Sir* Narasimha.

Aggarwal, Om Prakash, *rai sahib,* 1905-
   ₁*name derived from community*₁
   Refer from
Om-prakāṣa Agarvālā.
Om Parkash, Lala.
Prakash Aggarwal, Om.
Agarwala, Om Prakash.

Shastri, Gaurinath Bhattacharyya.
   ₁*academic title used as surname*₁
   Refer from
Bhattacharyya, Gaurinath, *sastri.*
Gaurinath Bhattacharyya Shastri.
Bhattacharjee, Gouri Nath.
Bhattacharji, Gauri Nath.
Gauri Nath Bhattacharjee, *sastri.*

III. Corporate Bodies as Authors[1]

71. General rule and specification.

Governments and their agencies, societies, institutions, firms, conferences, etc., are to be regarded as the authors of publications for which they, as corporate bodies, are responsible. Such material as official publications of governments; proceedings and reports of societies; official catalogs of libraries and museums; reports of institutions, firms, conferences, and other bodies is entered under the heading for the corporate body, even though the name of the individual preparing it is given.

Monographic works by individual officials, officers, members and employees of corporate bodies, when these works are not clearly administrative or routine in character, are preferably to be entered under personal author, even though issued by the corporate body. (Cf. 73C, 75C-D, 84C-D, 89C, E, H, 90A-B, 118A.)

Periodicals (as defined in the GLOSSARY) are entered according to the general rule (5C) even though issued by governments, societies or institutions.

Government Publications[2]

72. General rule.

Enter under countries or nations, states, cities, towns, and other government districts, official publications issued by them or by their authority.

France.
. . . Mandates. Communication from the French Government.

Great Britain.
Burma, statement of policy by His Majesty's Government.

For form of entry see IV. GEOGRAPHIC HEADINGS, especially 154.

A. Enter publications emanating from the various agencies of government under the names of the agencies (legislative bodies, courts,

---

[1] Cf. C. A. Cutter, *Rules for a dictionary catalog* (4th ed., rewritten; Washington, Govt. Print. Off., 1904), p. 39-41.
[2] Based on J. B. Childs, *Author entry for government publications* (Washington, Govt. Print. Off., 1939).

executive departments, bureaus, etc.) as subheadings (under country, or other jurisdiction) in the latest form in the vernacular.[3] Refer from variant forms.

> **Breslau.** *Statistisches Amt.*
> **China.** *Inspectorate General of Customs.*
>   *Refer from*
>   China. *Customs, Inspectorate General of.*
> **Finland.** *Lantdagen, 1809–1906. Ridderskapet och adeln.*
>   *Refer from*
>   Finland. *Ritaristo ja aateli.*
>   Finland. *Ridderskapet och adeln.*
> **Mexico.** *Departamento del Trabajo.*
>   *Refer from*
>   Mexico. *Trabajo, Departamento del.*
> **New York** (*County*) *Board of Supervisors.*
>   *Refer from*
>   New York (*County*) *Supervisors, Board of.*
> **New York** (*State*) *Dept. of Excise.*
>   *Refer from*
>   New York (*State*) *Excise, Dept. of.*

(1) Use for a subheading the name of the office rather than the title of the officer except where the title of the officer is the only name of the office.

> **U. S.** *Office of Education* not **U. S.** *Commissioner of Education.*
> *but*
> **Canada.** *Fuel Controller.*
> **Illinois.** *State Entomologist.*
> **Pennsylvania.** *Secretary of the Commonwealth.*

Make whenever necessary a reference from the name of the head of a department to the name of the office.

Exception.—Certain classes of institutions and other bodies created, maintained, controlled or owned by governments, but not direct agencies of government are, however, to be treated according to the rules governing these bodies as authors, e.g., colleges, universities, schools, libraries, museums, galleries, observatories, agricultural experiment stations, hospitals, asylums, prisons, theaters, chambers of commerce, botanical and zoological gardens, banks, business corporations, churches, societies, etc.[4] (Cf. 91-149.)

---

[3] For governments having more than one official language, prefer English if it is one of the official languages, e.g., Canada. The departments, bureaus, etc., of Finland may preferably be entered under the Swedish form of name, with reference from the Finnish form. Those of Switzerland are entered under the German form with reference from the French and Italian forms. For governments not using officially a Roman, Greek, or Slavic alphabet, prefer an English form of name.

[4] The Library of Congress does not extend this exception to institutions of the United States government. The headings for these are established according to the regular rules for government agencies, e.g.,

> **U. S.** *Army War College, Washington, D. C.*
> *not* Washington, D. C. Army War College.
> **U. S.** *Navy Yard, Boston*
> *not* Boston. Navy Yard.

B. Enter official gazettes directly under government without sub-division. Make added entry under title. Occasional exception may be made for entry under title when the publication has had separate existence as a newspaper or periodical (cf. 5C.), or has only semi-official standing as a gazette. In accordance with the practice in cataloging periodicals, make cross references for changes of title.

France.
Journal officiel de la République française.

Mexico.
. . . Gaceta diaria de México . . .

73. Sovereigns, presidents, governors, etc.

A. Enter collections of messages to legislative bodies, proclamations, executive orders, and similar documents of sovereigns, presidents, governors, etc., covering more than one administration, under the name of the country or other jurisdiction, followed by the name of the office. Make added entry for editors.

U. S. *President.*
. . . Inaugural addresses of the presidents of the United States . . . edited by John Vance Cheney.
I. Cheney, John Vance, 1848-1922, ed.

U. S. *President.*
Presidential messages and state papers; being the epoch-marking national documents of all the presidents from George Washington to Woodrow Wilson . . . edited by Julius W. Muller . . .
I. Muller, Julius Washington, 1867-   ed.

Gt. Brit. *Sovereigns, etc.*
. . . British royal proclamations relating to America, 1603-1783. Edited by Clarence S. Brigham, A. M.
I. Brigham, Clarence Saunders, 1877-   ed.

New York (*State*) *Governor.*
The executive budget . . .

New York (*City*) *Mayor.*
Message of the mayor to the Common Council . . .

B. For single messages to legislative bodies, proclamations, executive orders, etc., include in the heading the inclusive years of the administration or reign and, in parentheses, the name of the incumbent. Refer from the name of the incumbent.

Gt. Brit. *Sovereigns, etc., 1702-1714* (*Anne*)
A proclamation of Queen Anne for settling and ascertaining the current rates of foreign coins in America . . .
Refer from Anne, *Queen of Great Britain, 1665-1714.*

Gt. Brit. *Sovereigns, etc., 1558-1603 (Elizabeth)*
Queene Elizabeth's speech to her last Parliament.
Refer from Elizabeth, *Queen of England,* 1533-1603.

France. *Sovereigns, etc., 1643-1715 (Louis XIV)*
Declaration du Roy, sur le tarif des droits pour les ports de lettres . . .
Refer from Louis xiv, *King of France,* 1638-1715.

U. S. *President, 1913-1920 (Wilson)*
Executive order of President Wilson establishing defensive sea areas and regulations for carrying same into effect.
Refer from Wilson, Woodrow, *Pres. U. S.,* 1856-1924.

U. S. *President, 1933-1945 (Franklin D. Roosevelt)*
. . . Federal Communications Commission. Message of the President of the United States recommending that Congress create a new agency to be known as the Federal Communications Commission . . .
Refer from Roosevelt, Franklin Delano, *Pres. U. S.,* 1882-1945.

Uruguay. *Presidente, 1897-1903 (Cuestas)*
Manifiesto de S. E. el señor presidente provisional de la República O. del Uruguay don Juan L. Cuestas dirigida al país, á nacionales y extrangeros.
Refer from Cuestas, Juan Lindolfo, *Pres. Uruguay,* 1837-1905.

New York *(State) Governor, 1933-1942 (Lehman)*
. . . Special message of the Governor to the Legislature. Recommendations for the improvement of criminal law enforcement.
Refer from Lehman, Herbert Henry, 1878-

Boston. *Mayor, 1834-1835 (Lyman)*
Communication to the City Council, on the subject of introducing water into the city. Printed by order of the Common Council.
Refer from Lyman, Theodore, 1792-1849.

C. Enter other single addresses and collected editions of the papers of a single sovereign, president, governor, etc., under the individual as author.

Roosevelt, Theodore, *Pres. U. S.,* 1858-1919.
Address of President Roosevelt to the Deep Waterways Convention, Memphis, Tennessee, October 4, 1907.
Refer from U. S. *President, 1901-1909 (Roosevelt)*

Wilson, Woodrow, *Pres. U. S.,* 1856-1924.
Address of President Wilson delivered at Mount Vernon, July 4, 1918.
Refer from U. S. *President, 1913-1923 (Wilson)*

George V, *King of Great Britain,* 1865-1936.
The King to his people; being the speeches and messages of His Majesty King George the Fifth delivered between July 1911 and May 1935.
  i. Gt. Brit. Sovereigns, etc., 1910-1936 (George v)

Irigoyen, Hipólito, *Pres. Argentine Republic, 1852-1933.*
Discursos, escritos y polémicas del Dr. Hipólito Yrigoyen,
1878-1922 . . .
> *Refer from* Argentine Republic. *Presidente, 1916-1922*
> *(Irigoyen)*

Hoover, Herbert Clark, *Pres. U. S., 1874-*
The state papers and other public writings of Herbert Hoover,
collected and edited by William Starr Myers . . .
> I. U. S. President, 1929-1933 (Hoover) II. Myers, William Starr, 1877-

D. Enter the publications of officials or official bodies having governing power over a colony, protectorate, territory, etc., with or without a degree of autonomy, under the name of the territory over which they have jurisdiction, rather than under the name of the country to whose sovereignty they are subject. Use the title of the official or the name of the office as subheading.

> **Morocco** (*Spanish zone*) *Alta Comisaría de España.*
> **District of Columbia.** *Commissioners.*
> **Canada.** *Governor-general.*
> **Maranhão,** *Brazil (State) Interventoria Federal.*

Enter similarly the publications of officials or bodies governing occupied territory.

> **Cuba.** *Military Governor.*
> **Jersey.** *Militärischer Befehlshaber.*
> **Netherlands** (*Territory under German occupation, 1940-1945*)
> *Reichskommissar für die Besetzten Niederländischen Gebiete.*
> **France** (*Territory under German occupation, 1940-1944*) *Chef*
> *der Militärverwaltung in Frankreich.*
> **Germany** (*Territory under Allied occupation, 1945-*   *U. S.*
> *Zone*) *Military Governor.*

74. Legislative bodies.

Enter the proceedings of sessions, debates, reports, etc. (but not "acts" or laws), of legislative bodies under the name of the government with the name of the body as subheading, subdivided as needed by date of session and/or branch, committee, or other subordinate entity. In the case of the United States Congress, when dates are given, give also the number of the congress and the session.

> **Gt. Brit.** *Parliament.*
> **Gt. Brit.** *Parliament. Joint Select Committee on Nationality of*
> *Married Women.*
> **Gt. Brit.** *Parliament, 1766.*
> **Gt. Brit.** *Parliament, 1766. House of Commons.*
> **Gt. Brit.** *Parliament, 1766. House of Lords.*
> **Gt. Brit.** *Parliament. House of Commons. Select Committee on*
> *Finance.*
> **New York** (*State*) *Legislature.*
> **New York** (*State*) *Legislature. Joint Committee on Banking and*
> *Investment Trusts.*
> **New York** (*State*) *Legislature. 1908. Senate.*

> **New York** (*State*) *Legislature. Senate. Committee on Finance.*
> **U. S.** *Congress.*
> **U. S.** *Congress. Joint Committee on Internal Revenue Taxation.*
> **U. S.** *2d Cong., 1st sess., 1791-1792.*
> **U. S.** *52d Cong., 2d sess., 1892-1893. House.*
> **U. S.** *Congress. House.*
> **U. S.** *Congress. House. Committee on Labor.*
> **U. S.** *Congress. Senate. Library.*

75. Executive departments, etc.

Enter executive departments, ministries and secretariats as subheadings under the country or other jurisdiction.

> **U. S.** *Dept. of the Interior.*
>   *Refer from*
> **U. S.** *Interior, Dept. of the.*[5]
> **Argentine Republic.** *Ministerio de Guerra.*
>   *Refer from*
> Argentine Republic. *Guerra, Ministerio de.*

A. Bureaus or offices subordinate to a department. Enter bureaus or offices subordinate to an executive department, ministry or secretariat directly under the name of the jurisdiction, not as a subheading under the department, ministry or secretariat.

> **U. S.** *Bureau of Insular Affairs.*
>   *Refer from*
> **U. S.** *Insular Affairs, Bureau of.*
> **U. S.** *War Dept. Bureau of Insular Affairs.*
> **Italy.** *Direzione generale dei telegrafi.*
>   *Refer from*
> Italy. *Telegrafi, Direzione generale dei.*
> Italy. *Ministero dei lavori pubblici. Direzione generale dei telegrafi.*

When, however, the bureau or office does not have a distinctive name so that one of the same name might exist in another department, enter under the department with a reference from the bureau.

> **U. S.** *War Dept. Bureau of Public Relations.*
> **U. S.** *Treasury Dept. Bureau of Accounts.*
> **U. S.** *Interstate Commerce Commission. Bureau of Accounts.*

B. Divisions and other units. Divisions, regional offices and other units of departments, bureaus, commissions, etc., subordinate to these departments, bureaus, commissions, etc., are usually entered, if required, as subheadings to the departments, bureaus, commissions, etc.

> **U. S.** *Dept. of Agriculture. Division of Botany.*
> **U. S.** *Bureau of Animal Husbandry. Dairy Division.*
> **U. S.** *National Resources Planning Board. Region 8.*

---

[5] Many libraries use such subheadings in the inverted form (e.g., **U. S.** *Interior, Dept. of the*) or obtain the same arrangement by underlining the key word.

C. Reports, papers, etc., by an official.

(1) Enter under the department or other government agency administrative reports which are prepared by an official as a part of his routine duty. No added entry need be made under the name of an official for a report strictly administrative in character.

> **Massachusetts.** *Secretary of the Commonwealth.*
> Instructions relative to the registry and return of births, marriages and deaths in Massachusetts. By Francis DeWitt, secretary of the Commonwealth.

> **Oregon.** *Insurance Dept.*
> Fire prevention bulletin, 1915. By Harvey Wells, state insurance commissioner.

> **Oregon.** *Secretary of State.*
> . . . Constitutional provisions and statutes related to incorporated cities and towns . . . Compiled by Hal E. Ross, secretary of state.

(2) Enter under personal author[6] scientific papers, addresses, and other publications, not administrative or routine in character, but which are issued officially by the department to which the author is attached. Make added entry under the department.

> **Lamont, Robert Patterson,** 1867–
> . . . Unemployment and business stability. An address by Secretary of Commerce Robert P. Lamont before the Chamber of Commerce of the United States.
> At head of title: U. S. Department of Commerce.
> i. U. S. Dept. of Commerce. ii. Title.

> **Hoover, Herbert Clark,** *Pres. U. S.,* 1874–
> . . . The future of our foreign trade, by Herbert Hoover, Secretary of Commerce. An address given at a dinner in New York City.
> At head of title: Department of Commerce. Bureau of Foreign and Domestic Commerce. Washington.
> i. U. S. Bureau of Foreign and Domestic Commerce. ii. Title.

> **Veiller, Lawrence Turnure.**
> Tenement house legislation in New York, 1852–1900. Prepared for the Tenement House Commission of 1900. By Lawrence Veiller, secretary . . .
> i. New York (State) Tenement House Commission.

D. Reports not by an official.
Enter under the writer reports made to a department or other government agency by a person who is not an official, with added entry under the department or agency.

> **Hubert, Ernest Everett,** 1887–
> . . . Sap stains of wood and their prevention, by Ernest E. Hubert, professor of forestry, School of Forestry, University of

---

[6] The Library of Congress usually enters under personal author papers which appear in a series which has been entered under an official heading.

Idaho. Tenth report of a series on the marketing and use of lumber . . .

> At head of title: United States Department of Commerce. Wood utilization.
>
> I. U. S. Dept. of Commerce. II. Title.

E. Collection or series of reports. Enter a collection or series of reports to a department, by different persons, under the department. If the importance or manner of publication of the single reports warrants it, make an added entry or analytical entry for each under the author's name, even if he is an official.

> **U. S.** *Geological Survey.*
> . . . Reconnaissances in the Cape Nome and Norton Bay regions, Alaska, in 1900, by Alfred H. Brooks, George B. Richardson, Arthur J. Collier and Walter C. Mendenhall. Washington, Govt. Print. Off., 1901.
>
> I. Brooks, Alfred Hulse, 1871-1924. II. Collier, Arthur James, 1866- III. Mendenhall, Walter Curran, 1871-   IV. Richardson, George Burr, 1872-

76. Armies, navies, etc.

A. Enter reports of operations, orders, circulars, proclamations, dispatches, etc., emanating from armies, navies, marine corps, etc., under the country, with the name of the body as subheading in the vernacular.

> **U. S.** *Army.*
> **U. S.** *Navy.*
> **U. S.** *Marine Corps.*
> **France.** *Armée.*
> **Germany.** *Heer.*
> **Mexico.** *Ejército.*

B. Enter military units of armies or navies (such as commands, armies, corps, divisions, regiments, artillery and infantry) as subdivisions of the army, navy, etc., in the vernacular. Refer from any popular name.

> **U. S.** *Army. Antiaircraft Command.*
> **Gt. Brit.** *Navy. Sea Cadet Corps.*
> **U. S.** *Navy. 7th Amphibious Force.*
> **Gt. Brit.** *Army. Royal Gloucestershire Hussars.*
> **Germany.** *Heer. Panzer-Division Nr. 11.*
> **France.** *Armée. Artillerie.*

However, enter subdivisions of armies, navies, etc., which have names beginning with the name, or an adjective derived from the name, of the army, navy, etc., directly under the country. Refer from the indirect form.

> **U. S.** *Naval Air Transport Service.*
> *Refer from*
> U. S. *Navy. Naval Air Transport Service.*
> **Canada.** *Army Medical Corps.*
> *Refer from*
> Canada. *Army. Army Medical Corps.*

(1) In headings for the Army of the United States, and of Great Britain and her dominions designate Armies by number spelled out, corps by roman numerals, and divisions by arabic numerals.

> **U. S.** *Army. First Army.*
> **U. S.** *Army. IV Corps.*
> **Gt. Brit.** *Army. 7th Division.*

(2) In the headings for the Army of the United States, and of Great Britain and her dominions, enter regiments designated only by number within the various services (cavalry, infantry, etc.) under number, followed by the name of the service. The word regiment is not included in the heading. For other units (battalions, brigades, etc.) include the distinguishing word.

> **U. S.** *Army. 27th Cavalry.*
> **U. S.** *Army. 101st Cavalry Group.*

(3) In the present organization of the U. S. Army the regiments are numbered consecutively within each arm of the service. Besides the regular army regiments there were regiments of Negro troops and sharpshooters during the Civil War and volunteer regiments during the Spanish-American War. As the numbering of such regiments may duplicate that of the regular army a distinguishing word is added in the heading.

> **U. S.** *Army. 1st Cavalry.*   ₍regular army₎
> **U. S.** *Army. 1st Cavalry (Colored)*   ₍Civil War₎
> **U. S.** *Army. 1st Cavalry (Volunteer)* ₍Spanish-American War₎
> **U. S.** *Army. 2d Infantry.*
> **U. S.** *Army. 2d Infantry (Colored)*
> **U. S.** *Army. 2d Infantry (Sharpshooters)*

C. Military units which are not a part of the U. S. Army but were a part of the army conscripted by the states through the Civil War period are entered under the name of the state followed by the name of the unit. This heading is subdivided in the same manner as the present U. S. Army, except that dates of muster and discharge are added when possible. The greater number of such units are distinguished by ordinal numbers only. Those having distinctive names are treated in the same way as those known by ordinal numbers. Refer from popular names.

> **Delaware Infantry.** *1st Regt., 1776-1783.*
> **Tennessee Cavalry.** *2d Regt., 1862-1865.*
> **New York Infantry.** *8th Regt., 1861-1863.*
>   *Refer from*
>   New York Infantry. *Blenker's Rifles.*
>   Blenker's Rifles.
> **Illinois Infantry.** *United States Zouave Cadets, 1859-1860.*
>   *Refer from*
>   United States Zouave Cadets of Chicago.

134

77. State Guards and National Guard (U. S.).

    A. Enter the State Guard of each state or territory of the United States under the name of the state or territory to which it belongs.

> **Wisconsin.** *State Guard.*
> **Puerto Rico.** *State Guard.*

    B. Enter the National Guard of the United States, a military force maintained jointly by the several states and by the U. S. government, under the name of the state or territory in which it is organized.

> **Louisiana. National Guard.**
> **Puerto Rico. National Guard.**

During the two world wars the guard was drafted into the regular Army of the U. S., and was known by regular army designation. Previously, when the army was supplemented by a volunteer army conscripted by the states, many of the National Guard units became a part of the state organization and were known by the name of the state. (Cf. 76C.)

78. Embassies, legations, consulates, etc.

    Enter publications emanating from embassies, consulates, etc., under the nation represented followed by the name of the representing body. Include in the heading for embassies and legations the names of the countries to which they are assigned; for consulates, the names of the cities in which they are located.

> **Australia.** *High Commissioner in London.*
> **France.** *Consulat. Buenos Aires.*
> **Germany.** *Gesandtschaft. Switzerland.*
> **Gt. Brit.** *Consulate. Cairo.*
> **Gt. Brit.** *Embassy. U. S.*
> **Gt. Brit.** *Legation. China.*
> **U. S.** *Consulate. Amsterdam.*
> **U. S.** *Legation. Sweden.*

79. Delegation, delegates, delegate.

    Enter a delegation, delegates or delegate officially representing a country at a conference or congress, under the name of the conference or congress with a subheading for the delegation. The subheading will consist of the phrase "Delegation from [country]" unless the name of the conference or congress is not in English; the corresponding phrase in the language of the heading will then be used.

> **International American Conference.** *1st, Washington, D. C.,* 1889–1890. *Delegation from Haiti.*
> **International Economic Conference,** *Geneva,* 1927. *Delegation from the United States.*

80. Archives.

    A. Enter national, state, provincial, municipal, diocesan, parish and other local archives under the name of the country, state, city, diocese, etc., with the name of the archive as subheading. Add the name of the place where located, when necessary for clearness or distinction.

> **France.** *Archives nationales.*
> **Portugal.** *Arquivo Nacional.*
> **Netherlands** (*Kingdom, 1815-*) *Rijks Archief in Drenthe, Assen.*
> **Aube,** *France (Dept.) Archives.*
> **Augsburg.** *Stadtarchiv.*
> **U. S.** *National Archives.*

B. Enter archives of particular government departments as follows:
(1) Under the name of the country followed by the name of the archive, when the archive has a name of its own.

> **France.** *Archives de la guerre.*
>   *Refer from*
> France. *Ministère de la guerre. Archives.*

(2) Under the name of the ministry, department or bureau with the addition of the subheading ARCHIVES, when the archive does not have an independent name.

> **France.** *Ministère des travaux publics. Archives.*

C. Enter institutional, society, and family archives under institution, society, or family, with a subheading consisting either of the name of the archive or the word ARCHIVES.

> **Harvard University.** *Archives.*

81. Government commissions and committees.

A. Enter reports and recommendations of official commissions and committees, whether permanent or temporary, under the name of the country or other jurisdiction, with the name of the commission or committee as a subheading, directly under country or under the appointing department, legislative body, etc. (Cf. 74.) Refer from the name of the commission or committee.

> **U. S.** *Commission to Study the Proposed Highway to Alaska.*
> **U. S.** *Interstate Commerce Commission.*
> **U. S.** *Committee on Economic Security.*
> **Gt. Brit.** *Royal Commission on Local Taxation.*
> **France.** *Commission des affaires coloniales.*
> **France.** *Comité d'organisation du travail des métaux.*
> **U. S.** *Children's Bureau. National Commission on Children in Wartime.*

B. Enter an official commission to an exposition or exhibition under the name of the country sending it with the name of the commission as subheading. If the commission is mentioned only in general terms without an official name, use a subheading in the vernacular consisting of (*1*) the term signifying the commission, (*2*) the name of the exposition, (*3*) the place if it does not appear in the name, (*4*) the date of the exposition.

> **Austria.** *Central-Commission, Weltausstellung in Chicago, 1893.*
> **France.** *Commission, Exposition internationale de Chicago, 1893.*

> **Germany.** *Reichskommission, Weltausstellung in Chicago,* 1893.
> **New Jersey.** *Commission, Jamestown Exposition,* 1907.
> **Bolivia.** *Comisión Nacional, Exposición Internacional Panamá-Pacífico, San Francisco,* 1915.

For international commissions see 139A and C.

82. Special local government districts.

Enter special local government districts for harbor control and development, power development and distribution, sanitation, irrigation, education, etc., under their own names rather than under the governments creating them.

> **Minneapolis-Saint Paul Sanitary District.**
> **East Bay Municipal Utility District.**
> **Houston Independent School District.**
> **Mancomunidad Hidrográfica del Guadalquivir.**

In cases where districts are more generally known by the name of the authority or board in charge of them than by their own official designation, prefer entry under the governing body.

> **California Toll Bridge Authority.**
> **Dundee Harbour Trust** *not* Harbour District of Dundee.
> **Junta de las Obras del Puerto de Santander.**
> **Port of New York Authority** *not* Port of New York District.
> **Tennessee Valley Authority.**

83. Laws, Ancient and medieval.

Ancient and medieval laws (codes, compilations, special collections, extracts, etc.) are entered under the names or titles by which they are traditionally known as headings. These may be the name of the promulgator:

> **Hammurabi,** *King of Babylonia.*
> **Manu.**

or the name of the people governed by the laws:

> **Hittites.** *Laws, statutes, etc.*
> **Visigoths.** *Laws, statutes, etc.*

or the title (name) of the code:

> **Breviarum Alarici.**
> **Corpus juris civilis.**
> **Leges XII tabularum.**
> **Lex Romana Burgundionum.**
> **Sachsenspiegel.**
> **Salic law.**
> **Södermannalagen.**

84. Laws, Modern.

Enter laws, decrees, and other acts having the force of law under the country, state, or other jurisdiction with the form subheading LAWS, STATUTES, ETC.

Common forms of publication are:

137

General collections, compiled statutes, all laws in force at a
certain time.
General codes.
Civil codes.
  Code of civil procedure.
  Code of civil practice.
Penal codes.
  Code of criminal procedure.
  Code of criminal practice.
Judicial codes.
Political codes.
  (Chiefly American)
Commercial codes.
  (For countries other than the United States)
Official editions of a special act or acts on a particular subject
  (e.g., banks, income tax, etc.) whether annotated or un-
  annotated.
Nonofficial editions or compilations of acts not annotated or
  with annotations subordinate to the text of the law.
Official drafts (or legislative bills) for individual laws and codes.

A. Subdivision by reign, administration, etc. For the larger, long-
continued jurisdictions it may be desirable to segregate individual
acts (other than codes), or collections of acts enacted during a given
reign or executive administration or during a given legislative period,
by adding to the subheading LAWS, STATUTES, ETC. the inclusive dates
of the reign, administration, or legislative period, and in parentheses
the name of the incumbent executive or the designation of the legislative period.

> **France.** *Laws, statutes, etc., 1924-1931 (Doumergue)*
> **Gt. Brit.** *Laws, statutes, etc., 1837-1901 (Victoria)*
> **Spain.** *Laws, statutes, etc., 1814-1833 (Ferdinand VII)*

Make general references from legislative bodies to the subheading
LAWS, STATUTES, ETC.

B. Laws of territories, dependencies, etc. Enter the laws of states
and territories, including dependencies, with or without a degree of
autonomy, under the name of the jurisdiction or territory to which
they apply, rather than under the name of the country or countries
to whose sovereignty or suzerainty they have been successively subject
and whose lawmaking or executive powers have promulgated the laws.
Make added entry for the latter.

> **French Guiana.** *Laws, statutes, etc.*
>   Ordonnance du Roi, portant application du Code d'instruction
> criminelle à la Guiane française.
>   I. France. Laws, statutes, etc.

C. Annotated laws. Enter annotated editions or compilations of
acts under the annotator, publisher, or title, only when the text of the
acts is obviously subordinate to the annotations, following the same
principle as for entering other commentaries. (Cf. 29.)

Carr, Arthur Strettell Comyns, 1882-   ed.
Recent mining legislation, including the Coal mines act, 1930
(annotated) by A. S. Comyns Carr . . . and Wilfrid Fordham . . .
    I. Fordham, Wilfrid Gurney, joint ed. II. Gt. Brit.   Laws, statutes, etc.

Canada. *Laws, statutes, etc.*
The Insolvent act of 1875: with the rules of practice and
tariffs of fees . . . Annotated by Ivan Wotherspoon . . . with an
index and list of cases, by C. H. Stephens . . .
    I. Wotherspoon, Ivan Tolkein, ed. II. Stephens, Charles Henry.

D. Digests of laws. When the original text of the laws digested or
annotated is quoted only in part, or in a fragmentary manner, or when
the contribution of the digester or annotater forms the main feature
of the book, enter under the digester with added entry under the
name of the country.

Herty, Thomas.
A digest of the laws of the United States of America. Being a
complete system, (alphabetically arranged) of all the public acts
of Congress now in force—from the commencement of the federal government to the end of the third session of the Fifth
Congress, which terminated in March 1799, inclusive. By Thomas
Herty . . .
    I. U. S.   Laws, statutes, etc.

In doubtful cases prefer entry under country with added entry
under digester or annotater.

U. S. *Laws, statutes, etc.*
Digest of the general laws of the U. S. . . . by James Dunlop.
    I. Dunlop, James, 1795-1856, ed.

E. Ordinances. Enter local ordinances and bylaws, and likewise
compilations of local laws relating to a single city or other local government, under the name of the city or other local government with
form subheading ORDINANCES, ETC.

Cleveland. *Ordinances, etc.*

F. Laws of city states. Enter collections of the "statuti," "ordini,"
"leggi," "consuetudine," etc., of the Italian medieval city states, comuni,
etc., and similar collections of the "Stadtrechte" of the city states of
Germany, Switzerland, the Baltic states, etc., under the name of
the city with the subheading LAWS, STATUTES, ETC.

Bergamo. *Laws, statutes, etc.*
Statuta magnificæ civitatis Bergomi cum correctionibus, refor-
mationibus, & aliis decretis . . . in veteri non impressis, cum indice
alphabetico . . . pluribus . . . erroribus expurgata, & faciliori
lectioni accomodata per Bernardinum Riccium . . .
    I. Riccius, Bernardinus, ed.

Hamburg. *Laws, statutes, etc.*
Gesetz betreffend die Amortisation der Staatsschuld. Auf
Befehl e.H. Senats der Freien und Hansestadt Hamburg publicirt
den 29. Mai 1865.

85. Constitutions.

Enter constitutions, and official drafts of proposed constitutions, under the name of the country or state with the form subheading Constitution. Refer from country with subheading in the vernacular.

> U. S. *Constitution.*
>
> Ohio. *Constitution.*
>
> South Africa. *Constitution.*
> *Refer from*
> Gt. Brit. *Laws, statutes, etc.*
> South Africa Act, 1909.
>
> Switzerland. *Constitution.*
> *Refer from*
> Switzerland. *Bundesverfassung.*

86. Constitutional conventions.

A. Enter constitutional conventions of the states and territories of the United States under the name of the state or territory with subheading Constitutional Convention, followed by the date.

> New Hampshire. *Constitutional Convention, 1902.*

B. Enter constitutional conventions of foreign countries under the name of the country with the name of the body in the vernacular as subheading, followed by the date.

> Germany. *Nationalversammlung, 1919-1920.*
> Portugal. *Assembleia Nacional Constituinte de 1911.*

87. Charters.

Enter charters for colonial, provincial or local governments, and for other corporate bodies under the name of the government or body to whom the charter is granted. Make added entry or reference under the name of the sovereign power granting the charter, except under states or countries for municipal charters.

> New Orleans. *Charters.*
> Charter of the city of New Orleans. Act 159 of the General Assembly of the state of Louisiana, session of 1912, as expressly amended by acts of the Louisiana Legislature to and including the session of 1926. Commission form of government.
>
> Cincinnati, Hamilton and Dayton Railroad Company.
> Charter and by-laws of the Cincinnati, Hamilton and Dayton Rail Road Company.
> i. Ohio. Laws, statutes, etc.

88. Treaties.

A. Enter **single treaties,** conventions, executive agreements, and other exchanges of notes having the effect of treaties, under the party named first on the title page, with the form subheading Treaties, etc. followed by inclusive dates of reign or administration and the name of the executive incumbent in the year of signing. For certain governments, such as those of the British dominions, the subheading is fol-

140

lowed only by the year of signature. Make added entry under the other party or parties to the treaty. Added entries are also to be made, when necessary, for the countries with the subheadings DEPT. OF STATE; FOREIGN OFFICE; MINISTÈRE DES AFFAIRS ÉTRANGÈRES; etc., and for editors, compilers, translators, etc. When the treaty is commonly called by the place where it was signed, make a subject entry under the name of the place followed by the phrase TREATY OF and the year. Make references from any other appellations.

See also 118C (Concordats).

> **Canada.** *Treaties, etc., 1932.*
> . . . Trade agreement between Canada and New Zealand. Signed at Ottawa and Wellington April 23, 1932. In force May 24, 1932.
>> i. New Zealand. Treaties, etc., 1932. ii. Title.

> **Gt. Brit.** *Treaties, etc., 1760-1820 (George III)*
> The definitive treaty of peace and friendship between His Britannick Majesty, the most Christian King, and the King of Spain. Concluded at Paris the 10th day of February, 1763. To which the King of Portugal acceded on the same day. Published by authority.
>> 1. Paris, Treaty of, 1763. i. France. Treaties, etc., 1715-1774 (Louis xv) ii. Spain. Treaties, etc., 1759-1788 (Charles iii) iii. Portugal. Treaties, etc., 1750-1777 (Joseph i)

> **U. S.** *Treaties, etc., 1801-1809 (Jefferson)*
> Treaty and conventions, entered into and ratified by the United States of America and the French Republic relative to the cession of Louisiana.
>> 1. Paris, Treaty of, 1803. 2. Louisiana Purchase. i. France. Treaties, etc., 1799-1804 (Consulate)

B. Enter **multilateral treaties** or conventions signed at international conferences under the name of the conference.

> **International American Conference.** *4th, Buenos Aires, 1910.*
> . . . Convention between the United States and other powers on literary and artistic copyright. Signed at Buenos Aires, August 11, 1910.

> **International Conference for the Unification of Laws on Bills of Exchange, Promissory Notes and Cheques.** *1st, Geneva, 1930.*
> International convention on the stamp laws in connection with bills of exchange and promissory notes. Geneva, June 7, 1930. <The convention has not been ratified by His Majesty> . . .

C. Enter **collections of treaties** of several countries under the compiler.

> **Rockhill, William Woodville,** 1854-1914, *ed.*
> Treaties and conventions with or concerning China and Korea, 1894-1904, together with various state papers and documents affecting foreign interests. Edited by William Woodville Rockhill . . .
>> i. China. Treaties, etc. ii. Korea. Treaties, etc. iii. U. S. Treaties, etc.

141

D. Enter **collections of the treaties of a particular country** with more than one other country under the name of the country which is a party to all the treaties even when it is not the one mentioned first on the title page.

> **Portugal.** *Treaties, etc.*
> . . . Compilação até 31 de outubro de 1929 dos tratados e convenções comerciais em vigor entre Portugal e os outros paises. Autorizada por despacho ministerial de 8 de setembro de 1929.

> **U. S.** *Treaties, etc.*
> Treaties of amity and commerce, and of alliance eventual and defensive, between His Most Christian Majesty and the thirteen United States of America; the definitive treaty between Great-Britain and the thirteen United States of America; and the treaty of amity, commerce, and navigation, between His Britannic Majesty and the United States of America . . .
> I. France. Treaties, etc., 1774-1792 (Louis XVI) II. Gt. Brit. Treaties, etc., 1760-1820 (George III)

89. Courts.

A. Enter courts under their names (statutory titles) as subheadings under the countries, states, etc., from which they derive their authority.

> **Chicago.** *Municipal Court.*
> **France.** *Conseil d'État.*
> **France.** *Parlement (Paris)*
> **France.** *Parlement (Toulouse)*
> **Gt. Brit.** *High Court of Justice.*
> **Gt. Brit.** *High Court of Justice. King's Bench Division.*
> **New York** *(State) Court of Oyer and Terminer (Albany Co.)*
> **Pennsylvania.** *Orphans' Court (Allegheny Co.)*
> **Prussia.** *Oberlandesgericht, Breslau.*
> **Spain.** *Tribunal Supremo.*
> **U. S.** *Circuit Court (2d Circuit)*
> **U. S.** *District Court. Illinois (Northern District)*
> **U. S.** *Supreme Court.*

B. Enter **joint courts** of two or more governments under the name of the court followed by the name of the place if there is a permanent seat.[7] Refer from the name of the place.

> **Corte de Justicia Centro-americana,** *Cartago, Costa Rica.*
> **Hanseatisches Oberlandesgericht,** *Hamburg.*

C. Enter a single **opinion, decision,** or **charge** under the name of the court, with added entries under the name of the judge, parties to the suit, or other headings as the case may require. (Cf. footnote 8 rule 90B.) Collections of the opinions and other papers of a single judge are preferably to be entered under his name as personal author.

---

[7] Exception has been made by the Library of Congress for the Permanent Court of Arbitration and the Permanent Court of International Justice, both located at the Hague and entered under the place.

U. S. *Circuit Court* (*1st Circuit*)
The opinion of Judge Story in the case of William Allen vs. Joseph McKeen, treasurer of Bowdoin College, delivered in the Circuit Court of the United States, at the May term at Portland 1833.
I. Story, Joseph, 1779-1845. II. Allen, William, 1784-1868, plaintiff. III. McKeen, Joseph, 1787-1865, defendant.

U. S. *Circuit Court* (*8th Circuit*)
. . . Decision of John F. Philips, judge, in Temple lot case. The Reorganized Church of Jesus Christ of Latter Day Saints *versus* the Church of Christ, et al.
I. Philips, John Finis, 1834-1919. II. Reorganized Church of Jesus Christ of Latter Day Saints. III. Independence, Mo. Church of Christ. IV. Title: Temple lot case.

D. Enter **reports of decisions of a single court** under the name of the court, with added entry under the name of the reporter, editor, or collector, as the case may be.

New York (*State*) *Court of Appeals.*
Transcript appeals . . . The file of opinions in cases argued before the Court of Appeals of the State of New York, during the January term, 1867- ₍June term, 1868₎ From official copies certified by Joel Tiffany, state reporter.
I. Tiffany, Joel, 1811-1893, reporter. II. Title.

Gt. Brit. *Court for the Consideration of Crown Cases Reserved.*
Crown cases reserved for consideration, and decided by the twelve judges of England, from the year 1799 to the year 1824. By William Oldnall Russell and Edward Ryan . . . With references to the English common law reports.
I. Russell, Sir William Oldnall, 1785-1833, reporter. II. Ryan, Sir Edward, 1793-1875, reporter. III. Title.

E. Enter a **collection of decisions on a single subject** under the editor or compiler. If limited to a single court, make added entry under the court.

Powell, Thomas Reed, 1880-
Supreme Court decisions on federal power over commerce, 1910-1914, by Thomas Reed Powell . . .
I. U. S. Supreme Court.

F. Enter **reports of two courts published together** with collective title under the first named court with added entry for the second.

New York (*State*) *Supreme Court.*
Reports of cases argued and determined in the Supreme Court and in the Court for the Correction of Errors of the State of New York ₍1845-1848₎ By Hiram Denio . . .
I. New York (State) Court for the Trial of Impeachments and Correction of Errors. II. Denio, Hiram, 1799-1871, ed.

G. Enter **reports of three or more courts published together** with collective title under the name of country, state, etc., with the subheading COURTS. Make added entry for each court. If, however,

143

the reports are mainly those of one court and usually so cited, enter under that court with added entry for the others.

> **Pennsylvania.** *Courts.*
> Reports of cases adjudged in the courts of Common Pleas, Quarter Sessions, Oyer and Terminer, and Orphans' Court of the First Judicial District of Pennsylvania ₍1808-1841₎; with notes and references by John W. Ashmead and with citations from opinions of the Supreme Court, Superior Court and other courts of Pennsylvania. Collected by Charles A. Hawkins . . .
>
> ɪ. Ashmead, John Wayne, reporter. ɪɪ. Hawkins, Charles Augustus, 1859-   ɪɪɪ. Pennsylvania. Court of Common Pleas (Philadelphia Co.) ɪᴠ. Pennsylvania. Court of Quarter Sessions of the Peace (Philadelphia Co.) ᴠ. Pennsylvania. Court of Oyer and Terminer (Philadelphia Co.) ᴠɪ. Pennsylvania. Orphans' Court (Philadelphia Co.) ᴠɪɪ. Pennsylvania. Supreme Court. ᴠɪɪɪ. Pennsylvania. Superior Court.

H. Enter **digests of reports** under the digester; if anonymous, under the title. Make added entry under the name of the court or judge whenever the digest is limited to the reports of a particular court, and under the title of the collection or set of reports if it is frequently referred to by title.

> **Morrison, Robert Stewart,** 1843-1920.
> Colorado digest; containing the decisions of the Supreme Court, Court of Appeals, and federal courts of the state as reported in volume 1-25 Colorado reports, 1-13 Court of Appeals reports, the contemporaneous Pacific reporters, 1-100 Federal reporters, 101-178 U. S. reports and local reports, with table of cases digested, with their citations, and table of overruled cases, by R. S. Morrison . . .
>
> ɪ. Colorado. Supreme Court. ɪɪ. Colorado. Court of Appeals. ɪɪɪ. Title.

I. Enter **court rules**, plain text or annotated, under the name of the court.

> **U. S.** *Circuit Court of Appeals* (*2d Circuit*)
> Rules of the United States Circuit Court of Appeals for the Second Circuit, October 16, 1918.

J. Enter **grand juries** under their names (statutory titles) as subheadings under the county or parish.

> **Kings Co.,** *N. Y. Grand Jury.*
> **New York** (*County*) *Sheriff's Jury.*
> **Orleans Parish,** *La. Grand Jury.*

90. Trials.
A. Pleas and briefs. Enter a plea or brief printed separately under the lawyer who makes it. Make added entries for joint authors, parties to the suit, etc., as the case may require. (Cf. footnote 8 rule 90B.)

> **Whiting, William,** 1813-1873.
> Argument of William Whiting, esq., in the case of Ross Winans *v.* Orsamus Eaton et al. for an alleged infringement of his patent

for the eight-wheel railroad car. Before Hon. Samuel Nelson, justice of the United States Circuit Court for the Northern District of New York. Phonographically reported by Arthur Cannon . . .
    I. Winans, Ross, 1798-1877. II. Eaton, Orsamus.

In law cases where briefs and other records are numerous, the material may be made available under the parties to the case and under subject, using for practical convenience a factitious collective entry.

> **Atchison, Topeka and Santa Fé Railway Company, et al.,** *defendants.*
> (**Kansas and Public Utilities Commission for the State of Kansas,** *complainants*)
> Action brought under the Act to regulate commerce, of 1887.
> Before the Interstate Commerce Commission.
> Briefs and other records in this case, 1912-   not separately listed or cataloged are to be found on shelf: [Call no. of the collection]
>   I. Kansas, complainant. II. Kansas. Public Utilities Commission, complainant. III. U. S. Interstate Commerce Commission.

> **Eastman Kodak Company of New Jersey,** *defendant-appellant.*
> (**Goodwin Film and Camera Company,** *complainant-appellee*)
> Patent case.
> Briefs and other records in this case, 1913-   not separately listed or cataloged are to be found on shelf: [Call no. of the collection]
>   I. Goodwin Film and Camera Company, Newark, N. J., complainant-appellee.

B. Civil actions. Enter reports of civil actions under the party to the suit who is named first on the title page. Make added entry under the second party, under the court, and under the reporter if his name appears on the title page.[8]

> **Brooks, William,** 1803-1863, *complainant.*
> The case of William Brooks *versus* Ezekiel Byam and others, in equity, in the Circuit Court of the United States, for the First Circuit—district of Massachusetts. Before the Honorable Mr. Justice Story, the Honorable Judge Sprague, Simon Greenleaf, esq., Charles Sumner, esq., counsel for complainant. Franklin Dexter, esq., Eben'r Smith, Jr., esq., counsel for respondents.
>   I. Byam, Ezekiel, respondent. II. U. S. Circuit Court (1st Circuit) III. Title.

C. Contested elections. Proceed according to the rule for civil actions, but enter under author reports of committees, speeches in Congress, etc., upon contested elections, with added entries for the parties in the case if the reports, etc., include evidence. Make subject entries for the parties in the case when their names are not used as author or added entries.

---

[8] The number of added entries made for courts, judges, defendants other than the first will depend largely on the fullness of the catalog and the character of the library.

Rainey, Henry Thomas, 1860-1934.
Contested-election case of Henry T. Rainey *v.* Guy L. Shaw, from the Twentieth Congressional District of Illinois.
    I. Shaw, Guy Loren, 1881-   II. Title.

Mumford, William.
. . . Contested election case of Henry T. Rainey, *vs.* Guy L. Shaw. From the Twentieth Congressional District of Illinois. Statement, brief and argument for contestee. William Mumford, attorney for contestee.
    I. Rainey, Henry Thomas, 1860-1934. II. Shaw, Guy Loren, 1881- III. Title.

D. Crown, state, and criminal trials. Enter reports of crown, state and criminal proceedings under the name of the defendant. When there are several defendants, enter under the one named first on the title page with added entries for the others. If none are named on the title page, enter under the one best known in connection with the case, or, lacking such, under title. Make added entry for the court and for the reporter and editor.

O'Connell, Daniel, 1775-1847, *defendant.*
. . . A report of the proceedings on an indictment for a conspiracy, in the case of the Queen *v.* Daniel O'Connell, John O'Connell, Thomas Steele, Charles Gavan Duffy . . . in Michaelmas term, 1843, and Hilary term, 1844. By John Simpson Armstrong, and Edward Shirley Trevor.
    I. O'Connell, John, 1810-1858, defendant. II. Steele, Thomas, 1788-1848, defendant . . . VIII. Ray, Thomas Matthew, defendant. IX. Armstrong, John Simpson, reporter. X. Trevor, Edward Shirley, reporter. XI. Ireland. Court of King's Bench.

Burr, Aaron, 1756-1836, *defendant.*
Trial of Aaron Burr for treason; printed from the report taken in shorthand by David Robertson . . .
    Trial in the Circuit Court of the United States for the District of Virginia, Richmond, May 22-Sept. 1, 1807.
    I. Robertson, David, reporter. II. U. S. Circuit Court (4th Circuit)

Alley, Leavitt, *b.* 1816, *defendant.*
Report of the trial of Leavitt Alley, indicted for the murder of Abijah Ellis, in the Supreme Judicial Court of Massachusetts. Reported by Franklin Fiske Heard.
    I. Heard, Franklin Fiske, 1825-1889, reporter. II. Massachusetts. Supreme Judicial Court.

E. Impeachment trials. Enter reports of impeachment trials under the defendant, with subject entry for the office, and added entries for the legislative body sitting as the court of impeachment, and for the other parties, reporters, etc., whose connection with the case is such as to warrant entry under their names. Refer from the subject IMPEACHMENTS [LOCAL SUBDIVISION] to the name of the defendant.

Burdett, John S   *defendant.*
Proceedings of the Senate sitting for the trial of the impeachment of John S. Burdett, treasurer of the state of West Virginia. With evidence.

E. D. York, reporter of the evidence.

1. West Virginia. Treasurer's Office. I. West Virginia. Legislature, 1875. Senate. II. York, E. D., reporter.

Impeachments—West Virginia *see also* Burdett, John S., *defendant*.

F. Courts-martial and courts of inquiry. Enter reports of courts-martial and courts of inquiry under the defendant, with added entry for the court, followed by name of defendant and date of trial, and for the reporter, providing his name is given.

Hull, William, 1753-1825, *defendant*.
Report of the trial of Brig. General William Hull; commanding the North-Western Army of the United States. By a court martial held at Albany on Monday, 3d January, 1814, and succeeding days. Taken by Lieut. Col. Forbes . . .
I. U. S. Army. Courts-martial. Hull. 1814. II. Forbes, James Grant, reporter.

Everson, Alfred, *defendant*.
Proceedings of a naval general court-martial, in the case of Acting Master Alfred Everson, United States Navy, charged with assault with intent to kill James O'Neill, a fireman of the British steamer Nicholas I, and with maltreatment and cruelty.
I. U. S. Navy. Courts-martial. Everson. 1864.

Yancey, Robert, *defendant*.
Court martial held at Louisa courthouse, on the 10th of December, 1806, by order of Major General James Williams, for the trial of Lieutenant Colonel Robert Yancey, of the Fortieth Regiment of Virginia Militia.
I. Virginia. Militia. Courts-martial. Yancey. 1806.

Hall, Theron Edmund, 1821-1880, *defendant*.
Proceedings of a court of inquiry, convened at Aquia Landing, Va., March 13th, 1863, to examine into certain charges preferred against Captain T. E. Hall, assistant quartermaster.
I. U. S. Army. Courts of Inquiry. Hall. 1863.

G. Admiralty proceedings. Enter admiralty proceedings relating to vessels under the name of the vessel. Make added entry for the court and for the reporter if his name is mentioned.

Meteor (*Steamship*)
Report of the case of the steamship Meteor, libelled for alleged violation of the Neutrality act . . . Edited by F. V. Balch . . .
CONTENTS.—I. Proceedings in the District Court of the United States for the Southern District of New York.—II. Proceedings in the Circuit Court of the United States for the Southern District of New York in the Second Circuit, and in the Supreme Court of the United States.
I. Balch, Francis Vergnies, 1839-1898, ed. II. U. S. District Court. New York (Southern District) III. U. S. Circuit Court (2d Circuit) IV. U. S. Supreme Court.

H. Collected reports of trials. Enter collected reports of trials under the name of the compiler; if published anonymously, enter under title.

Howell, Thomas Bayley, 1768–1815, *ed.*
A complete collection of state trials and proceedings for high treason and other crimes and misdemeanors from the earliest period to the year 1783 . . . compiled by T. B. Howell . . .

Colección de las causas mas célebres, los mejores modelos de alegatos, acusaciones fiscales, interrogatorios y defensas, en lo civil y criminal, del foro francés, inglés, español y mexicano. 1854.

Societies and Institutions[9]

Definitions and specifications.—A society is an organization of persons associated together for the promotion of common purposes or objects, such as research, business, recreation, etc.

Included in the rules for societies are academies (learned societies), associations, and societies of all kinds, scientific, technical, educational, benevolent, moral, etc., even when strictly local or named from a country, state, province, or city; also clubs, gilds, orders of knighthood, secret societies, Greek letter fraternities, Young Men's and Young Women's Christian Associations, affiliated societies, political parties, religious sects, etc., as distinguished from institutions (establishments).

Institutions (establishments) are entities whose functions require a plant with buildings, apparatus, etc., as distinguished from bodies, organized groups of persons such as societies, associations, etc., whose duties may be performed equally well in one place or another. The necessity of having a permanent material equipment tends to identify the institution with a locality.

Included in the rules for institutions are colleges, universities, schools, libraries, museums, galleries, radio stations, observatories, laboratories, churches, monasteries, convents, hospitals, asylums, prisons, theaters, buildings, etc.

The designations academy, athenaeum, college, institute, lyceum, museum, etc., and similar terms in other languages are used interchangeably for cultural associations and educational institutions; these are to be entered as societies or as institutions according to the nature of their organization.

91. General rule (Societies).

Enter a society under the first word (not an article, cf. 93A) of its latest corporate name, with reference from any other name by which it is known and from the place where its headquarters are established. (Cf. B, p. 150.)

---

[9] The rules for corporate entry as applied to Societies and Institutions are based on U. S. Library of Congress, Catalog Division, *Guide to the cataloguing of the serial publications of societies and institutions,* compiled by Harriet W. Pierson (2d ed.; Washington, Govt. Print. Off., 1931).

Academy of Natural Sciences of Philadelphia.
Refer from
Philadelphia. Academy of Natural Sciences.
College of Physicians of Philadelphia.
Refer from
Philadelphia. College of Physicians.
Colegio de Abogados de Lima.
Refer from
Lima. Colegio de Abogados.

A. Change of name.

(1) When a society has changed its name, enter under the latest form, with references from earlier forms.[10]

Accademia di scienze, lettere e belle arti di Palermo.
Refer from
Accademia palermitana.
Accademia di scienze e lettere, *Palermo.*
Académie d'agriculture de France, *Paris.*
Refer from
Société royale d'agriculture de la généralité de Paris.
Société royale d'agriculture de Paris.
Société d'agriculture du département de la Seine.
Société royale et centrale d'agriculture, *Paris.*
Société nationale et centrale d'agriculture, *Paris.*
Société impériale et centrale d'agriculture, *Paris.*
Société centrale d'agriculture de France, *Paris.*
Société nationale d'agriculture de France, *Paris.*

(2) When two or more societies which have had an independent existence unite to form a new society, enter each under its own name up to the time of union, with *see also* references to and from the new body.

Royal Society of Victoria, *Melbourne.*
In 1855 the Philosophical Society of Victoria (founded 1854) and the Victorian Institute for the Advancement of Science (founded 1854) united to form the Philosophical Institute of Victoria; in 1859 the name of the latter was changed to Royal Society of Victoria.
In 1887 the society absorbed the Microscopical Society of Victoria.

Entries to be made under

Philosophical Society of Victoria.
with see also reference to
Royal Society of Victoria, *Melbourne.*
Victorian Institute for the Advancement of Science, *Melbourne.*
with see also reference to
Royal Society of Victoria, *Melbourne.*
Royal Society of Victoria, *Melbourne*
with see also references to
Philosophical Society of Victoria.

---

[10] The heading established for a corporate body is used for all the publications, whether or not another form appears in some of the titles; necessary references are made. In case of subsequent changes of name, all entries and references are revised to conform to the new name.

Victorian Institute for the Advancement of Science, *Melbourne.*
　Refer from
Philosophical Institute of Victoria.

B. Use of place in heading.

(1) If the name of the place does not appear in the corporate name, add it in the established form (cf. 153) when the activities of the society are local or when the location is an aid to identification for societies of nondistinctive or similar names. Refer from the place.

Civic Symphony Orchestra Society, *Fort Wayne, Ind.*
　Refer from
Fort Wayne, Ind.　Civic Symphony Orchestra Society.

Club Católico, *Montevideo.*
　Refer from
Montevideo.　Club Católico.

Asociación Amigos del Museo, *Buenos Aires.*
　Refer from
Buenos Aires.　Asociación Amigos del Museo.

Société d'histoire du droit, *Paris.*
　Refer from
Paris.　Société d'histoire du droit.

Society of Comparative Legislation, *London.*
　Refer from
London.　Society of Comparative Legislation.

Sociedad de Psiquiatría, *Montevideo.*
　Refer from
Montevideo.　Sociedad de Psiquiatría.

(2) The city is not added, ordinarily, to the names of societies whose headquarters have changed, or whose membership is nationwide and whose branches may be located in different places. In general, for national societies of the United States prefer the omission of the city; for foreign societies, the addition of the city may serve also to distinguish the country to which the society belongs. Reference may be made for established headquarters, even though not used in the heading.

American Library Association.
American Library Association. *Division of Cataloging and Classification.*
American Philosophical Association.
Wissenschaftliche Gesellschaft für Luftfahrt.
Archäologisches Institut des Deutschen Reichs.
Royal Asiatic Society of Great Britain and Ireland.
but
American Philosophical Society, *Philadelphia.*
Institution of Civil Engineers, *London.*
Asociación Nacional de Ingenieros Agrónomos, *Madrid.*
Asociación Sudamericana de Paz Universal, *Buenos Aires.*
Sociedad Nacional de Minería, *Lima.*
Sociedad Nacional de Minería, *Santiago de Chile.*

(3) When necessary for identification, in cases where headquarters of a society are not given, the name of the country, state, province, etc., is added.

> **Asociación Nacional de Abogados** (*Mexico*)
> **National Council for Maternity and Child Welfare** (*Gt. Brit.*)
> **Labor Party** (*Australia*)
> **State Association of Superintendents of the Poor** (*Michigan*)
> **State Association of Miners** (*Kansas*)
> **Agricultural Society of New Castle County** (*Delaware*)
> **Children's Aid Society** (*Ontario*)
> **Friends of the University Library** (*University of Toledo*)

If the name of state or other geographical division is inserted in the body of the heading, it is ordinarily abbreviated.

> **Montgomery County (Md.) Agricultural Society.**
> **Sangamon County (Ill.) Bar Association.**

C. Identical name and place. When two or more societies in the same place have the same name distinguish them by dates in the heading.

> **Scientific Society of San Antonio.** (*Founded 1892*)
> **Scientific Society of San Antonio.** (*Founded 1904*)
> **Cincinnati Medical Society.** (*Founded 1819*)
> **Cincinnati Medical Society.** (*Founded 1831*)
> **Cincinnati Medical Society.** (*Founded 1851*)

The general rule applies to all bodies included in the specification for societies unless the subsequent rules (94-130) provide exceptions, variations or special rulings.

For additional rulings on the form of headings see 93.

92. General rule (Institutions).
Enter an institution (using the latest name) under the name of the place in which it is located.

> **Boston. Public Library.**
> **Manila. Ateneo.**
>   *Refer from*
>   Ateneo de Manila.
> **Philadelphia. Children's Hospital.**
>   *Refer from*
>   Children's Hospital of Philadelphia.
> **Gratz. Anna-Kinderspital.**
>   *Refer from*
>   Anna-Kinderspital, *Gratz.*
> **Paris. Musée national du Louvre.**
>   *Refer from*
>   Musée national du Louvre, *Paris.*
>   Louvre, Musée national du, *Paris.*
>   France. Musée national du Louvre, *Paris.*

Hamburg. Institut für Allgemeine Botanik.
Refer from
Institut für Allgemeine Botanik, *Hamburg.*

Newark, N. J. Radio station WOR.
Refer from
WOR (Radio station) *Newark, N. J.*

Asunción. "Radio Prieto" (ZP9)
Refer from
"Radio Prieto" (ZP9) *Asunción.*
ZP9 "Radio Prieto," *Asunción.*

Louvain. Université catholique.
Refer from
Université catholique, *Louvain.*

Greenwich, Eng. Royal Observatory.
Refer from
Royal Observatory, *Greenwich.*
Gt. Brit. Royal Observatory, *Greenwich.*

Kalocsa, Hungary. Haynald Observatorium.
Refer from
Haynald Observatorium, *Kalocsa, Hungary.*

Exceptions.—

A. Names beginning with a proper noun or proper adjective.[11] Enter an institution of the United States or of the British Empire whose name begins with a proper noun or a proper adjective under the first word of its name and refer from the place where it is located. Add the name of the place to the heading if it does not occur in the name of the institution, unless the institution is so well known as to make the addition of the place unnecessary. For countries other than the United States and the British Empire follow the general rule of entry under place. (For state institutions see 104.)

Corcoran Gallery of Art, *Washington, D. C.*
Refer from
Washington, D. C. Corcoran Gallery of Art.

Carnegie Institution of Washington.
Refer from
Washington, D. C. Carnegie Institution of Washington.

Smithsonian Institution.
Refer from
Washington, D. C. Smithsonian Institution.

British Museum.
Refer from
London. British Museum.

Dartmouth College.
Refer from
Hanover, N. H. Dartmouth College.

---

[11] This exception has not been applied to tax-supported schools (see 107) nor to Carnegie, Passmore-Edwards, and similar public libraries which because of their number as well as the nature of their grants and endowments, tend to become better known, at least outside of their immediate neighborhood, by the name of the city in which they are located than by their own name. Where only the building is a private donation, the library being otherwise endowed and supported by public taxation the presumption is particularly strong in favor of entry under the place.

> **Passavant Memorial Hospital,** *Chicago.*
> *Refer from*
> Chicago. Passavant Memorial Hospital.

To avoid doubt or complications in the order of filing, it has been found expedient to write the names of institutions beginning with the name of a place (city) in the form of entry under place, with subdivision.

> **San Francisco. Museum of Art.**
> *not* San Francisco Museum of Art.

Exception may be made, however, in names long established and well known.

> **Boston Athenaeum.**

Initials of personal names occurring at the beginning of the name of an institution are omitted, but forenames when given in full are included. (Cf. 93C.)

> **Smiley Public Library,** *Redlands, Calif.*
> *Refer from*
> A. K. Smiley Public Library, *Redlands, Calif.*
> Redlands, Calif. A. K. Smiley Public Library.
> Redlands, Calif. Smiley Public Library.
> **Enoch Pratt Free Library,** *Baltimore.*
> *Refer from*
> Pratt Free Library, *Baltimore.*
> Baltimore. Enoch Pratt Free Library.
> **Brigham Young University,** *Provo, Utah.*
> *Refer from*
> Provo, Utah. Brigham Young University.
> **Peter Bent Brigham Hospital,** *Boston.*
> *Refer from*
> Boston. Peter Bent Brigham Hospital.

Colleges and other institutions named after Luther may be regarded as a group and entered under the conventional rather than the official form of name LUTHER COLLEGE, followed by name of place, with references from the official form.

> **Luther College,** *New Ulm, Minn.*
> *Refer from*
> Dr. Martin Luther College.
> Martin Luther College.
> New Ulm, Minn. Dr. Martin Luther College.

B. Minor variations in names. French municipal libraries are variously and irregularly called Bibliothèque; Bibliothèque communale; Bibliothèque de la ville; Bibliothèque municipale; Bibliothèque publique. These are preferably to be entered under the designation BIBLIOTHÈQUE MUNICIPALE in agreement with the practice adopted by the *Annuaire des bibliothèques et des archives,* e.g.,

Reims. Bibliothèque municipale.

Follow the general rule, however, for libraries having a distinctive individual name, e.g.,

Aix. Bibliothèque Méjanes.

or for important libraries that have issued publications tending to make another form distinctive for the library in question, e.g.,

Lyon. Bibliothèque de la ville.

93. Entry word (Societies or institutions).

A. Retain the initial article in heading only when necessary for clearness, and disregard it in filing.

> **The Players,** *Detroit.*
>> *Refer from*
>> Detroit. The Players.
>
> **The Club,** *London.*
>> *Refer from*
>> London. The Club.
>
> **The Typophiles,** *New York.*
>> *Refer from*
>> New York. The Typophiles.
>
> **Les Français de Grande-Bretagne,** *London.*
>> *Refer from*
>> London. Les Français de Grande-Bretagne.

B. Omit from the name of a society or institution the adjective or abbreviation of an adjective denoting royal privilege,[12] except (*1*) when it forms the distinguishing part of the name and (*2*) in English names. In foreign names the adjective denoting a national body is not to be abbreviated.[13] Adjectives denoting pontifical privilege are not omitted.

---

[12] Academies especially reflect in such adjectives the changes in the political history of the countries to which they belong. Thus the academy of Berlin has had the following successive changes of name:

> **Societät der Wissenschaften.**
> **Königliche Societät der Wissenschaften.**
> **Churfürstlich Brandenburgische Societät der Wissenschaften.**
> **Preussische und Churfürstlich Brandenburgische Societät der Wissenschaften.**
> **Academia Regia Scientiarum Berolinensis.**
> **Königliche Akademie der Wissenschaften.**
> **Académie royale des sciences et belles-lettres.**
> **Königlich-preussische Akademie der Wissenschaften zu Berlin.**
> **Preussische Akademie der Wissenschaften.**

In view of the many changes, a shorter form is to be preferred, with references from other forms.

> **Akademie der Wissenschaften,** *Berlin.*

[13] National institutions which include in their names the name of the country, and therefore tend to become better known by the name of the country than by that of the place where they are located, may be entered under the name of the country. The name of the city or town is to be added in the heading. In doubtful cases enter under the city or town. This exception is to be confined to the higher institutions of learning, such as universities, libraries, etc. Secondary schools are better under the name of the city.

Footnote continued on next page.

Accademia di scienze, lettere ed arti degli agiati in Rovereto.
(*not* I. R. Accademia . . .)
Refer from
Imperiale Regia Accademia di scienze, lettere ed arti degli agiati in Rovereto.
Regia Accademia di scienze, lettere ed arti degli agiati in Rovereto.
Rovereto. Accademia di scienze, lettere ed arti degli agiati.

Danske videnskabernes selskab, *Copenhagen.*
(*not* K. Danske . . .)
Refer from
Kongelige Danske videnskabernes selskab, *Copenhagen.*
Copenhagen. K. Danske videnskabernes selskab.

Florence. Galleria degli Uffizi.
Refer from
Reale Galleria degli Uffizi, *Florence.*
Uffizi, Galleria degli, *Florence.*

but

Royal Society of Edinburgh.
Refer from
Edinburgh. Royal Society.

London. National Gallery.
Refer from
National Gallery, *London.*

Hague. Koninklijke Bibliotheek.
Refer from
Koninklijke Bibliotheek, *The Hague.*
Bibliothèque royale de la Haye.

Leyden. Rijksuniversiteit.
Refer from
Rijksuniversiteit, *Leyden.*

Pontificia Accademia romana di archeologia.
Refer from
Accademia romana di archeologia.

Rome. Pontificio Istituto orientale.
Refer from
Pontificio Istituto orientale, *Rome.*
Istituto orientale, *Rome.*

Footnote continued from preceding page.

Chile. Universidad, *Santiago.*
Refer from
Santiago de Chile. Universidad de Chile.

Venezuela. Universidad Central, *Caracas.*
Refer from
Caracas. Universidad Central de Venezuela.

Peru. Biblioteca Nacional, *Lima.*
Refer from
Lima. Biblioteca Nacional del Perú.

Victoria, Australia. Public Library, Museums and National Gallery, *Melbourne.*
Refer from
Melbourne. Public Library, Museums and National Gallery of Victoria.

New South Wales. Public Library, *Sydney.*
Refer from
Sydney. Public Library of New South Wales.

but

San José, Costa Rica. Liceo de Costa Rica.
Refer from
Liceo de Costa Rica, *San José.*
Costa Rica, Liceo de, *San José.*

C. Names beginning with a title of honor, distinction, or address. Titles of honor, distinction, or address occurring at the beginning of the name of a society or institution are to be retained; if, however, they occur in an abbreviated form, they may be omitted. Refer from form not used.

> **Judge Baker Guidance Center,** *Boston.*
> *Refer from*
> Baker Guidance Center, *Boston.*
> Boston. Judge Baker Guidance Center.
>
> **Bishop White Prayer Book Society.**
>
> **Sir Walter Raleigh Monument Association.**
> *Refer from*
> Raleigh Monument Association.
>
> **Kaiser Wilhelm-Gesellschaft zur Förderung der Wissenschaften,** *Berlin.*
> *Refer from*
> Berlin. Kaiser Wilhelm-Gesellschaft zur Förderung der Wissenschaften.
>
> **Herzl Zion Club,** *New York.*
> *Refer from*
> Dr. Herzl Zion Club, *New York.*
> New York. Herzl Zion Club.
> New York. Dr. Herzl Zion Club.
>
> **Birmingham, Eng. King Edward's School.**
> *Refer from*
> King Edward's School, *Birmingham, Eng.*
>
> **Washington, D. C. Miss Madeira's School.**
> *Refer from*
> Miss Madeira's School, *Washington, D. C.*
> Madeira's School, *Washington, D. C.*
>
> **Leyden. Rijksuniversiteit.** *Jan van der Hoeven-Stichting voor Theoretische Biologie van Dier en Mensch.*
> *Refer from*
> Prof. Dr. Jan van der Hoeven-Stichting voor Theoretische Biologie van Dier en Mensch, verbonden aan der Rijksuniversiteit te Leiden.
> Jan van der Hoeven-Stichting voor Theoretische Biologie van Dier en Mensch, verbonden aan der Rijksuniversiteit te Leiden.
> Hoeven-Stichting voor Theoretische Biologie van Dier en Mensch, verbonden aan der Rijksuniversiteit te Leiden.
> Leyden. Rijksuniversiteit. *Prof. Dr. Jan van der Hoeven-Stichting voor Biologie van Dier en Mensch.*

D. Names beginning with a numeral. Enter a society whose corporate name begins with a numeral under that name, with the numeral spelled out in the vernacular.

For 3 October-Vereeniging write:

> **Drie October-Vereeniging,** *Leyden.*
> *Refer from*
> October-Vereeniging, *Leyden.*
> Leyden. Drie October-Vereeniging.
> Leyden. October-Vereeniging.

E. Names made up of initial letters or syllables of the actual name. Enter a society using a name made up of initial letters or syllables of its actual name or initials of the principal words so combined as to make a short, convenient form, under that form if it represents the usage of the society. Refer from full name.

> **Scapa Society,** *London.*
> > *Refer from*
> > Society for Checking the Abuses of Public Advertising, *London.*
> > Public Advertising, Society for Checking the Abuses of. London. Scapa Society.

but

> **Federation of Allied Legions.**
> > *with references from*
> > Fédération interalliée des anciens combattants.
> > FIDAC [*i.e.* Fédération interalliée des anciens combattants]
> > F.I.D.A.C. [*i.e.* Fédération interalliée des anciens combattants]

F. Names containing initials. Enter a society whose corporate name contains initials under the form of name used by the society, with explanation of the initials in brackets when necessary for clearness.

> **Sällskapet D.B.W.** [*i.e.* **de badande vännerna**] *Visby, Sweden.*
> > *Refer from*
> > D.B.W. sällskapet, *Visby, Sweden.*
> > D.B.V. sällskapet, *Visby, Sweden.*
> > Visby, Sweden. Sällskapet D.B.W.

> **K.F.R. Society,** *Washington, D. C.*
> > *Refer from*
> > Washington, D. C. K.F.R. Society.

94. Corporate names practically unknown.

A society or institution[14] whose full corporate name is so little used as to be practically unknown may be entered by a shorter better-known form.

> **American Philosophical Society,** *Philadelphia.*
> > *Refer from*
> > American Philosophical Society held at Philadelphia for Promoting Useful Knowledge.

> **Cymmrodorion Society,** *London.*
> > *Refer from*
> > Honourable Society of Cymmrodorion.

> **Deutsche Akademie,** *Munich.*
> > *Refer from*
> > Akademie zur Wissenschaftlichen Erforschung und zur Pflege des Deutschtums: Deutsche Akademie.

> **Glasgow North American Colonial Society.**
> > *Refer from*
> > Society (in connection with the Established Church of Scotland) for Promoting the Religious Interests of Scottish Settlers in British North America.

---

[14] Among institutions, the universities of continental Europe, in particular, are known by short forms.

National Research Council (*Canada*)
Refer from
Honorary Advisory Council for Scientific and Industrial Research (*Canada*)

Harvard University.
[*Corporate name: President and Fellows of Harvard College*]

Bari (City) Università.
Refer from
Università degli studi "Benito Mussolini," *Bari*.

Brünn. Universita.
Refer from
Masarykova Universita, *Brünn*.

Oslo. Universitet.
Refer from
Kongelige Frederiks universitet, *Oslo*.

Heidelberg. Universität.
Refer from
Grossherzogliche Ruprecht-Karls Universität zu Heidelberg.

Riga. Universitate.
Refer from
Latvijas Universitate, *Riga*.

95. Incorporated societies.

Omit in the heading for an incorporated society the term indicating incorporation, unless that term is the initial word of the name, or forms a distinguishing part of it. (For firms, business corporations, etc., cf. 144.)

The practice of incorporated societies differs in the matter of using in their statutory names the term "incorporated" ("inc.") or its equivalent in other languages. Many incorporated societies omit in their names the term indicating incorporation; others which may have existed for a long period before incorporation, add the designation "incorporated" ("inc." etc.) upon the adoption of their charter.

American Ethnological Society, *New York*.
not American Ethnological Society, inc.

Society of Engineers, *London*.
not Society of Engineers (incorporated)

Automobiltechnische Gesellschaft.
not Automobiltechnische Gesellschaft E.V.

Deutsche Gesellschaft für Kunst und Wissenschaft in Bromberg.
not Deutsche Gesellschaft für Kunst und Wissenschaft in Bromberg (eingetragener Verein)

but

Incorporated Gas Institute, *London*.

Incorporated Society of Authors, Playwrights and Composers, *London*.

96. Political parties.

Enter official publications (platforms, proceedings, manifestoes, campaign books, etc.) of political parties under the name of the party.

158

When necessary for identification, add the name of the country in parentheses. (Cf. 91B(3).)

> **Labor Party** (*Gt. Brit.*)
> *Refer from*
> Labour Party (*Gt. Brit.*)
>
> **Nationalsozialistische Deutsche Arbeiter-Partei.**
> *Refer from*
> National Socialist German Labor Party.
> Nazi Party.
> N.S.D.A.P.
>
> **Partido Autonomista Puerto-riqueño.**
>
> **Partito socialista italiano.**
> *Refer from*
> Socialist Party (*Italy*)
>
> **Republican Party.** *National Committee, 1932-1936.*
>
> **Democratic Party.** *National Convention, Chicago, 1884.*
>
> **Democratic Party.** *Pennsylvania.*
>
> **Republican Party.** *New York (State) 6th Congressional District.*
>
> **Republican Party.** *Rhode Island. State Central Committee.*

The publications of the Republican and Democratic congressional committees are to be entered under the names of these committees, not under the parties.

> **Republican Congressional Committee,** 1901-1903.

97. International societies.

Enter a society extending through many lands, or having authorized names in many languages, under the English form if it is used officially (i.e., if it appears on any of the society's publications); otherwise under that official form of the name which occurs most frequently, with reference from all other forms.

> **International Maritime Association.**
> *Refer from*
> Association internationale de la marine.
>
> **International Council for the Study of the Sea.**
> *Refer from*
> Conseil permanent international pour l'exploration de la mer.
> Central-Ausschuss für die Internationale Meeresforschung.
>
> **Comité international des poids et mesures.**
> *Refer from*
> International Commission of Weights and Measures.
>
> **Red Cross.**
> [*for general works*]
>
> **Red Cross.** *U. S. American National Red Cross.*
> *Refer from*
> American National Red Cross.
>
> **Red Cross.** *Denmark. Foreningen Dansk Røde kors.*
> *Refer from*
> Foreningen Dansk Røde kors.
> Dansk Røde kors.

      Red Cross. *Gt. Brit. British Red Cross Society. County of London Branch.*
        Refer from
      British Red Cross Society.

      Rotary International.
        [for the international association]
      Rotary International. *Country or regional subdivision, e.g.,*
        Rotary International. *Brazil.*

But local rotary clubs are entered according to the general rule (91) under their own names.

      Rotary Club, *Washington, D. C.*

98. Orders of knighthood, secret orders, etc.

    Enter orders of knighthood, both those of medieval and modern times, also secret orders and other similar organizations, under their names; but enter the American Knights Templars and other regular masonic bodies under the heading FREEMASONS.

    A. Medieval orders (including orders still in existence) are usually entered under an English form of the name.

      Teutonic Knights.
        Refer from
      Deutscher Orden.
      Deutscher Ritter.
      Orden der Ritter des Hospitals St. Marien des Deutschen Hauses.
      Templars.
        Refer from
      Knights Templars (*Monastic and military order*)
      Order of the Golden Fleece.
        Refer from
      Golden Fleece, Order of the.

    B. Modern orders are entered under their names in the vernacular with references from significant words of the name or from other forms.

      Légion d'honneur.
        Refer from
      Legion of Honor (*National order of France*)
      Order of the Legion of Honor.
      Elefantordenen.
        Refer from
      Order of the Elephant.
      Elephant, Order of the.

    C. Masonic bodies are entered under the form heading FREE-MASONS,[15] followed by place according to the following examples:

---

[15] Outline of masonic organization.
"Blue Lodge." 1st–3rd degrees.
    Local: Lodges having name or number, usually both.
    State: Grand lodges.

Footnote continued on next page.

(1) Masons of a state or place in general, unorganized:

Freemasons. *Massachusetts.*
Freemasons. *Galena, Ill.*

(2) "Blue Lodge" bodies:

Freemasons. *France. Grand Orient.*
Freemasons. *New York (State) Grand Lodge.*
Freemasons. *New Hampshire. 5th Masonic District.*
Freemasons. *Roxbury, Mass. Washington Lodge.*
Freemasons. *Lancaster, Pa. Lodge No. 43.*

Such special headings as the following may be made when required:

Freemasons. *Maryland. Grand Stewards' Lodge.*
Freemasons. *U. S.   Conference of Grand Masters, Cedar Rapids, Iowa, 1918.*

Footnote continued from preceding page.

 U. S.: No central body.
  Conventions and meetings of grand masters have been held, but these have
   no official status.
 Other countries: Grand lodges under various names.
  In the United States some states are divided, for administrative purposes,
 into numbered masonic districts; in England, into provinces. In Maryland and
 New York is found a kind of executive committee of the Grand Lodge called
 the Grand Stewards' Lodge.

Royal Arch Masons. 4th-7th degrees.
 Local: Chapters with name or number like "Blue Lodge."
 State: Grand chapters.
 U. S.: General Grand Chapter.
  States are subdivided as in the "Blue Lodges."
 Other countries (England, Scotland, Canada): Chapters and grand chapters.

Royal and Select Masters. "Cryptic Masons." 8th-10th degrees.
  In some states these degrees are conferred by the chapter.
 Local: Councils.
 State: Grand Council.
 U. S.: General Grand Council.
 Other countries (England, Canada): Councils and grand councils.

Knights Templars. 11th-13th degrees.
 Local: Commanderies.
 State: Grand Commandery.
 U. S.: Grand Encampment.

These four bodies, the "Blue Lodge" (Freemasons proper), Royal Arch Masons,
Cryptic Masons, and Knights Templars, make up what is sometimes called the "York
Rite" as distinguished from the Scottish Rite.

Ancient Accepted Scottish Rite. 4th-33d degrees.
 Local:
  Northern Jurisdiction
   Lodge of Perfection. 4th-14th degrees.
   Council of Princes of Jerusalem. 15th-16th degrees.
   Chapter of Rose Croix. 17th-18th degrees.
   Consistory of Sublime Princes of the Royal Secret. 19th-32d degrees.
  Southern Jurisdiction
   Lodge of Perfection. 4th-14th degrees.
   Chapter of Rose Cross. 15th-18th degrees.
   Council of Kadosh. 19th-30th degrees.
   Consistory of Sublime Princes of the Royal Secret. 31st-32d degrees.
  In the United States and Great Britain the 1st-3d degrees are conferred only
  by the "Blue Lodge." The 33d degree, Sovereign grand inspector general,
  is conferred by the Supreme Council.
 State:
  In some states are found Councils of deliberation; in some, Grand consis-
  tories; some have no state organization.
 U. S.:
  No national body; instead there are two Supreme councils for the Northern
  and Southern jurisdictions.
  There are also two "clandestine" Supreme councils for the U. S. A., whose
  publications can only be distinguished by noting carefully the names of
  the officers.

(3) Royal Arch Masons. For Chapter masonry add ROYAL ARCH MASONS after name of place.

For unorganized Royal Arch Masons in general, or those of a state or place:

> **Freemasons.** *Royal Arch Masons.*
> **Freemasons.** *Boston. Royal Arch Masons.*

For national, state or local bodies:

> **Freemasons.** *U. S. Royal Arch Masons. General Grand Chapter.*
> **Freemasons.** *Maine. Royal Arch Masons. Grand Chapter.*
> **Freemasons.** *Bridgewater, Mass. Royal Arch Masons. Harmony Chapter.*
> **Freemasons.** *Binghamton, N. Y. Royal Arch Masons. Chapter No. 139.*

The exact name of the Grand Chapter varies slightly in the different states, e.g., Virginia calls it the Supreme Grand Royal Arch Chapter; some states say Grand Royal Arch Chapter, others the Grand Chapter of Royal Arch Masons. Make headings uniform as indicated and bring out any variations in the title or a note. Make cross references when necessary.

(4) Royal and Select Masters. Treat bodies of Cryptic Masons (Councils of Royal and Select Masters) like Royal Arch Masons.

> **Freemasons.** *U. S. Royal and Select Masters. General Grand Council.*
> **Freemasons.** *Maine. Royal and Select Masters. Grand Council.*
> **Freemasons.** *Portland, Me. Royal and Select Masters. Portland Council No. 4.*

(5) Knights Templars. Treat Knights Templars like Royal Arch Masons.

> **Freemasons.** *U. S. Knights Templars. Grand Encampment.*
> **Freemasons.** *Maine. Knights Templars. Grand Commandery.*
> **Freemasons.** *Boston. Knights Templars. Boston Commandery.*

(6) Scottish Rite. Treat Scottish Rite bodies like Royal Arch Masons.

> **Freemasons.** *U. S. Scottish Rite. Supreme Council for the Southern Jurisdiction.*
> **Freemasons.** *U. S. Scottish Rite. Supreme Council for the Northern Jurisdiction.*
> **Freemasons.** *Massachusetts. Scottish Rite. Council of Deliberation.*
> **Freemasons.** *Boston. Scottish Rite. Massachusetts Consistory.*
> **Freemasons.** *Boston. Scottish Rite. Giles F. Yates Council of Princes of Jerusalem.*
> **Freemasons.** *Boston. Scottish Rite. Mount Olivet Chapter of Rose Croix.*
> **Freemasons.** *Boston. Scottish Rite. Boston Lafayette Lodge of Perfection.*
> **Freemasons.** *District of Columbia. Scottish Rite. Robert de Bruce Council, Knights Kadosh.*

(7) Other masonic and related bodies.[16] Enter the Eastern Star and Mystic Shrine under their own names, not under Freemasons. Their organization is like that of "Blue Lodges" and may be treated in the same way.

For Negro bodies add (Negro)

Freemasons. *District of Columbia. Grand Lodge (Negro)*

Other related bodies may be treated like Royal Arch Masons.

Freemasons. *District of Columbia. Masonic Veteran Association.*
Freemasons. *U. S. Red Cross of Constantine.*

Schismatic grand lodges and other "clandestine" bodies may be entered like regular bodies. The distinction can generally be brought out in the name.

Freemasons. *New York (State) St. John's Grand Lodge.*

D. American secret societies are preferably to be entered under that part of the name by which they are commonly known.

The following selected examples are offered merely as a guide to form of entry. Libraries with much material in this class will need to work out a scheme of organization for the various societies similar to that given above for Freemasons.

Elks, Benevolent and Protective Order of.
  Refer from
Benevolent and Protective Order of Elks.
B.P.O.E.
Elks, Benevolent and Protective Order of. *Grand Forum.*
Elks, Benevolent and Protective Order of. *Missouri Elks Association.*
  Refer from
Missouri Elks Association.
Elks, Benevolent and Protective Order of. *Augusta Lodge No. 205.*
Odd Fellows, Independent Order of.
  Refer from
Independent Order of Odd Fellows.
I.O.O.F.
Odd Fellows, Independent Order of. *Sovereign Grand Lodge.*
Odd Fellows, Independent Order of. *Maryland. Grand Encampment.*
Odd Fellows, Independent Order of. *Illinois. Grand Lodge.*
Odd Fellows, Independent Order of. *Chatham Village, N. Y. Morning Star Lodge, No. 128.*

---

[16] The Eastern Star, Mystic Shrine and Red Cross of Constantine draw their members from Masons and their families, but have no official connection with masonic bodies. There are other "rites" or bodies, such as the Rite of Mizraim, some of which are recognized and some not. Colored grand lodges exist in many states but are not recognized by most white masonic bodies. In some states, also, "clandestine" or non-recognized lodges and grand lodges exist.

Odd Fellows, Independent Order of. *Daughters of Rebekah.*
Refer from
Daughters of Rebekah.
Rebekah, Daughters of.

Odd Fellows, Independent Order of. *Patriarchs Militant.*
Refer from
Patriarchs Militant.

Odd Fellows, Independent Order of. *Patriarchs Militant. Ladies Auxiliary.*

99. Federated societies.

Enter local branches of federated societies under the name of the general organization when this forms part of the name of the local society. On the other hand, local branches having individual names which do not include the name of the general organization are to be entered as independent bodies according to the regular rule for societies, with a reference from the name of the general organization.

Daughters of the American Revolution. *Massachusetts. Col. Timothy Bigelow Chapter, Worcester.*

International Musical Society. *North American Section.*
but
Associazione dei musicologi italiani.
[*which functions as the Italian section*]
Refer from
International Musical Society. *Italian Section.*

Akademiia nauk SSSR. *Dal'nevostochnyĭ filial, Vladivostok.*
Refer from
Dal'nevostochnyĭ filial Akademii nauk SSSR., *Vladivostok.*

Phi Beta Kappa. *New York Delta, Columbia University.*
Refer from
. Columbia University. *Phi Beta Kappa.*

Phi Beta Kappa. *New York Theta, Cornell University.*
Refer from
Cornell University. *Phi Beta Kappa.*

Psi Upsilon. *Chi Chapter, Cornell University.*

Psi Upsilon. *Gamma Chapter, Amherst College.*

100. Affiliated societies.

Enter affiliated societies under their own names without reference from the larger organization with which they are affiliated.

American Association of Law Libraries.
[*which is affiliated with the American Library Association*]
Archaeological Society of Washington, *Washington, D. C.*
[*which is affiliated with the Archaeological Institute of America*]

101. Societies related to, but not an integral part of, a larger organization.

A. College or university societies. Enter societies of students, of faculty, or of both under the name of the institution. Refer from the name of the society.

For Greek letter societies see 99.

Columbia University. Philolexian Society.
> *Refer from*
> Philolexian Society, *Columbia University.*

Oxford. University. Oxford Union Society.
> *Refer from*
> Oxford Union Society.

Michigan. University. Michigan Union.
> *Refer from*
> Michigan Union.

Yale University. Elizabethan Club.
> *Refer from*
> Elizabethan Club of Yale University.

Michigan. University. *Medical School. Victor C. Vaughan Society.*
> *Refer from*
> Victor C. Vaughan Society, *Medical School, University of Michigan.*

B. Alumni organizations.

(1) Enter general alumni associations, funds, etc., under the name of the school, college, or university.

Yale University. Society of the Alumni.
> *Refer from*
> Society of the Alumni of Yale University.

Smith College. Alumnae Association.
> *Refer from*
> Alumnae Association of Smith College.

Paris. École commerciale. Association des anciens élèves.
> *Refer from*
> Association des anciens élèves de l'École commerciale de Paris.

Illinois College, Jacksonville. Alumni Fund Association.
> *Refer from*
> Illinois College Alumni Fund Association.

Columbia University. *School of Law. Alumni Association.*

Exception.—When the association of alumni comprises a professional group better known under its name, entry may be made under the name of the association, with reference from the name of the institution.

Association des ingénieurs sortis de l'École de Liège.
> *Refer from*
> Liège. École des arts et manufactures et des mines. Association des ingénieurs sortis de l'École de Liège.

Association des ingénieurs-techniciens de Charleroi.
> *Refer from*
> Charleroi. Université de travail. Association des ingénieurs-techniciens de Charleroi.

(2) Enter local associations of alumni under their own names.

Harvard Club of New York City.
Harvard Club of Rhode Island.

165

102. Institutions forming an integral part of a larger organization.

Enter the various faculties, colleges, professional schools, laboratories, libraries, chapels, museums, observatories, hospitals, shops, etc., which form an integral part of a university or other institution under the larger institution with the name of the particular entity as subheading.

> **Oxford. University.** *Balliol College.*
> *Refer from*
> Balliol College.
>
> **Yale University.** *Sheffield Scientific School.*
> *Refer from*
> Sheffield Scientific School.
>
> **Bologna. Università degli studi.** *Scuola di farmacia.*
>
> **Toulouse. Université.** *Faculté de droit.*
>
> **Vatican.** *Biblioteca vaticana. Gabinetto numismatico.*
>
> **Harvard University.** *Peabody Museum of American Archaeology and Ethnology.*
> *Refer from*
> Peabody Museum of American Archaeology and Ethnology.
>
> **Chicago. University.** *Hull Physiological Laboratory.*
> *Refer from*
> Hull Physiological Laboratory.
>
> **Berlin. Universität.** *Institut für Meereskunde.*
> *Refer from*
> Institut für Meereskunde, *Berlin.*
> Berlin. Institut für Meereskunde.
>
> **Paris. Université.** *Bibliothèque.*
>
> **Williams College.** *Thompson Memorial Chapel.*
> *Refer from*
> Thompson Memorial Chapel, *Williamstown, Mass.*
> Williamstown, Mass. Thompson Memorial Chapel.
>
> **Michigan. University.** *Observatory.*
>
> **Wisconsin. University.** *Washburn Observatory.*
> *Refer from*
> Washburn Observatory, *Madison, Wis.*
> Madison, Wis. Washburn Observatory.

Exceptions.—

A. Exception may be made in the case of an observatory which is much more likely to be looked for under its own name than under that of the place or of the institution of which it forms a part.

> **Lick Observatory.**
> *Refer from*
> California. University. *Lick Observatory.*
> Mt. Hamilton, Calif. Lick Observatory.
>
> **Allegheny Observatory.**
> *Refer from*
> Allegheny, Pa. Western University of Pennsylvania. *Allegheny Observatory.*

Yerkes Observatory.
Refer from
Chicago. University. *Yerkes Observatory.*
Williams Bay, Wis. Yerkes Observatory.

B. Colleges or professional schools whose names begin with a proper noun or proper adjective may be entered under their own names, particularly if they are situated at a distance from the university of which they form a part, have merely a nominal connection with it, or for other reasons are unlikely to be looked for under its name. Cases in point are some of the American schools which, originally independent, have later affiliated with or become departments of a university.

St. Ignatius College, *Chicago.*
Refer from
St. Louis University. *St. Ignatius College.*

Barnard College, *New York.*
Refer from
Columbia University. *Barnard College.*

103. Institutions located in suburbs later absorbed in a metropolitan area.

When an institution located in a place (town or city) and identified with it has been entered under the name of that place, the entry may remain in that form until the place itself has become absorbed in a larger unit and is known only as a subdivision of a metropolitan area, e.g.,

Charlottenburg. Städtische Volksbücherei.

eventually

Berlin. Stadtbücherei, *Charlottenburg.*

Entries are made under the earlier heading for the period when Charlottenburg was an independent corporation; under the later heading, from the date when it became a part of the Berlin metropolitan area. The two headings are connected by references.

When churches and other institutions located in a section of a city which was formerly independent have become identified with the larger metropolis, they are entered under the latter. (Cf. 124C.)

Philadelphia. Trinity Lutheran Church, *Germantown.*

104. State and provincial institutions (U. S. and Canada).

Enter state and provincial institutions of the United States and Canada under the name of the state or province. The name of the state or province is to be followed by a period and the next word capitalized.

Illinois. Asylum for Insane Criminals, *Chester.*
Refer from
Asylum for Insane Criminals, *Chester, Ill.*
Chester, Ill. Asylum for Insane Criminals.

167

Massachusetts. State Library, *Boston.*
 Refer from
 State Library of Massachusetts, *Boston.*
 Boston. State Library of Massachusetts.

Ohio. State University, *Columbus.*
 Refer from
 Columbus. Ohio State University.

Manitoba. Deaf and Dumb Institute, *Winnipeg.*
 Refer from
 Deaf and Dumb Institute, *Winnipeg.*
 Winnipeg. Deaf and Dumb Institute.

Ontario. Institution for the Education of the Blind, *Brantford.*
 Refer from
 Institution for the Education of the Blind, *Brantford, Ont.*
 Brantford, Ont. Institution for the Education of the Blind.

Texas. Sam Houston State Teachers' College, *Huntsville.*
 Refer from
 Sam Houston State Teachers' College, *Huntsville, Tex.*
 Huntsville, Tex. Sam Houston State Teachers' College.

When the name of the institution begins with the name of the city in which it is located, transpose the name of the city to the end of the entry.

California. State Hospital, *Stockton.*
 Refer from
 Stockton, Calif. State Hospital.
 California. Stockton State Hospital.

There are certain institutions which, although not strictly official, i.e., maintained and controlled by the state, are, on account of their names, most frequently looked for under the name of the state. These may best be entered according to the above rule.

Pennsylvania. University.
 Refer from
 University of Pennsylvania, *Philadelphia.*
 Philadelphia. University of Pennsylvania.

Exception may be made in favor of entry under its own name for a state institution having a distinctive name which gives no indication of its relation to the state.

Miami University, *Oxford, Ohio.*
 Refer from
 Ohio. Miami University, *Oxford.*
 Oxford, Ohio. Miami University.

105. American state historical and agricultural societies.
 Enter American state historical and agricultural societies under the name of the state whether or not it is the first word of the name of the society. If the corporate name begins with the name of the state, the corporate form is to be followed; if not, the name of the state is to be followed by a period.

Ohio State Archaeological and Historical Society.

South Carolina. State Agricultural Society.
  Refer from
  State Agricultural Society of South Carolina.
but
Historical and Philosophical Society of Ohio.
  [*not a state society*]
  Refer from
  Ohio, Historical and Philosophical Society of.

Enter American state societies which are also state boards under the name of the society, with reference from the state.

West Virginia Humane Society.
  Refer from
  West Virginia. *State Board* (*West Virginia Humane Society*)

106. Agricultural experiment stations.
  A. Enter agricultural experiment stations of the United States under the name of the state or territory in which they are organized. Include in the heading the name of the place where the station is located. Refer from the university or college of which the station may form a department, from the name of the station, if it is at all distinctive, and from the name of the place where it is located.

New York. Agricultural Experiment Station, *Geneva.*
  Refer from
  Geneva, N. Y. Agricultural Experiment Station.
New York. Agricultural Experiment Station, *Ithaca.*
  Refer from
  Cornell University. *Agricultural Experiment Station.*
  Ithaca, N. Y. Agricultural Experiment Station.
Puerto Rico. Federal Experiment Station, *Mayagüez.*
  Refer from
  Mayagüez, P. R. (City) Agricultural Experiment Station.
  Mayagüez, P. R. (City) Federal Experiment Station.
Missouri. Fruit Experiment Station, *Mountain Grove.*
  Refer from
  Mountain Grove, Mo. Fruit Experiment Station.
Missouri. State Poultry Experiment Station, *Mountain Grove.*
  Refer from
  Mountain Grove, Mo. State Poultry Experiment Station.

  B. Enter Canadian agricultural experiment stations under CANADA. Include the name of the place in the heading.

Canada. Experimental Station, *Harrow, Ont.*
  Refer from
  Harrow, Ont. Experimental Station.

  C. Enter foreign agricultural experiment stations according to the general rule for institutions. (92)

Gembloux, Belgium. Station agronomique de l'État.
  Refer from
  Belgium. *Ministère de l'agriculture. Station agronomique de l'État, Gembloux.*
  Belgium. Station agronomique de l'État, *Gembloux.*

Santiago de las Vegas, Cuba. Estación Central Agronómica.
Refer from
Cuba. *Secretaría de Agricultura. Estación Central Agronómica.*
Cuba. Estación Central Agronómica, *Santiago de las Vegas.*

Bhadgáon, India. Khándesh Experimental Farm.
Refer from
Khándesh Experimental Farm, *Bhadgáon.*

107. Public schools.

Enter all elementary and secondary schools supported by taxation under the name of the place and refer from the name of the school if distinctive.

New York. Morris High School.
Refer from
Morris High School, *New York.*

Minneapolis. Lincoln School.
Refer from
Lincoln School, *Minneapolis.*

Brooklyn. Public School 48.

Paris. Lycée Janson-de-Sailly.
Refer from
Lycée Janson-de-Sailly, *Paris.*
Janson-de-Sailly, Lycée, *Paris.*

Leipzig. Thomasschule.
Refer from
Thomasschule, *Leipzig.*

Edinburgh. Sciennes School.
Refer from
Sciennes School, *Edinburgh.*

For the entry of institutions of higher learning see 104.

108. Private and endowed schools.

A. Enter American and British private and endowed schools under the name when this begins with a proper noun or proper adjective, otherwise under the place.

Balliol School, *Utica, N. Y.*
Refer from
Utica, N. Y. Balliol School.

Copeland School, *Saratoga Springs, N. Y.*
Refer from
Saratoga Springs, N. Y. Copeland School.

St. Peter's College, *Westminster.*
Refer from
Westminster. St. Peter's College.
Westminster School, *London.*
London. Westminster School.

but

Washington, D. C. National Cathedral School for Girls.
with references from
Cathedral School for Girls, *Washington, D. C.*
National Cathedral School for Girls, *Washington, D. C.*

When a school is known only by the name of the proprietor, enter under his name.

>   **Chesborough (A. J.) school.**

B. Enter foreign private schools under the place, with reference from the name of the school or the proprietor.

>   **Oslo. Nissens Skole.**
>   *Refer from*
>   Nissens Skole, *Oslo.*
>   **Milan. Istituto privato Robiati.**
>   *Refer from*
>   Istituto privato Robiati, *Milan.*
>   Robiati, Ambrogio (*see also*)

109. Indian schools (U. S.)
   A. Enter Indian schools of the U. S. Indian Service and denominational and private schools which receive government support, under the name of the place where located. Refer from the name of the school. For information and lists of schools cf. reports of the Commissioner of Indian Affairs.

>   **Carlisle, Pa.   United States Indian School.**
>   **Pipestone, Minn.   Indian Training School.**
>   **Phoenix, Ariz.   United States Indian Vocational School.**
>   **Morris, Minn.   Indian School.**

B. Private Indian schools not a part of the U. S. Indian Service and not receiving government support are to be entered according to the rule for American private schools. (108)

110. Radio stations.
   Enter radio stations, regardless of their ownership or sponsorship, under the name of the place in which they are located, followed by the name of the station. If the name is limited to call letters, the designation RADIO STATION, or its foreign equivalent, precedes the call letters. Refer from the name or call letters.

>   **Cincinnati.   Radio station WKRC.**
>   *Refer from*
>   WKRC (*Radio station*) *Cincinnati.*
>   **Ames, Iowa.   Radio station WOI.**
>   *Refer from*
>   WOI (*Radio station*) *Ames, Iowa.*
>   **Vatican (City) Stazione radio HVJ.**
>   *Refer from*
>   HVJ (*Stazione radio*) *Vatican (City)*
>   **Guatemala (City) Radio Nacional.**
>   *Refer from*
>   Radiodifusoro Nacional de Guatemala.
>   **Rabat, Morocco.   Radio Maroc.**
>   *Refer from*
>   Radio Maroc, *Rabat, Morocco.*

111. University and union league clubs.

Enter university and union league clubs under the place where they are located, with reference from the name.

> **Washington, D. C. University Club.**
> *Refer from*
> University Club, *Washington, D. C.*

> **Chicago. Union League Club.**
> *Refer from*
> Union League Club of Chicago.

112. Volunteer fire companies and associations.

Enter volunteer fire companies and associations under the name of the place with reference from the name of the company or association.

> **Philadelphia. Hibernia Fire Company.**
> *Refer from*
> Hibernia Fire Company, *Philadelphia.*

> **Chambersburg, Pa. Friendship Fire Company.**
> *Refer from*
> Friendship Fire Company, *Chambersburg, Pa.*

> **Gloucester, Mass. Steam Fire Association.**
> *Refer from*
> Steam Fire Association, *Gloucester, Mass.*

For treatment of the official fire departments of cities or towns see 72.

113. Mercantile library associations.

Enter mercantile library associations, library companies, etc., under the place, with reference from the name of the association.

> **Boston. Mercantile Library Association.**
> *Refer from*
> Mercantile Library Association of Boston.

> **Philadelphia. Mercantile Library Company.**
> *Refer from*
> Mercantile Library Company, *Philadelphia.*

114. Gilds.

Enter gilds under the name of the place, with the name of the company as subheading.

> **London. Merchant Taylors' Company.**
> *Refer from*
> Merchant Taylors' Company, *London.*

> **Dunfermline, Scot. Weavers' Incorporation.**
> *Refer from*
> Weavers' Incorporation, *Dunfermline.*

> **Sheffield, England. Cutlers' Company.**
> *Refer from*
> Cutlers' Company, *Sheffield.*

Religious Societies and Institutions

115. Churches not organized within national bounds.

For ancient churches, the Eastern churches (including the independent units of the Orthodox Eastern communion) and all churches not organized as corporate bodies within national bounds, adopt the most commonly accepted English form of name as the official entry, and use this form for all subject headings.

> **Moravian Church.**
> **Armenian Church.**
> **Orthodox Eastern Church.**
> **Catholic Church.**[17]

116. Catholic and Eastern churches.
    A. Local ecclesiastical units.

(1) Enter ecclesiastical provinces, archdioceses, and other regional districts of Catholic and Eastern churches under the name of the see city, or region for which they are named, adding, in parentheses, the type of jurisdiction, followed by the designation of the office or board.

> **Baltimore** (*Ecclesiastical Province*)
> **Danzig** (*Diocese*) *Bishop.*
> **Harrisburg,** *Pa.* (*Diocese*)
> **Philadelphia** (*Archdiocese*) *Diocesan Board.*

If two or more jurisdictions have come to exist in the same city, add a distinguishing adjective denoting rite.

> **Pittsburgh** (*Diocese, Catholic Byzantine*)
> **Pittsburgh** (*Diocese, Catholic*)

(2) Enter the historic patriarchates under the name of the patriarchal city, adding in parentheses the type of jurisdiction, adding also a distinguishing adjective denoting rite where necessary.

> **Alexandria,** *Egypt* (*Patriarchate*)
> **Alexandria,** *Egypt* (*Patriarchate, Coptic*)
> **Antioch** (*Patriarchate*)
>   [*Used for early material*]
> **Antioch** (*Patriarchate, Syrian Jacobite*)
> **Antioch** (*Patriarchate, Orthodox Melkite*)
> **Antioch** (*Patriarchate, Maronite*)
> **Antioch** (*Patriarchate, Catholic Syrian*)
> **Antioch and all the East** (*Patriarchate, Catholic Melkite*)

Disregard patriarchates that are purely titular.

> **Lisbon** (*Archdiocese*)

---

[17] In English and American Protestant usage, Roman Catholic Church is the more usual and in many cases the legal designation. The Library of Congress uses the shorter form, Catholic Church, a designation preferred by Catholics themselves, and this form, having been established on the printed cards, is consistently followed in these rules.

(3) Enter modern patriarchates, the patriarch of which is the ecclesiastical head of a national church (cf. 116B(2)) under the name of the church, followed by the title (in English).

> **Orthodox Eastern Church, Russian.** *Patriarch.*
> **Orthodox Eastern Church, Rumanian.** *Patriarch.*
> **Orthodox Eastern Church, Yugoslavian.** *Patriarch.*
> Refer from the patriarchal city.
>> **Moscow** (*Patriarchate*)
>> *see*
>> **Orthodox Eastern Church, Russian.** *Patriarch.*

B. Orthodox Eastern Church.

(1) Enter those autocephalous units of the Orthodox Eastern Church which are continuations of ancient patriarchates or archdioceses under the name of the patriarchate or archdiocese.

> **Alexandria,** *Egypt* (*Patriarchate, Orthodox*)
> **Cyprus** (*Archdiocese*)[18]

(2) Enter those autocephalous units of the Orthodox Eastern Church which are organized on a national basis under the name of the church followed by the adjective form of the national name.[19]

> **Orthodox Eastern Church, Russian.**
> **Orthodox Eastern Church, Greek.**

(3) Enter the Basilian monastery at Mt. Sinai, which has independent status as a church of the Byzantine rite, under the heading appropriate to it as a monastery.

> **Sinai. Saint Catharine** (*Basilian monastery*)

C. Lesser Eastern churches.
As the lesser Eastern churches are organized as patriarchal jurisdictions, enter all official publications emanating from the patriarchate under the name of the patriarchate.[20] Use the popular name of the church as the author heading only where a form subheading is used.

> **Alexandria,** *Egypt* (*Patriarchate, Coptic*)
> [*For an official document issued by the Coptic Patriarchate of Alexandria*]
>
> **Coptic Church.** *Liturgy and ritual.*
> Coptic morning service for the Lord's day . . .

D. Eastern churches in communion with Rome.
Enter Eastern churches in communion with Rome under CATHOLIC CHURCH, adding subheading designating rite and, in the case of the Byzantine Catholics,

---

[18] Now demoted to a diocese.

[19] The alternative to this type of entry would be direct entry under the national church, e.g., RUSSIAN CHURCH, BULGARIAN CHURCH (ORTHODOX), GREEK CHURCH (SYNOD OF GREECE).

[20] This is not contradicted by rule 116A(3), because in all these cases the claim to the title is based on succession from the historic patriarchates of the early church.

adding to the name of the rite the adjective denoting the country or language group.

> **Catholic Church.** *Armenian rite.*
> *Ethiopic rite.*
> *Syrian rite.*
> *Byzantine rite.*
> *Byzantine rite (Bulgarian)*
> *Byzantine rite (Russian)*

E. Ecclesiastical documents.

(1) Enter early documents, whether proceeding from general or local officials, directly under the name of the person with added entry, if necessary, under the name of the church body or local ecclesiastical unit. This applies to all documents issued by the Church fathers[21] which as a rule need no added entry under the name of the church or local ecclesiastical unit.

> **Clemens** *Romanus.*
> Epistle of Saint Clement, Bishop of Rome . . .

> **Joannes I,** *Patriarch of Antioch, d.* 648.
> Joannis Episcopi Antiocheni ad Cyrillum Alexandrinum epistola finito Concilio Ephesino scripta.
>   I. Antioch (Patriarchate)

(2) Enter post-patristic official Catholic and Eastern ecclesiastical documents under the name of the church, or the local ecclesiastical unit.

> **Catholic Church.**
> **Mainz** (*Archdiocese*)
> **Etchmiadzin** (*Armenian catholicate*)

F. Liturgies.

Enter liturgies of the Eastern and Latin rites, including the early forms, under the name chosen for the church, adding the form subheading LITURGY AND RITUAL. Use this subheading without modification for collections of two or more books. For collections containing texts translated into a nonliturgical language, add adjective denoting language.[22]

> **Orthodox Eastern Church.** *Liturgy and ritual.*
> **Orthodox Eastern Church.** *Liturgy and ritual. English.*
> **Catholic Church.** *Liturgy and ritual.*
> **Catholic Church.** *Liturgy and ritual. English.*

---

[21] Limit the use of the term Church fathers to the time of Gregory the Great for Latin fathers and to the time of John of Damascus for Greek fathers and the fathers of the lesser Eastern churches.

[22] The liturgical language of the Catholic Church in the West (Patriarchate of Rome) is Latin and for that reason the term Latin rite is used. There are six distinct rites in Latin, of which the Roman, Ambrosian, and Mozarabic are still in use; whereas the African, Gallican, and the so-called Celtic rites are defunct. The Roman rite is extant in four forms: (1) Early pre-Tridentine, (2) Standardized revision by Pope Pius v authorized for general use, (3) Forms in use by various monastic orders called Regular use, (4) Forms which have grown up about certain local churches called Local use.

(1) Enter specific service books of the Orthodox Eastern Church, either in Greek or in any other liturgical language, under the heading ORTHODOX EASTERN CHURCH. LITURGY AND RITUAL, followed by the name of the book preferably in Greek. For translations into liturgical or nonliturgical languages add adjective denoting language.

> **Orthodox Eastern Church.** *Liturgy and ritual. Leitourgikon.*[23]
> **Orthodox Eastern Church.** *Liturgy and ritual. Menaion. English.*

(2) For the lesser Eastern churches, use the form which seems to be the best specific designation for the particular book, either the vernacular, Latin, or an English translation.

> **Armenian Church.** *Liturgy and ritual. Dagharan.*

(3) Enter Eastern liturgies edited for use in Eastern churches in communion with Rome under the name established for the particular rite with subheading LITURGY AND RITUAL. Make added entry under the name of the corresponding non-Catholic group using this same liturgy; refer from CATHOLIC CHURCH. LITURGY AND RITUAL. [NAME OF RITE]

> **Catholic Church.** *Armenian rite. Liturgy and ritual. Mystery*
> *manual of the sacred oblation.*
> Liturgia armena transportata in italiano sino dal 1816 cura del p. Gabriele Avedichian.
>   I. Armenian Church. Liturgy and ritual. Mystery manual of the sacred oblation.
>   *with reference:*
> **Catholic Church.** *Liturgy and ritual. Armenian rite*
>   see
> **Catholic Church.** *Armenian rite. Liturgy and ritual.*

(4) Enter separate books of the Latin rite[24] (all rites in Latin or Roman rite only) under the heading CATHOLIC CHURCH. LITURGY AND RITUAL, followed by the name of the book.

> **Catholic Church.** *Liturgy and ritual. Missal.*
> **Catholic Church.** *Liturgy and ritual. Memoriale rituum.*

(5) Enter collections of Latin service books of the Roman rite used in a specific locality under the usual heading, CATHOLIC CHURCH. LITURGY AND RITUAL, adding the name of the place. Refer from the place with subheading LITURGY AND RITUAL.

---

[23] The Eucharistic liturgy of the various Eastern rites is frequently designated as the "Liturgy." Prefer, however, the specific name of the liturgical book if it can be easily determined. Some forms are found in Jeannette M. Lynn, *An alternative classification for Catholic books* (Chicago, American Library Association, 1937).

[24] Since the Council of Trent, the basic official liturgical books have been the Missal, the Breviary, the Ritual, the Pontifical, the Ceremonial of bishops, the Martyrology, the Memoriale rituum and the Caeremoniale Romanum (for papal ceremonies only).

> **Catholic Church.** *Liturgy and ritual. Salisbury.*
>   The use of Sarum . . .
>   *Refer from*
>   Salisbury (*Diocese*) *Liturgy and ritual.*
>   Sarum use.[25]

For individual service books make added entry with the place as second subheading.

> **Catholic Church.** *Liturgy and ritual. Missal.*
>   Missale ad usum insignis ecclesiae Eboracencis . . .
>   1. Catholic Church. Liturgy and ritual. York.

> **Catholic Church.** *Liturgy and ritual. Ordines.*[26]
>   Ordinale Exon . . .
>   1. Catholic Church. Liturgy and ritual. Exeter.

Exception.—In entering modern directories for use in a specific locality include both the name of the book and the name of the place in the heading, and make added entry with the place as second subheading.[27]

> **Catholic Church.** *Liturgy and ritual. Directory. Treves* (*Diocese*)
>   Directorium Dioecesis Treverensis; seu, Ordo divini officii recitandi missaeque celebrandae . . .
>   1. Catholic Church. Liturgy and ritual. Treves (Diocese)

(6) Enter collections of Latin liturgical books of the Roman rite for a monastic order under the usual heading, CATHOLIC CHURCH. LITURGY AND RITUAL, followed by the name of the order. Refer from the name of the order with subheading LITURGY AND RITUAL.

> **Catholic Church.** *Liturgy and ritual. Benedictine.*
>   *Refer from*
>   Benedictines. *Liturgy and ritual.*

For individual books, make added entry with the order as second subheading.

> **Catholic Church.** *Liturgy and ritual. Breviary.*
>   Breviarium Romanum ad usum Ordinis Carmelitarum Discalcatorum . . .
>   1. Catholic Church. Liturgy and ritual. Carmelite.

Exception.—In entering directories for the use of a monastic order, include the name of the book and the name of the order in the heading.

> **Catholic Church.** *Liturgy and ritual. Directory. Benedictine.*
>   *with added entry:*
>   1. Catholic Church. Liturgy and ritual. Benedictine.

---

[25] These local variations of the Roman rite are frequently called rites, but are more correctly designated by the term *use*.

[26] The subheading ORDINES is used for older compilations of texts giving liturgical directions (often including prayers and worship forms) variously called ordo, ordines, ordines romani, ordinarium, consuetudines, etc.

[27] The subheading DIRECTORY is used for the annual official book of directions for priests, the Ordo divini officii recitandi.

For local monastic service books, make one added entry with the order as second subheading and another with place as second subheading.

> **Catholic Church.** *Liturgy and ritual. Missal.*
> The missal of S. Augustine's Abbey, Canterbury.
>   I. Catholic Church. Liturgy and ritual. Benedictine. II. Catholic Church. Liturgy and ritual. Canterbury.

(7) Enter collections of Latin liturgical books in a rite other than Roman under the usual heading, CATHOLIC CHURCH. LITURGY AND RITUAL, followed by the name of the rite.

> **Catholic Church.** *Liturgy and ritual. Ambrosian rite.*
>   *Refer from*
> Ambrosian rite.
> Milan, Liturgy of.
> Catholic Church. *Liturgy and ritual. Milan (see also)*

For individual service books, make added entry with the rite as second subheading.

> **Catholic Church.** *Liturgy and ritual. Breviary.*
> Breviarium Ambrosianum . . .
>   I. Catholic Church. Liturgy and ritual. Ambrosian rite.

(8) Enter collections of Latin liturgical books translated into any language under the usual heading, CATHOLIC CHURCH. LITURGY AND RITUAL, followed by the name of the language.

> **Catholic Church.** *Liturgy and ritual. English.*

For translations of individual service books, add the name of the language to the heading and make added entry for the language.

> **Catholic Church.** *Liturgy and ritual. Breviary. English.*
>   *with added entry:*
> Catholic Church. Liturgy and ritual. English.

117. Canon law (Catholic and Eastern churches).

These rules cover the canon law of Catholic and Eastern churches. The documents containing the canon law of such Protestant churches as use this term are entered under the name of the denomination concerned, using such subheadings as the circumstances require.

A. General principles.

(1) The decrees, canons, statutes, etc., of individual councils and synods are entered under the heading appropriate to the council or synod involved. (Cf. 119.)

(2) The decrees, etc., issued by individual executives (archbishops, bishops, metropolitans, popes, etc.) are entered under the name of the official in the early period and under the name of the office in the later period. (Cf. 116E.)

(3) Single laws, constitutions, etc., governing a particular body

178

are entered under the name of the body with the name of the law, constitution, etc., as subheading.

(4) Compilations of unknown source and having a specific name are entered according to the rules for anonymous classics. (33)

(5) Compilations known under the name of the individual compiler are entered under his name, but if the compilation is made by an executive in his official capacity, enter under the office.

(6) Compilations that have a particular name and are in force in a particular body are entered under the name of the body with the name of the compilation as subheading.

(7) Miscellaneous compilations of laws in force in any particular body are entered as form headings under the name of the body. Such form headings, however, are not to be used as added entries to assemble texts that may be entered under other headings.

B. Early undivided church. Enter documents considered to be sources of canon law as anonymous classics under their conventional name, unless they are the compilations of individuals or the decrees of early councils. For councils of the early church see 119A.

> **Apostolic canons.**
> **Apostolic constitutions.**
> **Didascalia apostolorum.**
>
> *but*
>
> **Hippolytus,** *Saint, fl.* 217–235.
> Traditio apostolica.

C. Eastern churches.

(1) Enter miscellaneous compilations of law of the Orthodox Eastern Church, the Coptic and other separate Eastern churches under the name of the church followed by the form heading CANONS, NOMO-CANONS, DECREES, ETC.

> **Orthodox Eastern Church.** *Canons, nomocanons, decrees, etc.*

(2) Enter single and collected laws, that can be given a more definite treatment, in accordance with the general principles set forth above (117A (1-6).)

D. Catholic Church. Enter collections of canons, decretals, constitutions, bullaria, etc., of the Catholic Church as follows:

(1) Collections other than those specified in the following paragraphs, and not limited to the decretals, constitutions, etc., of a single pontificate under

> **Catholic Church.** *Canons, decretals, etc.*

(2) Editions of the Decretum of Gratian under

> **Gratianus,** *the Canonist, d. before* 1160.

(3) Editions of the Decretales ("Compilatio nova," "Extravagantes") of Gregory IX under

> **Catholic Church.** *Pope, 1227-1241 (Gregorius IX)*

(4) Editions of the Decretales ("Liber sextus") compiled by order of Boniface VIII under

    Catholic Church. *Pope, 1294-1303 (Bonifacius VIII)*

(5) Editions of the Decretales ("Liber septimus," "Clementinae") of Clemens V, promulgated by John XXII, under

    Catholic Church. *Pope, 1305-1314 (Clemens V)*

(6) Editions of the Decretales extravagantes ("Extravagantes") of John XXII under

    Catholic Church. *Pope, 1316-1334 (Johannes XXII)*

(7) Editions of combinations of (2)-(6), first published Rome, 1582, by authority of the "Correctores Romani," under

    Catholic Church. *Corpus juris canonici.*
      Refer from
    Corpus juris canonici.

(8) Editions of the new official codification promulgated by Benedictus XV, 1917, taking effect May 19, 1918, under

    Catholic Church. *Codex juris canonici.*
      Refer from
    Codex juris canonici.

Special parts, extracts, selections, etc., from the Codex, dealing with particular subjects are entered under

    Catholic Church. *Codex juris canonici [inclusive numbers of the canons and title of the book (Liber) or other subdivisions (Pars, Sectio, Titulus, Caput, Articulus) as the case may be].*
    Catholic Church. *Codex juris canonici. C. 726-1551: De rebus.*
    Catholic Church. *Codex juris canonici. C. 731-1153: De sacramentis.*
    Catholic Church. *Codex juris canonici. C. 1395-1405: De prohibitione librorum.*

(9) For editions of the constitutions, decretals, etc., of a single pontificate see 118A.

(10) Editions of the partially spurious collection attributed to Isidorus Mercator (9th century) with genuine decretals in the form of the Collectio "Hispana" under

    Decretales pseudo-Isidorianae.

For collections prior to Pseudo-Isidor, cf. Friedrich Maassen, *Geschichte der Quellen und der Literatur des canonischen Rechts* (Gratz, Leuschner & Lubensky, 1870).

118. Catholic Church (special rules).
    A. Pope and Holy See.
    (1) Enter under CATHOLIC CHURCH with subheading POPE *(1)*

ecclesiastical documents proceeding from the Holy See;[28] (2) documents proceeding from the pope alone, e.g., collections of bulls, encyclicals, apostolic letters, etc.

> **Catholic Church.** *Pope.*
> Magnum bullarium Romanum . . .

(2) Enter collections of documents issued during a single pontificate under CATHOLIC CHURCH. POPE followed by the dates of the pontificate, and, in parentheses, the name of the pope.

> **Catholic Church.** *Pope, 1585-1590 (Sixtus V)*
> Bullarii; sive, Collectionis constitutionum annis quattuor sui pontificatus editarum a S.D.N. Sixto Quinto . . .

(3) Enter single bulls, encyclicals, and other documents as in the preceding rule, with the addition in the heading of the first Latin word[29] or words of the text by which it is officially known, and the date of issue in parentheses.

> **Catholic Church.** *Pope, 1846-1878 (Pius IX) Ineffabilis Deus (8 Dec. 1854)*

B. Congregations, etc. Enter under CATHOLIC CHURCH with subheading for the congregation, tribunal, or office, documents issuing from such sources. Use the Latin form of name as officially used in the Acta apostolicae sedis, omitting the word sacra which is a prefix of honor.

> **Catholic Church.** *Congregatio Sacrorum Rituum.*
> **Catholic Church.** *Poenitentiaria Apostolica.*

For particular documents officially cited by first words of text, the first Latin word or words of the text may be included in the heading, followed by the date of issue in parentheses.

> **Catholic Church.** *Congregatio Consistorialis. Maxima cura (20 Aug. 1910)*

C. Concordats.

(1) Enter collections of concordats, "modus vivendi," or other agreements concluded between the Holy See and secular governing bodies under the heading CATHOLIC CHURCH with subheading TREATIES, ETC. Refer from CATHOLIC CHURCH. CONCORDATS. Make added entry for compiler.

> **Catholic Church.** *Treaties, etc.*
> Raccolta di concordati su materie ecclesiastiche tra la Santa Sede e le autorita civili.
> I. Mercati, Angelo, comp.

---

[28] The term Holy See embraces the pope and the congregations, tribunals, and offices of the Roman Curia.

[29] Occasionally the pope uses a language other than Latin; use the original language in the heading.

(2) Enter single concordats or agreements under the heading CATHOLIC CHURCH. TREATIES, ETC., adding the dates of the pontificate and, in parentheses, the name of the pope. Make added entry for the secular party or parties to the agreement under the name of the country with subheading TREATIES, ETC. (Cf. 88.) Make added entry or, preferably, *see also* reference under the heading CATHOLIC CHURCH. POPE, followed by the dates of the pontificate and, in parentheses, the name of the pope.

> **Catholic Church.** *Treaties, etc., 1922-1939 (Pius XI)*
> Die Lateran-Verträge zwischen dem Heiligen Stuhl und Italien vom 11. Februar 1929 . . .
>   i. Italy. Treaties, etc., 1900-   (Victor Emmanuel iii)
>   *with reference:*
> **Catholic Church.** *Pope, 1922-1939 (Pius XI)*
>   *see also*
> **Catholic Church.** *Treaties, etc., 1922-1939 (Pius XI)*

(3) Enter early concordats arranged between bishops and secular authorities under the heading for the ecclesiastical jurisdiction authorizing the concordat, with added entry for the secular governmental body which is party to the contract.

D. Indulgences.

(1) Enter indulgences granted by the pope under CATHOLIC CHURCH. POPE, in accordance with rule 118A.

(2) Enter indulgences granted by authorities other than the pope under the name of the jurisdiction in which they are applicable in accordance with rule 116E(2).

(3) Enter indulgences granted by cardinals applicable in their "titular churches" in Rome under the name of the church with added entry under the name of the cardinal.

> **Rome (City)**   **San Nicola in Carcere** *(Church)*

(4) Enter indulgences granted by cardinals applicable to ecclesiastical societies or institutions not within their jurisdiction under the name of the cardinal.

> **Mundelein, George William,** *Cardinal,* 1872-1939.

(5) Enter collections of indulgenced prayers (except those collections which are issued by the Roman Poenitentiaria Apostolica) under the compiler.

> **Seeböck, Philibert,** 1839-1914, *comp.*
> Vollständiges Ablass-Gebetbuch ausschliesslich aus authentischen Ablassgebeten zusammengestellt von P. Philibert Seeböck . . .

(6) Enter collections of indulgenced prayers issued by the Roman Poenitentiaria Apostolica, under the heading CATHOLIC CHURCH. POENITENTIARIA APOSTOLICA.

Catholic Church. *Poenitentiaria Apostolica.*
    . . . Collection of prayers and good works to which the Roman
pontiffs have attached indulgences in favor of all the faithful or
of a certain group of persons, 1899 to 1928; translated and edited
from the official versions by Rev. Richard E. Power . . . under
authority from the Sacred Apostolic Penitentiary . . .
    At head of title: Official Vatican manual of indulgenced prayers.
    I. Power, Richard E., tr.

119. Councils and synods.

A. Enter documents proceeding from early councils of the undivided church, from all general or ecumenical councils both of the
Latin and Eastern churches and from all early patriarchal, primatial
and national councils and local synods prior to the Council of Trent,
under the name by which the council or synod is known, inverting the
place name if necesary so that place name is the entry word. Add
to this the date of the meeting and place where held if place is not
included in the heading.

> **Nicaea, Council of,** 325.
> **Trent, Council of,** 1545-1563.
> **Vatican Council,** 1872.
> **Elvira, Synod of,** *ca.* 300.

B. Enter provincial councils and archdiocesan and diocesan synods
of Catholic ecclesiastical administrative areas under the heading used
for the area, adding subheading CouncIL for ecclesiastical provinces
and Synod for archdioceses and dioceses.

> **Paderborn** (*Archdiocese*) *Synod,* 1688.
> **Mainz** (*Ecclesiastical province*) *Council,* 1540.
> **Westminster** (*Ecclesiastical province*) *Council,* 1852.

If the synod is not held in the see of the ordinary the name of the
place is added to the entry after the date and reference is made from
the place in which the synod was held.

> **Leavenworth,** *Kan.* (*Diocese*) *Synod.* *3d, 1922, Kansas City,*
> *Kan.*

C. Enter plenary councils under the uniform heading CatholIC
ChurCH IN [NAME OF COUNTRY] with subheading Plenary CouncIL
followed by the place and date of meeting. Refer from the name of
the place.

> **Catholic Church in the U. S.** *Plenary Council. 1st, Baltimore,*
> 1852.
>   *Refer from*
> Baltimore, Council of, 1852.
> Baltimore, Plenary Council of, 1852.
> **Catholic Church in Spanish America.** *Plenary Council. 1st,*
> *Rome,* 1899.
>   *Refer from*
> Rome, Council of, 1899.
> Rome, Plenary Council of, 1899.

120. Protestant denominations.

A. Denominations with corporate names. Enter modern denominational bodies organized within national bounds, including the autonomous units of the Church of England, under the latest corporate name[30] in the vernacular of the country.[31]

> **Church of England.**
> **Nippon Seikokwai.**
> **Nederlandsche Hervormde Kerk.**
> **Églises reformées de France.**
> **Svenska kyrkan.**
> **Reformed Church in America.**
> **Presbyterian Church in the U. S. A.**
> **Protestant Episcopal Church in the U. S. A.**
> **Church in Wales.**

When two or more denominations have identical names, add, in parentheses, some distinguishing word or phrase.

> **Church of God** (*Adventist*)
> **Church of God** (*Apostolic*)
> **Church of God** (*New Dunkers*)
> **Church of God** (*Headquarters at Anderson, Ind.*)
> **Friends, Society of** (*Hicksite*)
> **Presbyterian Church in the U. S. A.** (*Old school*)
> **Presbyterian Church in the U. S. A.** (*New school*)

B. Denominations without corporate names (state or national churches). Enter Protestant denominational bodies organized as state or national churches but without a distinctive corporate name under a conventional form of name in the vernacular of the country.

This applies to:

(1) Swiss cantonal churches (French and German cantons).

> **Église nationale de Genève** ₍de Neuchâtel, etc.₎
> **Evangelisch-reformierte Kirche des Kantons Aargau** ₍Berne, etc.₎

(2) German state churches prior to their reorganization into more or less self-governing bodies in the nineteenth century.

> **Evangelische Landeskirche in Nassau-Saarbrücken.**
> **Evangelisch-lutherische Landeskirche in Reuss (Jüngere Linie)**
> **Evangelisch-reformierte Landeskirche in Lippe.**

C. Denominational bodies congregational in polity.

(1) Enter general and regional organizations of denominational bodies congregational in polity under their own names.

---

[30] In a few exceptional cases an inverted form of heading has been used in order to make the distinctive word in the name the entry word, e.g., Friends, Society of; Churches of God in North America, General Eldership of.

[31] Small libraries may prefer the English form for Oriental and East European churches, e.g., Episcopal church in Japan, instead of Nippon Seikokwai, but the vernacular is the better practice for scholarly collections.

>American Unitarian Association.
>General Council of Congregational Christian Churches.
>Congregational Union of England and Wales.
>Northern Baptist Convention.
>Southern Baptist Convention.
>Central Eastern Swedish Baptist Conference.

(2) Enter state, provincial, and lesser Baptist, Congregational, and Unitarian[32] local organizations as subheadings under the form headings BAPTISTS, CONGREGATIONAL CHURCHES, UNITARIAN CHURCHES, subdivided by country or state. In each case refer from the name of the local organization.

>**Baptists.** *Pennsylvania. Philadelphia Baptist Association.*
> *Refer from*
>Philadelphia Baptist Association.
>**Baptists.** *Alabama. Colored Bethlehem Baptist Association.*
> *Refer from*
>Colored Bethlehem Baptist Association.
>Bethlehem Baptist Association (Negro)
>**Primitive Baptists.** *Texas. Salem Association of Primitive Baptists.*
> *Refer from*
>Salem Association of Primitive Baptists.
>**Congregational Churches in Connecticut.** *South Consociation of Litchfield County.*
> *Refer from*
>South Consociation of Litchfield County.
>**Congregational Churches in Oregon.** *Conference.*
> *Refer from*
>Oregon Congregational Conference.

But enter local organizations of the Society of Friends as subheadings under the name of the society.

>**Friends, Society of.** *Philadelphia Yearly Meeting.*

D. Legislative and administrative departments and organizations.
(1) Enter the legislative and administrative departments and organizations of a denominational body under the name of the denomination.

>**Presbyterian Church in the U. S. A.** *General Assembly.*
>**Methodist Episcopal Church.** *General Conference.*
>**Church of England.** *National Assembly.*
>**Presbyterian Church in the U. S. A.** *Board of Foreign Missions.*
>**Protestant Episcopal Church in the U. S. A.** *National Council.*

(2) Enter societies functioning solely as a department of or through the denominational body as subheading under the name of the denomination, or of the department to which they are subsidiary. (Cf. 128.)

---

[32] The Library of Congress enters Unitarian local bodies directly under their own names.

> **Evangelical Lutheran Synod of East Pennsylvania.** *Women's Home and Foreign Missionary Society.*
> **Presbyterian Church in the U. S. A.** *Synodical of South Carolina.*
> [*A women's organization*]
> **Protestant Episcopal Church in the U. S. A.** *National Council. Women's Auxiliary.*

E. **Local administrative units.** Enter local administrative units into which a denominational body divides itself, variously known as provinces, dioceses, synods, presbyteries, classes, conferences, missions, missionary districts, etc., under a heading consisting of the name of the denomination followed by the name of the administrative unit in the plural, followed by the locality.[33]

> **Church of England in Canada.** *Dioceses. Huron.*
> **Protestant Episcopal Church in the U. S. A.** *Dioceses. New York.*
> **Presbyterian Church in the U. S. A.** *Synods. New York.*
> **Presbyterian Church in the U. S. A.** *Presbyteries. Pittsburgh.*
> **Methodist Episcopal Church.** *Conferences. Baltimore.*
> **Evangelical Lutheran Ministerium of Pennsylvania and Adjacent States.** *Conferences. Reading.*
> **Evangelical Lutheran Synod of Iowa and Other States.** *Districts. Northern District.*
> **Reformed Church in the U. S.** *Classes. Eastern Ohio.*
> **Methodist Episcopal Church.** *Missions and missionary conferences. New Mexico Spanish Mission.*

Exceptions.—

(1) Enter dioceses of the Church of England in Great Britain (in conformity with the usage for the Catholic Church) under the name of the see city with the qualification Diocese, or Province, added in parentheses.

> **London** (*Diocese*)
> **York** (*Province*)

(2) Enter overseas dioceses not organized into autonomous churches under the heading Church of England with subheading Dioceses, followed by the word Overseas in parentheses and the name of the locality.

> **Church of England.** *Dioceses (Overseas) Bermuda.*

(3) The Lutheran synods that entered and now comprise the United Lutheran Church in America are entered under their own names, because of their long independent history and their earlier membership in larger bodies.

> **Evangelical Lutheran Synod of Pennsylvania and Adjacent States.**
> **Illinois Synod of the United Lutheran Church in America.**

---

[33] The Library of Congress makes an exception for the dioceses of the Protestant Episcopal Church in the U. S. A., using the following form:
> **Protestant Episcopal Church in the U. S. A.** *New York (Diocese)*

F. Local ecclesiastical councils. Enter councils called by local Baptist, Congregational, Unitarian, etc., churches, or at the request of a local church by a local association of churches, under the name of the church or association issuing the call for the council.

> **Brooklyn. Plymouth Church.** *Advisory Council,* 1876.
> Proceedings of the Advisory Council of Congregational churches and ministers called by the Plymouth Church of Brooklyn, N. Y., and held in Brooklyn from the 15th to the 24th of February, 1876.

G. Creeds, hymnals, and service books.

(1) Enter creeds, hymnals, and service books issued by a local church or for its use under the name of the church.

> **Boston. King's Chapel.**
> Liturgy collected for the use of King's Chapel.

(2) Enter creeds, hymnals, and service books issued by denominational bodies under the name of the body. Add the name of the creed or hymnal in the heading only if essential for the arrangement of large groups of material; the name of a service book, if added, follows the subheading LITURGY AND RITUAL.

> **Presbyterian Church in the U. S. A.**
> The hymnal . . .
> **United Lutheran Church in America.** *Liturgy and ritual.*
> Common service book . . .
> **Church of England.** *Liturgy and ritual. Coronation service.*
> **Church of England.** *Book of common prayer.*[34]

121. Creeds, hymnals, and service books (Jewish).

Enter Jewish creeds, hymnals, and service books under the heading JEWS. LITURGY AND RITUAL.

No single Jewish organization represents all Jews, but the continuity of liturgical rites and forms justifies an entry in this form.

> **Jews.** *Liturgy and ritual.*
> Prayer book; abridged for Jews in the armed forces of the United States.
>
> **Jews.** *Liturgy and ritual. Hagadah. 1934.*
> The Haggadah. A new edition, with English translation, introduction, and notes by Cecil Roth.
> I. Jews. Liturgy and ritual. Hagadah. English. 1934. II. Roth, Cecil, 1899-   ed. and tr.

122. Religious orders.

Enter religious orders under a conventional short form of name in English, if the order extends over more than one country and is known by an English name.

---

[34] By exception the Book of common prayer is entered directly under the name of the church without the subheading LITURGY AND RITUAL.

Jesuits *not* Society of Jesus.
Benedictines *not* Order of St. Benedict.
Poor Clares.
Sisters of the Holy Cross.
Ursulines.
Brigittines.
Mekhitarists.

Exceptions, variations, and further specifications.—

A. Enter religious orders under their full name if a conventional form of name has not come into English use.

Congregation of the Holy Cross.
Congregation of the Sacred Hearts of Jesus and Mary.
Society of the Divine Word.

This will apply especially to orders of women that have episcopal approbation only.

B. Enter religious orders known historically only under the Latin form under that name.

Humiliati.
Reformati.

C. Enter religious orders operating in foreign countries and unknown under an English name, under a vernacular form.

Hijas de Jesús.
Sœurs de Saint-Augustin.
Sœurs des prisons de la Congrégation de Marie-Joseph.
Instituto de las Esclavas del Corazón de Jesús.

This will apply primarily to congregations and institutes operating solely under the approval of the local bishop and not having received pontifical approbation.

D. Enter "second" orders, i.e., orders of women taking solemn vows and following the same rule as the corresponding male orders save for necessary adaptations, and without a distinctive name, under the adjectival form of the name of the order followed by the word NUNS.[35]

Benedictine Nuns.
　Refer from
　Benedictines. *Second Order.*
but
Poor Clares.
　with reference from
　Franciscans. *Second Order.*

E. Enter "third" orders, i.e., organizations of lay people living in the world but observing as far as possible the rules of an order, whenever they have no name of their own, as subheadings under the names of the "first" orders.

---

[35] This unusual procedure is necessary because the English language no longer permits the feminine endings, as for instance, "Benedictinesses."

Franciscans. *Third Order.*

It must be noted that many of these "third" orders by making simple vows and leading a conventual life have become "religious."

Sisters of the Third Order of St. Francis of the Perpetual Adoration.

F. Enter reform movements no longer under the jurisdiction of the order proper and having their own rules, under their own names. Refer from the parent order.

Capuchins.
with reference: Franciscans *see also* Capuchins.
Olivetans.
with reference: Benedictines *see also* Olivetans.

G. Enter orders similar in name and customarily distinguished by addition of the name of the location of the mother house under their names with addition of location of the mother house by means of a preposition, or by a comma, or by enclosure in parentheses.[36]

Sisters of Bon Secours of Paris.
Sisters of Notre Dame de Namur.
Sisters of St. Joseph of Carondelet.
Sisters of Charity of Cincinnati, Ohio.

H. Enter subdivisions into which an order is divided as subheadings under the order but in the language of the territory where they are principally operative.

Jesuits. *Missouri Province.*
Jesuits. *Provincia de Andalucía.*
Dominicans. *Provincia de Buenos Aires.*
Benedictines. *Bursfelder Kongregation.*
Benedictine Nuns. *Congregation of Saint Scholastica.*
Benedictines. *Congrégation de Cluny.*[37]

(1) Enter documents issued by a regional group which does not have an official jurisdictional status under the name of the order with subdivision for the region.

Jesuits. *Spain.*

123. Monasteries, abbeys, convents, etc.
A. Enter monasteries, abbeys, convents, priories, etc., (other than those of the United States and the British Empire whose names begin with a proper noun or a proper adjective, cf. 123C), which are located in a city or town, under the name of the place. Give the name of the institution in the vernacular followed in parentheses and in English

---

[36] Cf. practice observed in the *Annuario pontificio* (Città del Vaticano) in listing the orders of which a cardinal may be the protector.
[37] The Library of Congress has entered Cluniacs under their own name on the strength of popular usage.

by the particular type of institution combined with the name of the order.[38] Refer from the name of the institution.

> **Angers, France. Saint-Aubin** (*Benedictine abbey*)
>   *Refer from*
>   Saint-Aubin (*Benedictine abbey*) Angers.
> **Rijnsburg, Netherlands. Sint Maria** (*Abbey of Benedictine nuns*)
>   *Refer from*
>   Sint Maria (*Abbey of Benedictine nuns*) Rijnsburg, Netherlands.
> **Vienna. Unsere Liebe Frau zu den Schotten** (*Benedictine abbey*)
>   *Refer from*
>   Unsere Liebe Frau zu den Schotten (*Benedictine abbey*) Vienna.
> **Florence. San Onofrio** (*Convent*)
>   *Refer from*
>   San Onofrio (*Convent*) Florence.

(1) If the specific name of the institution cannot be ascertained, use the descriptive name of the institution combined with that of the order.

> **Barcelona. Monasterio Domenico.**
> **Rheinfelden. Johanniterkommende.**
> **New Orleans. Ursuline convent.**

(2) When a village or town has grown up around a monastic institution and bears the same name, the entry consists of the name of the place followed by the type of institution combined with the order in parentheses and in English.

> **Fulda,** *Ger.* (*Benedictine abbey*)
> **Einsiedeln,** *Switzerland* (*Benedictine abbey*)
> **St. Gall,** *Switzerland* (*Benedictine abbey*)

as distinct from

> **Fulda,** *Ger.* (*City*)
> **Einsiedeln,** *Switzerland* (*City*)
> **St. Gall,** *Switzerland* (*City*)
> **St. Gall,** *Switzerland* (*Canton*)

When it is necessary to add the name of the province after the name of the country in order to distinguish one town from another with the same name, to avoid successive parentheses in the heading, give

---

[38] The terms monastery, convent, abbey, priory, in themselves do not indicate whether the institution is one of male or female religious. In popular English usage, however, a monastery is a house for men, and a convent is one for women. In accord with this usage, monastery is used for an institution for male religious and convent for an institution for female religious whenever either word is called for in the explanatory phrase following the name. In the case of abbeys and priories, the forms Benedictine abbey, Dominican priory, etc., indicate houses of men but such circumlocutions as Priory of Augustinian canonesses, Abbey of Benedictine nuns, etc., are necessary to indicate houses of women.

the descriptive name of the institution in the vernacular and without parentheses.

> **Eldena, Ger. (Pomerania) Cisterzienserkloster.**
> *not* **Eldena,** *Ger.* *(Pomerania)* *(Cistercian abbey)*

(3) When a village or town has grown up around a monastic institution and bears a different name, enter under the name of the monastery followed by the name of the place.

> **Averbode** *(Premonstratensian abbey) Testelt, Belgium.*

B. Enter a monastery or other monastic institution not located in a city, town, or village under its own name. Add the name of the province or other similar geographic designation and name of country if necessary for purposes of identification.

> **Grande-Chartreuse** *(Monastery)*
> **Monte Cassino** *(Benedictine abbey)*
> **Santa María** *(Augustinian abbey) Estany, Spain.*

C. Enter abbeys, priories, etc., of the United States and the British Empire, whose names begin with a proper noun or a proper adjective, under the first word of their names. If the name of the place does not occur in the name of the institution, add it in the heading and refer from it. If the name includes the name of the place in which the institution is located, the country may be added if necessary to distinguish between two institutions having the same name. Give the particular type of institution in parentheses if it is not evident from the name.

> **Ely Abbey.**
> **Tintern Abbey.**
> **St. Augustine's Abbey,** *Canterbury.*
> **St. Augustine's Abbey,** *Ramsgate.*
> **St. Benedict's Abbey,** *Atchison, Kan.*
> **Bangor Abbey** *(Ireland)*
> **Bangor Abbey** *(Wales)*

124. Churches, cathedrals, etc.[39]

Enter churches, cathedrals, basilicas, chapels, baptisteries, etc., also synagogues, in accordance with the general rule (92), under the name of the place in which they are located, with exceptions as specified in 124K-L, 125C. Refer from the name or names by which the church, congregation, parish, etc., is known.[40]

---

[39] The term "church" for the purpose of these rules may be defined as a local establishment for the public observance of Christian worship. It covers (1) the edifice used for the purposes of the establishment, whether denominated cathedral, church, meeting-house, or other term; (2) the organization functioning as the establishment, whether called church, parish, society, congregation, or other name (but cf. 125A); (3) the geographical territory to which the activities of the establishment are limited, usually denominated parish.

[40] A general reference may serve the same purpose in some cases, e.g.,
First Congregational Church.
   Congregational churches designated merely by number are entered under place, *e.g.,* Moline, Ill. First Congregational Church.

Philadelphia. Church of the Epiphany.
Refer from
Church of the Epiphany, *Philadelphia.*
Tenafly, N. J. Tenafly Presbyterian Church.
Refer from
Tenafly Presbyterian Church, *Tenafly, N. J.*
Hamburg. Israelitischer Tempel.
Refer from
Israelitischer Tempel, *Hamburg.*
Washington, D. C. Cathedral of Saint Peter and Saint Paul.
Refer from
Cathedral of Saint Peter and Saint Paul, *Washington, D. C.*
National Cathedral, *Washington, D. C.*
Washington, D. C. National Cathedral.
New York. Trinity Church.
Refer from
Trinity Church, *New York.*
Trinity Corporation, *New York.*
Corporation of Trinity Church in New York City.
New York. Trinity Corporation.
Verona. Duomo di Santa Maria Matricolare.
Refer from
Duomo di Santa Maria Matricolare, *Verona.*
Santa Maria Matricolare, Duomo di, *Verona.*
Lisbon. Basilica do Santissimo Coração de Jesus.
Refer from
Basilica do Santissimo Coração de Jesus, *Lisbon.*
Santissimo Coração de Jesus, Basilica do, *Lisbon.*

A. If the word church, cathedral,[41] etc., does not occur in the name, add the appropriate designation in English and in parentheses.

Paris. Notre Dame (*Cathedral*)
Florence. San Giovanni (*Baptistery*)
Pavia. San Michele Maggiore (*Basilica*)
Mainz. St. Martin (*Cathedral*)
Xanten, Ger. Sankt Victor (*Church*)

But add without parentheses an explanatory word presupposed by the use of the name of the church in the possessive case.

Bath, Eng. St. Michael's Church.
not Bath, Eng. St. Michael's (*Church*)
Quedlinburg, Ger. St. Servatiikirche.

B. For British cathedrals known familiarly by the name of the city, the word CATHEDRAL (or MINSTER) is used in composition with the name of the city.

York Minster.
Winchester Cathedral.

---

[41] The German word "Dom" is used not only for a cathedral, but also for the principal church in any city. When it is necessary to add an explanatory word to the name in the heading, use CATHEDRAL for churches that are the seat of a bishop, and CHURCH for others.

but
London. St. Paul's Cathedral.
Dublin. Cathedral Church of the Holy Trinity.

C. When it is necessary to distinguish between two or more churches of the same name in a city, add the name of the denomination or the name of the locality within the city, or both.

Baltimore. St. James's Church (*Catholic*)
New York. St. Peter's Church, *Manhattan* (*Catholic*)
New York. St. Peter's Church, *Manhattan* (*Protestant Episcopal*)
London. St. Paul's Church, *Covent Garden.*

D. When it is necessary to distinguish between different church edifices used concurrently or successively by the same church organization, include the name or address of the individual church in the heading.

New York. Collegiate Church. *Fifth Ave. and 48th Street.*
New York. Collegiate Church. *West End Ave. and 77th Street.*

E. Congregational churches, especially in New England, that call themselves "Church of Christ" or "First Church of Christ" of a given city, frequently add the word Congregational to the name for the purpose of popular identification (e.g., First Church of Christ, Congregational) or incorporate the word in the name and drop "of Christ" (e.g., First Congregational Church). When usage on publications of the same institution varies, prefer the form "Church of Christ" because it is the historical name and retains local coloring. If it is necessary to add the denominational adjective for identification, give it in parentheses following the usage for explanatory terms. Refer from forms used but not adopted as heading.

East Haddam, Conn. First Church of Christ (*Congregational*)

F. When a church changes its denominational affiliation without changing its name, add in parentheses the denominational adjective of the new relationship.

Ipswich, Mass. Independent Congregational Church (*Unitarian*)

G. If the name of a church cannot be ascertained, or if it is not commonly known and very rarely used, enter under the name of the place followed by the generic term in the vernacular. Refer from the specific name when known.

Tortosa, Spain. Catedral.
Bologna. Cattedrale.
Pisa. Battistero.
Chaumont, France. Église.
Santillana, Spain. Iglesia Colegial.

H. Enter a church established to minister to the needs of foreign

193

residents, under the name of the city followed by the name of the church in the language in which it functions.

> **Geneva. English Church.**
> **Paris. American Church.**
> **Philadelphia. Église épiscopale française du St. Sauveur.**

I. Enter a church organized by foreign immigrants who are potential citizens of the adopted country, under the name of the church in the adopted language with reference from the original name.

> **St. Louis. Trinity Lutheran Church.**
> *Refer from*
> St. Louis. Erste Deutsche Evangelisch-lutherische Gemeinde U. A. C.
> Deutsche Evangelisch-lutherische Gemeinde U. A. C. in St. Louis.
> Trinity Lutheran Church, *St. Louis.*

J. For churches in the Holy Land, in which the interest is universal throughout Christendom, use the conventional English form of the name.

> **Jerusalem. Church of the Holy Sepulcher.**
> **Bethlehem. Church of the Nativity.**

K. Enter Spanish missions (e.g., those in California and the Southwest) directly under their names.

> **San Gabriel Mission.**
> **San Carlos Borromeo Mission.**
> **San Xavier del Bac Mission.**

L. Enter churches, chapels, etc., located in the open country under their own names followed by the name of the geographical territory (i.e., township, county, state) in which they are located.

> **Bever Creek Church,** *Henry Co., Va.*
> **Mount Pisgah Church** *(Presbyterian) Woodford Co., Ky.*
> **Macedonia Christian Church,** *Taylor Township, Orange Co., Va.*

125. Church vs. parish,[42] **society, etc.**

A. In older New England churches of congregational polity when local congregational constituencies embrace two separate organizations, one (the church) consisting of members in full and regular standing, the other (the society of the church or parish) consisting of all members of the parish who do or do not have full membership, both organizations must be considered and entered under their own names.

> **New Haven. First Church.**
> *[Used for edifice and for First church society—members in good standing]*

---

[42] By parish as used in this section is understood *ecclesiastical parish.* Parishes constituting political divisions, corresponding to townships, or similar districts are entered under their names, e.g., BEAUMONT, ENG. (PARISH); BRISTOL, VA. (PARISH); ASCENSION PARISH, LA.

> **New Haven. First Ecclesiastical Society.**
> [*Used for the parish organization including both members in full
> church standing and members of the parish not in full communion*]

B. When in addition to the parish church, there are within the parish subsidiary chapels at different locations, use the name of the parish church in the heading for material involving the whole parish or the parish church. If the chapels have distinctive names of their own, use these in headings where they are concerned. Connect entries by appropriate references.

> **Washington, D. C. St. Alban's Church.**
> *Refer from*
> St. Alban's Church, *Washington, D. C.*
> Washington, D. C. St. Alban's Parish.
> **Washington, D. C. St. David's Chapel.**
> *Refer from*
> St. David's Chapel, *Washington, D. C.*
> *and refer to and from*
> Washington, D. C. St. Alban's Church.

C. Enter under the name of the parish those "larger parishes" composed of several congregations, each with its own church, which set up or do not set up a larger organization, but have one common pastor. Make separate headings when required for each individual unit and correlate with the "larger parish" by means of cross references.

> **New Ringgold Parish,** *Schuylkill Co., Pa.*
> [*This parish consists of four congregations: Christ Church, Mc-
> Keansburg; Frieden's Church, New Ringgold; Zion Church,
> Lewiston Valley; and Zion Church, Tuscarora*]
> *Refer to and from*
> McKeansburg, Pa. Christ Church.
> New Ringgold, Pa. Frieden's Church.
> Tuscarora, Pa. Zion Church.
> Zion Church, *Lewiston Valley, Pa.*
> [*Open country*]

126. Subsidiary church institutions.

A. Enter the churches of monasteries, abbeys, convents, etc., as subheadings under the heading appropriate to these institutions, using the word church in the vernacular. If the church has a name different from that of the institution to which it belongs, use this name as subheading. If the monastic institution dies out, but the church continues in use as a parish church, follow the rule for monasteries if the church has no special name; but if the church has a name of its own, follow the rules for churches, in which case a separate entry is made for the monastic establishment.

> **Ottobeuron,** *Ger.* (*Benedictine abbey*) *Kirche.*

B. Enter altars, baptisteries, chapels, etc., subsidiary to the main church edifice, as subheadings under the heading appropriate to the main edifice. If the subheading consists of a distinctive name, refer from it and from the place with it as a direct subheading.

Fréjus, France. Notre Dame et Saint Léonce (*Cathedral*) *Baptistère.*

Augsburg. St. Anna (*Church*) *Fuggerkapelle.*
  Refer from
  Fuggerkapelle, *Augsburg.*
  Augsburg. Fuggerkapelle.

Florence. San Marco (*Church*) *Capella di Santo Antonio.*
  Refer from
  Capella di Santo Antonio, *Florence.*
  Florence. Capella di Santo Antonio.

C. Enter cathedral and collegiate chapters as subheadings under the heading for the cathedral or collegiate church with which they are connected by adding the word chapter in the vernacular.

Passau. Dom. *Kapitel.*
Le Mans. Saint Julien (*Cathedral*) *Chapitre.*

For cathedral chapters, refer from the name of the diocese.

Passau (*Diocese*) *Cathedral Chapter*
  see
Passau. Dom. *Kapitel.*

D. Enter the variously named boards of executives of a church (trustees, elders, deacons, church wardens, vestry, church council, etc.), also special committees appointed by the church, as subheadings under the heading used for the church.

New York. Trinity Church. *Men's Committee.*
Savannah. Independent Presbyterian Church. *Flower Committee.*

E. Enter Sunday schools, Bible classes, etc., that is, all institutions whose purpose is to advance the religious knowledge of the church members, as subheadings under the heading used for the church.

Chicago. Third Presbyterian Church. *Sunday School.*
Philadelphia. Church of Our Redeemer. *Christian Workers' Bible Class.*
Providence. First Baptist Church. *Sunday School. Library.*

For schools conducted by churches that provide religious and secular instruction see PRIVATE AND ENDOWED SCHOOLS. (108)

For church auxiliary societies see 128.

F. Enter the publications of unorganized groups of church members under the heading used for the church with subheading MEMBERS, or the term that is used in the publication itself.

Wayne, Neb. Methodist Episcopal Church. Members and Friends.
Rochester, N. Y. Lake Avenue Memorial Baptist Church. Ladies.
Ishpeming, Mich. Grace Church. Women.

127. Denominational societies with local units.

Enter denominational or interdenominational religious societies, confraternities, sodalities, etc., under their names; regional groups of such societies under the name of the society with the name of the regional group as subheading; but enter local congregational or parish units of these societies as subheadings under the heading for the church in which they function.

> **Epworth League.**
> **Still Pond, Md. Methodist Episcopal Church. Epworth League.**
> **Society of St. Vincent de Paul.** *U. S.* ₎*Bolivia, France, etc.*₎
> **Society of St. Vincent de Paul.** *U. S. Central Council of Phila-*
> *delphia.*

128. Church auxiliary societies.

Enter church auxiliary societies as subheadings under the heading for the church in which they function. (Cf. 120D, 126D-F.)

> **Wilmington, Del. Holy Trinity Church. Ladies Parish Aid So-**
> **ciety.**
> **Evanston, Ill. First Methodist Episcopal Church. Queen Esther**
> **Circle.**
> **Omaha. Temple Israel. Sisterhood.**

129. Temples.

In general, follow the same rules of entry for temples as for churches, except that for ancient temples, especially those in extinct cities when they are known only from archaeological remains, use the English form of name.

A. Enter a temple dedicated to a special deity under the name of the city followed by the words TEMPLE OF ₎NAME OF DEITY₎.

> **Dandara, Egypt. Temple of Hathor.**
> *Refer from*
> Hathor, Temple of, *Dandara, Egypt.*
> **Ephesus. Temple of Artemis.**
> *Refer from*
> Artemis, Temple of, *Ephesus.*

B. Enter a temple named after the builder as in A. above, using the name of the builder instead of the name of the special deity.

> **Abydos, Egypt. Temple of Rameses I.**
> *Refer from*
> Rameses ɪ, Temple of, *Abydos, Egypt.*

C. Enter the temple of a foreign ethnic deity under the name of the city followed by the ethnic adjective governing the word temple.

> **Rome (City)   Syrian Temple.**

D. Enter a temple having a specific name under the city followed by the name of the temple, adding the word TEMPLE in parentheses if necessary for clarity. Refer from the specific name.

Kedu, Java. Tjandi Mendoet.
Refer from
Tjandi Mendoet, *Kedu, Java.*
Hanoi, Indochina. Chên Wu Pagoda.
Refer from
Chên Wu Pagoda, *Hanoi, Indochina.*
Cheribon, Java. Tiao-Kak-Sie (*Temple*)
Refer from
Tiao-Kak-Sie (*Temple*) *Cheribon, Java.*

E. Enter a temple having no particular designation under the name of the city followed by the word TEMPLE.

Amritsar (City) Temple.
Madura, India (City) Temple.

F. Enter a temple located in the open country under its own name with the word TEMPLE added in parentheses if necessary.

Ramesseum.
Angkor Vat (*Temple*)

130. Mosques.

The same general rules which apply to temples apply also to mosques, i.e., enter under the place followed by the name of the mosque. Use the vernacular if that form of name is generally used in western literature, otherwise use the English form of the name. Refer from the name of the mosque.

Samarkand. Gur Emir (*Mosque*)
Refer from
Gur Emir (*Mosque*) *Samarkand.*
Istanbul. St. Sophia.
Refer from
Istanbul. Hagia Sophia.
Hagia Sophia, *Istanbul.*
St. Sophia, *Istanbul.*
Kairwan. Mosque of Sidi Okba.
Refer from
Sidi Okba, Mosque of, *Kairwan.*

Miscellaneous Bodies Not Included
in the Specifications for Societies
and Institutions

This section includes conferences, congresses, exhibitions, and other occasional meetings; firms, and other business concerns; committees and classes of citizens; foundations and endowments; parks, cemeteries, etc.

131. Diplomatic congresses.[43]

Enter diplomatic congresses or conferences for the negotiation of a peace between belligerent powers, and all other official congresses or conferences commonly known by the name of the place of meeting, and noncontinuing, under the name of the place of meeting. (Cf. 88.)

> **Rastatt. Congress, 1797-1799.**
> **Vienna. Congress, 1814-1815.**
> **Berlin. Congress, 1878.**
> **Paris. Peace Conference, 1919.**
> **Moscow. Conference, 1943.**

In more recent years many conferences and congresses have been called for the purpose of discussion, mutual understanding, and the promotion of international agreement; some of them are consultative only; others lead to international pacts and treaties. It is preferable to enter congresses of this nature under their names, as they frequently form a continuing sequence, held at intervals in different places.

The conventions or agreements resulting from international conferences are entered under the name of the conference.[44] (Cf. 88B.)

> **Imperial Conference,** *London,* **1930.**
> **Imperial Economic Conference,** *Ottawa,* **1932.**

---

[43] Diplomatic congresses are meetings of plenipotentiaries for the discussion and settlement of international affairs. They are called at the invitation of one nation, with the concurrence of the participating governments. Such congresses have frequently been convoked for the negotiation of a peace between belligerent powers and the redistribution of territory which, in most cases, is one of the conditions of peace. Many of the earlier diplomatic congresses had no distinctive name, but were known by the name of the city in which they were held. The more recent congresses usually have descriptive names but are nevertheless known by the name of the city.

[44] For special treatment of an involved and interrelated series of international conferences and resulting agreements, revisions, etc., see Library of Congress information cards under the following headings:

> International Telegraph Conference (36-23352)
> International Radiotelegraph Conference (36-23357)
> International Telegraph Union (36-23353)
> International Telegraph Bureau, *Bern* (36-15303)
> International Radiotelegraph Bureau, *Bern* (36-23371)
> International Radiotelegraph Union (36-23367)
> International Telecommunication Bureau, *Bern* (36-23372)
> European Radio Conference (36-29054)

132. International meetings.

Enter international meetings, conferences, and congresses, of private persons, under their English names provided the English name has appeared in any of the publications of the conference. In other cases enter under the name in the language in which most of the publications have appeared, or when this cannot be ascertained, under the name by which the conference is best known. Make references from all other forms of name, and from the place where each congress has been held.

International Congress of Orientalists.
  Refer from
  Orientalists, International Congress of.
  Congrès international des Orientalistes.
  Internationaler Orientalisten Congress. etc., etc.

International Geographical Congress. *1st, Antwerp,* 1871.
  Refer from
  Congrès international pour le progrès des sciences géographiques, cosmographiques et commerciales.
  Congrès international de géographie.
  Antwerp. Congrès international pour le progrès des sciences géographiques, cosmographiques et commerciales. *1st,* 1871.

International Geographical Congress. *2d, Paris,* 1875.
  Refer from
  Paris. Congrès international de géographie. *2d,* 1875.

International Geographical Congress. *3d, Venice,* 1881.
  Refer from
  Congresso geografico internazionale.
  Congresso internazionale geografico.
  Venice. Congresso geografico internazionale. *3d,* 1881.

International Geographical Congress. *4th, Paris,* 1889.
  Refer from
  Paris. Congrès international de géographie. *4th,* 1889.

International Geographical Congress. *5th, Bern,* 1891.
  Refer from
  Bern. Congrès international de géographie. *5th,* 1891.

International Geographical Congress. *6th, London,* 1895.
  Refer from
  London. International Geographical Congress. *6th,* 1895.

International Geographical Congress. *7th, Berlin,* 1899.
  Refer from
  Internationaler Geographen-Kongress.
  Berlin. Internationaler Geographen-Kongress. *7th,* 1899.

International Geographical Congress. *8th, Washington, D. C.,* 1904.
  Refer from
  Washington, D. C. International Geographical Congress. *8th,* 1904.

International Geographical Congress. *9th, Geneva,* 1908.
  Refer from
  Geneva. Congrès international de géographie. *9th,* 1908.

International Geographical Congress. *10th, Rome,* 1913.
  Refer from
Rome (City) Congresso internazionale di geografia. *10th,* 1913.
  etc., etc.

A. If the numbering of the congresses is very irregular, the numbers are to be omitted from the heading, and an information card, stating the sequence of the congresses, is to be made.

International Congress of Hygiene and Demography.
  ₍1st₎ Brussels, 1852 (Congrès général d'hygiène)
  ₍2d₎ Brussels, 1876 (Congrès international d'hygiène)
  ₍3d₎ Paris, 1878 (Congrès international d'hygiène)
  ₍4th₎ Turin, 1880.
  ₍5th₎ Geneva, 1882 (Congrès international d'hygiène et démographie)
  ₍6th₎ The Hague,1884 (Congrès international d'hygiène et de démographie)
  ₍7th₎ Vienna, 1887 (Internationaler Congress . . .)
  ₍8th₎ Paris, 1889.
  ₍9th₎ London, 1891 (International Congress . . .)
  ₍10th₎ Budapest, 1894 (Nemzetközi Kzegészégi és Demografiai Congressus)
  ₍11th₎ Madrid, 1898 (Congreso Internacional de Higiene y Demografía)
  ₍12th₎ Paris, 1900.
  ₍13th₎ Brussels, 1903.
  ₍14th₎ Berlin, 1907.
  ₍15th₎ Washington, 1912.

The first three congresses (1852, 1876, 1878) were originally not numbered; the congresses held 1880-1900 were numbered 3d-10th with reference to the Brussels congress, 1876 as the first, and leaving out of the count, the Brussels congress, 1852, and the Paris congress, 1889. At the Brussels congress, 1903, the present numbering was adopted. (The place and date only are used in the heading)

B. The sessions of any one congress may be held successively in two or more different places.

When held in two places, the names of both cities are to be used in the heading, with reference from the name of each.

International Congress of Refrigeration. *3d, Washington, D. C., and Chicago,* 1913.
  Refer from
Washington, D. C. International Congress of Refrigeration. *3d,* 1913.
Chicago. International Congress of Refrigeration. *3d,* 1913.

When held in more than two places, the place of headquarters is to be used in the heading, followed by "etc.," with reference from the name of each city, if not more than three. A note of the places entertaining the congress is to be given, if not included in the title of the publication.

Congreso Internacional de la Prensa Técnica y Profesional. *5th, Barcelona, etc.,* 1929.
  Refer from
Barcelona. Congreso Internacional de la Prensa Técnica y Profesional. *5th,* 1929.
Madrid. Congreso Internacional de la Prensa Técnica y Profesional. *5th,* 1929.
Seville. Congreso Internacional de la Prensa Técnica y Profesional. *5th,* 1929.

When there are many places visited in the course of a meeting and the publications of the congress bear only the name of the country, the principal (usually the first) place of meeting is to be used in the heading, with reference from that name and also from the name of the country.

> **International Geological Congress.** *15th, Pretoria, etc., 1929.*
> *Refer from*
> Pretoria. International Geological Congress. *15th,* 1929.
> South Africa. International Geological Congress. *15th,* 1929.
> International Geological Congress. *15th, South Africa,* 1929.

133. Congresses of groups of states having similar language or culture.
Enter congresses of groups of states having similar language, or culture (e.g., the Scandinavian countries, or countries of South America) under the language in which most of the publications have appeared. If this cannot be ascertained, enter under the language of the country inaugurating the series.

No definite decision as to the final best form of entry can be made until a considerable body of material has been assembled. In the meanwhile references must be relied upon to make the entries readily available.

> **Nordiske Juristmøde.**
> *Refer from*
> Nordiska Juristmötet.
> **Nordiske Biblioteksmøde.**
> *Refer from*
> Nordiske Biblioteksstaevne.
> Nordiska Biblioteksmötet.
> Nordiske Bibliotekmøte.
> **Congreso Internacional de Historia de América.**
> *Refer from*
> Congresso Internacional de Historia da America.

134. National congresses.
Enter national congresses under the vernacular form of the name.

> **Congrès des ingénieurs en chef des associations de propriétaires d'appareils à vapeur.**
> Compte rendu des séances du 1.-   Congrès des ingénieurs en chef des associations de propriétaires d'appareils à vapeur.

In the following examples there is record of only two conferences, both held in the same year, and two entries are preferable.

> **National Conference on Inheritance and Estate Taxation.** *1st, Washington, D. C., Feb., 1925.*
> Proceedings of National Conference on Inheritance and Estate Taxation held at . . . Washington, D. C., February 19-20, 1925.

> **National Conference on Inheritance and Estate Taxation.** *2d, New Orleans, Nov., 1925.*
> Proceedings of the second National Conference on Inheritance and Estate Taxation held at . . . New Orleans, Louisiana, Tuesday, November 10, 1925.

135. Institutes, conferences, conventions, etc.

A. Enter institutes, meetings, conferences, etc., under the name of the meeting, except when they are meetings of the members of a society or other body and have no distinctive name of their own.

> **Pacific Northwest Regional Planning Conference.**
> **Illinois Farmers' Institute.**
> *but*
> **International Co-operative Alliance.** *2d congress, Paris,* 1896.
> **Baptist Training Union.** *Southwide conference. 4th, Birmingham, Ala.,* 1925.

B. If the institute or meeting is held at some institution (college, university, etc.) add the name of the institution to the heading.

> **Institute of Politics,** *Williams College,* 1932.
> **Conference on Higher Education,** *University of Oregon,* 1934.
> **Indiana Fire School,** *Purdue University, Lafayette, Ind.*

Care should be taken not to confuse with such conferences, the "institutes," "workshops," etc., which are departments or seminars in departments of academic institutions, and which are entered as such.

> **Minnesota. University.** *Institute of Child Welfare.*
> **Puerto Rico. University.** *Institute of Tropical Agriculture, Mayagüez.*

C. If the institute or meeting is associated with a particular city, add the name of the city to the heading. If the meeting is held only once, or the heading applies to only one meeting, add the date also.

> **Institute of War Medicine and Surgery for Dentists,** *Chicago,* 1942.

D. If no name can be found for the meeting, enter it under the place and supply a name descriptive of the character of the meeting.

> **Syracuse, N. Y. Convention of mechanics and others,** 1850.
> **Boston. Women's rights meeting,** 1859.

136. Exhibitions, etc.

A. General exhibitions. Enter general exhibitions, fairs, bazaars, etc., under the name of the place where they are held, and refer from the official title and any other names by which the exhibition is generally known.

> **Philadelphia. Centennial Exhibition,** 1876.
> **New Orleans. World's Industrial and Cotton Centennial Exposition,** 1884–1885.
> **Chicago. World's Columbian Exposition,** 1893.
> **Buffalo. Pan-American Exposition,** 1901.
> **London. Franco-British Exhibition,** 1908.
> **St. Louis. Louisiana Purchase Exposition,** 1904.
> **Paris. Exposition coloniale internationale,** 1931.
> **London. Lewis Carroll Centenary Exhibition,** 1932.
> **London. International Exhibition of Chinese Art,** 1931.

This rule applies to the official publications of an exhibition. Catalogs or descriptions of exhibits and other material published by commissions from the contributing countries, business firms, or other contributors, are to be entered under the bodies or persons issuing them. (Cf. 81B.)

> **U. S.** *Board of Management of Government Exhibit, Tennessee Centennial Exposition,* 1897.
> . . . Report on the United States government exhibit at the Tennessee Centennial Exposition, Nashville, 1897.

> **China.** *Organizing Committee, International Exhibition of Chinese Art, London,* 1935-1936.
> Illustrated catalogue of Chinese government exhibits for the International Exhibition of Chinese Art in London.

B. Exhibitions held by societies or other bodies. Enter exhibitions, fairs, bazaars, etc., held by or under the auspices of some society or institution[45] or in connection with an international or other congress, especially when they are numbered and occur at more or less regular intervals in different places, under the name of the body or congress, with reference from the name of the place and from the name of the exhibition when this is at all distinctive.

> **Grolier Club,** *New York.*
> Catalogue of an exhibition of French engravings of the eighteenth century . . . exhibited at the Grolier Club . . . MDCCCCV.

> **Franklin Institute,** *Philadelphia.*
> Report of the . . . exhibition of American manufactures, held in the city of Philadelphia . . . by the Franklin Institute.

> **California State Agricultural Society.**
> Official report . . . annual agricultural fair.

> **Licking County (Ohio) Agricultural Society.**
> Premium list and regulations for the annual fair.

> **Public Works of Art Project.**
> National exhibition of art, by the Public Works of Art Project, April 24, 1934 to May 20, 1934 (inclusive) the Corcoran Gallery of Art, Washington, District of Columbia.
> I. Corcoran Gallery of Art, Washington, D. C.

137. Pre-congress or pre-exhibition publications.

Enter pre-congress or pre-exhibition publications under the body responsible for their preparation, if such body can be ascertained. If, however, the authorship cannot be determined, enter under the congress or exhibition.

> **International Child Welfare Association.** *11th session, Brussels,* 1935.
> . . . Documents préparatoires . . . ₍Bruxelles? 1935₎

---

[45] An exhibition held in the galleries or exhibition rooms of a society or institution is not necessarily held under the auspices of the society or institution.

National Conference on Street and Highway Safety. *2d, Washington, D. C., 1926.*
... Report₍s₎ ... issued for consideration in advance of the National Conference on Street and Highway Safety.

New York. World's Fair, 1939-1940.
Feria Mundial de Nueva York, 1939. Nueva York, 1936.

If the congress or exhibition for which the publications were prepared is not held, add to the heading the words PROJECTED, NOT HELD in parentheses.

International Congress of Architects. *15th, Washington, D. C., 1939.* (*Projected, not held*)

138. Festivals.

A. Enter festivals, athletic contests, etc., if held regularly in one place, under the name of the place, with reference from the name of the festival. Exception is made for festivals, etc., held under the auspices of an institution, which are entered as subheadings under the name of the institution.

Asheville, N. C. Music Festival.
Baldwin-Wallace College, *Berea, Ohio. Conservatory of Music.*
Bach Festival.
Refer from
Bach Festival of the Baldwin-Wallace Conservatory of Music.

B. Enter festivals, etc., held at different places under their own names.

Olympic Games, *Athens,* 1906.
Niederrheinisches Musikfest.

C. Enter those held under the auspices of a society according to the above provisions except when the name of the festival is not distinctive. Such festivals are entered under the name of the society without subheading.

Limestone Choral Society.
Annual music festival.

Cincinnati Musical Festival Association.
Music festival at Cincinnati.

Refer from the name of the sponsoring society to festivals, etc., entered under their own names.

Neue Bachgesellschaft. *Deutsches Bachfest*
see
Deutsches Bachfest.

139. Commissions and committees.

A. Enter autonomous commissions and committees, international,

national or local, under their names, adding the place of headquarters only when necessary for identification.

> **International Commission for Air Navigation.**
> **International Commission for the Study of Clouds.**
> **Commission on Post-war Training and Adjustment.**
> **Committee on International Economic Policy.**
> **Committee for Refugee Education,** *New York.*

For official commissions of governments see C. below and 81.

B. Enter commissions, committees and delegations appointed by corporate bodies to perform particular functions, either permanent or temporary, as a subheading under the name of the appointing body, with references as required. (Cf. 81.)

> **American Council on Public Affairs.** *Committee on Economic Defense.*
> > *Refer from*
> > Committee on Economic Defense, American Council on Public Affairs.
>
> **Social Science Research Council.** *Committee on Personality and Culture.*
> > *Refer from*
> > Committee on Personality and Culture, Social Science Research Council.
>
> **London. Royal College of Physicians.** *Planning Committee.*
> > ⌊*no reference needed*⌋

The extent to which subdivision is made for routine committees depends partly on the prominence given to the committee in the publication and partly on the amount of material published either by a committee or by the whole body.

C. Enter joint commissions, committees or boards of two or more governments or organizations under their own names, with either added entries or references for each of the governments or bodies.

> **Mixed Claims Commission** (*U. S. and Germany*)
> **Joint Board of Engineers on St. Lawrence Waterway Project** (*U. S. and Canada*)
> **Interstate Joint Interim Legislative Committee Relating to Problems of the Interstate Columbia River Area.**
> **Commission européenne du Danube,** *Galati,* 1856-
> **Palisades Interstate Park Commission** (*New York and New Jersey*)
> **Joint Committee of the National Association of Manufacturers and National Industrial Council.**

140. Committees and meetings of citizens.

Enter reports of meetings or committees of citizens not belonging to any named body or class and having no definite name, under the name of the place with subheading CITIZENS. Make reference or added entry under the name of the chairman or first signer.

206

The subheading CITIZENS which is, in effect, a form subdivision, is used in English regardless of the language of the country in which the meeting takes place.

Albany. Citizens.
Proceedings of a meeting of citizens of the city of Albany, held Nov. 27, 1847, for the purpose of promoting a system of literary and scientific international exchanges.

Westchester Co., N. Y. Citizens.
The Post Office for the people, not for politicians and liquor dealers. The conspiracy against the residents near Katonah exposed, and the bargain for Whitlock's appointment disapproved. The proceedings of citizens of Westchester Co., New York, at Putney's Hall, Katonah, March 27, 1862.

Geneva. Citizens.
Le recrutement forcé des Serbes par les Bulgares; protestations publiques de Genève et Lausanne.
   I. Lausanne. Citizens.

141. Classes of citizens.

Enter anonymous publications of any class of citizens (not organized) under the name of the place with the name of the class as subheading in English, preferably, except in cases where it is not possible to give a satisfactory English equivalent for a concise foreign phrase. If the class is not clearly defined, prefer title entry.

Albany. Bar.
Memoir of William A. Jackson, a member of the Albany bar . . .
Published by the bar of the city of Albany.

Baltimore. Merchants.
The memorial of the merchants & traders of the city of Baltimore . . .

Geneva. American residents.
Celebration of the ninetieth anniversary of American independance [!] in Geneva (Suisse) July 4th, 1866 . . .

London. Women.
A true copie of the petition of the gentlewomen, and tradesmens-wives, in and about the City of London. Delivered to . . . the House of Commons in Parliament, the 4th of February, 1641 . . .

Paris. Maîtres techniques.
Le travail du fer pratique, 56 objets choisis suivant une progression géometrique. Les tours de main complétés par un vocabulaire des mots techniques présenté par les maîtres techniques de la ville de Paris . . .

142. Boards, trustees, etc.

Enter bodies whose legal names begin with such words as Board, Corporation, Trustees, under the names of the institutions or bodies over which they exercise supervision.

Harvard University. *Board of Overseers.*
British Museum. *Trustees.*

If, however, a board is organized to administer the combined funds of several bodies, enter it under its own name.

Board of Trustees of the Relief and Red Cross Funds.

143. Foundations, endowments, funds.

Enter foundations and endowments, funds, etc., under their names. Retain, at the beginning of the name of a foundation, forenames and titles of honor, distinction or address which are given in full; initials of forenames and abbreviations of titles may be omitted. (Cf. 92A, 93C.) Refer from place, and from the exact name if not used as the heading.

> **Nobelstiftelsen,** *Stockholm.*
>
> **Carlsbergfondet,** *Copenhagen.*
>
> **Teyler's Stichting,** *Haarlem.*
>
> **Fondation egyptologique Reine Elisabeth,** *Brussels.*
>
> **Fondation Thiers,** *Paris.*
>
> **Fondazione Leonardo per la cultura italiana,** *Rome.*
>
> **Russell Sage Foundation,** *New York.*
>
> **Julius Rosenwald Fund.**
> > *Refer from*
> > Rosenwald Fund.
>
> **Baron de Hirsch Fund.**
>
> **Kellogg Foundation,** *Battle Creek, Mich.*
> > *Refer from*
> > W. K. Kellogg Foundation.
> > Kellogg (W. K.) Foundation.

Endowments and special funds of institutions (universities, colleges, etc.) are usually to be entered under the institution, with a reference from the name of the fund. (Cf. 101B.)

> **Smithsonian Institution.** *Hodgkins Fund.*
> > *Refer from*
> > Hodgkins Fund.
>
> **Michigan. University.** *Harris Memorial Trust.*
> > *Refer from*
> > Harris Memorial Trust.
>
> **Yale University.** *John Addison Porter Prize.*
> > *Refer from*
> > John Addison Porter Prize.

144. Firms, business corporations, etc.

Enter firms, business corporations (including those owned by governments), hotels,[46] railway companies, etc., under the corporate name. The terms incorporated (inc.), limited (ltd.), etc., or their equivalents

---

[46] Hotels, while they may be considered as institutions, are better treated as firms, corporations, or business concerns and therefore entered under their names. A subject reference is invariably made from the name of the city, subdivision HOTELS, TAVERNS, ETC.

if included in the corporate name are to be retained. Add the place in the heading for firms located in one city only, but not for those with branches.

> **British Broadcasting Corporation.**
>
> **General Electric Company.**
>
> **Home Owners' Loan Corporation.**
> *Refer from*
> U. S. *Home Owners' Loan Corporation.*
>
> **Greene-Cananea Copper Company.**
>
> **New York, New Haven and Hartford Railroad Company.**
>
> **International Harvester Company of America (incorporated)**
>
> **Sears, Roebuck and Company.**
>
> **Safeway Stores, inc.**
>
> **Hamilton Watch Company,** *Lancaster, Pa.*
>
> **Ambassador Hotel,** *Washington, D. C.*
> *with see also reference from subject*
> Washington, D. C.—*Hotels, taverns, etc.*

A. If the name begins with the forename or initials of a personal name, enter under surname, giving forenames or initials according to the usage of the firm or corporation. If the inversion brings them *within* the corporate name, inclose them within parentheses rather than commas.

> **Feather (William) Company,** *Cleveland.*
> *Refer from*
> William Feather Company, *Cleveland.*
>
> **Harris (M.) and Sons,** *London.*
> *Refer from*
> M. Harris and Sons, *London.*
>
> **Hostmann (Chr.)-Steinberg'sche Farbenfabriken G.m.b.H.,**
> **Celle.**
> *Refer from*
> Chr. Hostmann-Steinberg'sche Farbenfabriken G.m.b.H.,
> *Celle.*
> Celle. Chr. Hostmann-Steinberg'sche Farbenfabriken G.m.b.H.
>
> **Du Pont de Nemours (E. I.) Powder Company.**
> *Refer from*
> E. I. Du Pont de Nemours Powder Company.
>
> **Knight (Emerson B.) inc.,** *Indianapolis.*
> *Refer from*
> Emerson B. Knight, inc., *Indianapolis.*
>
> **Loew's, inc.**
>
> **Asch, ltd.**
>
> **Vickers (Aviation) limited.**
>
> **Henley's (W. T.) Telegraph Works Co., ltd.**
> *Refer from*
> W. T. Henley's Telegraph Works Co., ltd.

Exception.—Entry under forename may be preferred in a few cases, favoring customary use.

> **Marshall Field and Company.**
> *Refer from*
> Field (Marshall) and Company.

B. The names of many foreign firms begin with the words or abbreviations denoting a joint stock company. It is preferable in these cases to use an inverted form making entry under the first distinctive word, with reference from the actual name.

> **Elektrometall, Aktiebolaget,** *Stockholm.*
> *Refer from*
> Aktiebolaget Elektrometall, *Stockholm.*
> **Göteborgssystemet, Aktiebolaget,** *Stockholm.*
> *Refer from*
> Aktiebolaget Göteborgssystemet i Stockholm.
> **Norsk varekrigsforsikring, A/S.**
> *Refer from*
> A/S Norske varekrigsforsikring.
> **Svenska teknologföreningens förlag, Aktiebolaget,** *Stockholm.*
> *Refer from*
> Aktiebolaget Svenska teknologföreningens förlag.

C. If a firm is known only by the name of the owner or founder, add the designation FIRM to the heading to distinguish it from the same name as personal entry.

> **Witte, Friedrich,** *firm, Rostock.*

D. In dealing with a large number of entries, where slight changes in the name are frequent, the following form of heading may prove serviceable.

> **Scribner,** *firm, publishers, New York.*
> (1905. *Charles Scribner's Sons*)
> *Refer from*
> Charles Scribner's Sons.
> **Leavitt,** *firm, auctioneers, New York.*
> (1865. *Geo. A. Leavitt*)
> *Refer from*
> Leavitt, Geo. A., *firm, New York.*

The second line consists of the date of publication of the book cataloged and the form of name then in use.

145. Banks.

Enter banking institutions including government owned and controlled banks under firm, association, or corporate name.

> **Bank of England.**
> **Banque de France,** *Paris.*
> *Refer from*
> Paris. Banque de France.

Cassa di risparmio delle provincie Lombarde, *Milan.*
Refer from
Milan. Cassa di risparmio delle provincie Lombarde.

Chase National Bank of the City of New York.
Refer from
New York. Chase National Bank.

Commonwealth Bank of Australia, *Sydney.*
Refer from
Sydney. Commonwealth Bank of Australia.

Finlands bank, *Helsingfors.*
Refer from
Helsingfors. Finlands bank.

Suffolk Bank, *Boston.*
Refer from
Boston. Suffolk Bank.

Sveriges riksbank.
Refer from
Sweden. Riksbanken.
Rikets Ständers bank.

Enter national banks in the United States designated merely by number or without any special designation, under the place.

Philadelphia. First National Bank.
Geneva, N. Y. National Bank.

146. **Chambers of commerce, boards of trade, stock, produce, and other exchanges.**
A. Enter chambers of commerce devoted mainly to the promotion of business interests of a definite political division under the name of the place[47] (country, state, province, city, etc.).

Amsterdam. Kamer van Koophandel en Fabrieken.
Refer from
Kammer van Koophandel en Fabrieken, *Amsterdam.*

Kansas City, Mo. Chamber of Commerce.
Refer from
Chamber of Commerce of Kansas City, Mo.

New York. Chamber of Commerce of the State of New York.
Refer from
Chamber of Commerce of the State of New York.

Parma (Province) Camera di commercio e industria.
Refer from
Camera di commercio e industria della provincia di Parma.

Costa Rica. Cámara de Comercio, *San José.*
Refer from
Cámara de Comercio de Costa Rica.
San José, Costa Rica. Cámara de Comercio de Costa Rica.

(1) If the area is larger than national, or if the body is an association

---

[47] The Library of Congress enters the Chamber of Commerce of the United States of America under its name.

or union of chambers of commerce, or if the name begins with a national adjective, entry under the name of the body is preferred.

> **Vsesoíuznaía torgovaía palata.**
> **Uniunea Camerelor de Comerţ şi de Industrie,** *Bucharest.*
> **Canadian Chamber of Commerce.**
>> *Refer from*
>> Canada. Chamber of Commerce.
>> Montreal. Canadian Chamber of Commerce.

(2) If the region represented is not identical with a political or geographical division, enter under the name of the body.

> **Niederrheinische Industrie- und Handelskammer Duisburg-Wesel zu Duisburg-Ruhrort.**
>> *Refer from*
>> Duisburg, Ger. Niederrheinische Industrie- und Handels-kammer Duisburg-Wesel zu Duisburg-Ruhrort.
>> Ruhrort, Ger. Niederrheinische Industrie- und Handels-kammer Duisburg-Wesel zu Duisburg-Ruhrort.

(3) Enter chambers of commerce serving national interests in foreign countries under the name of the body.

> **British Chamber of Commerce in Brazil,** *Rio de Janeiro.*
>> *Refer from*
>> Rio de Janeiro. British Chamber of Commerce in Brazil.
> **Chambre de commerce belge aux États-Unis.**
> **Cámara Oficial Española de Comercio en los Estados Unidos Mexicanos.**
>> *Refer from*
>> Mexico. Cámara Oficial Española de Comercio.

(4) Enter associations and clubs functioning as chambers of commerce under the name of the body.

> **Merchants' Association of New York.**
>> *Refer from*
>> New York. Merchants' Association.
> **Long Island Association.**

B. Enter boards of trade, stock, produce, and other exchanges, under the place (city, etc.).

> **Boston. Board of Trade.**
>> *Refer from*
>> Board of Trade of Boston.
> **Montreal. Stock Exchange.**
>> *Refer from*
>> Stock Exchange of Montreal.
> **Salt Lake City. Stock and Mining Exchange.**
>> *Refer from*
>> Stock and Mining Exchange of Salt Lake City.
>> Salt Lake Stock and Mining Exchange.

Vienna. Börse.
Refer from
Wiener Börse.
Vienna. Wiener Börse.

São Paulo, Brazil (City)   Bolsa de Mercadorias.
Refer from
Bolsa de Mercadorias de São Paulo.

147. Parks.

Enter reports and other material of official character under the name of the administrative body having charge of the park, as subheading under the jurisdiction (country, state, or city).

For subject entry, city parks are entered under the name of the city, subheading PARKS whether the name of the park be distinctive (beginning with a proper noun or adjective) or not, e.g., BOSTON-PARKS-FRANKLIN PARK. National, state and regional parks are entered under their names if distinctive, e.g., YELLOWSTONE NATIONAL PARK.

U. S. *National Park Service.*
Circular of general information regarding Yellowstone National Park.
For earlier reports see: U. S. *Superintendent of Yellowstone National Park.*
1. Yellowstone National Park.

Canada. *Dept. of the Interior. Dominion Parks Branch.*
The call of untrodden ways.
1. Jasper Park, Alberta.

District of Columbia. *Commissioners.*
Report upon improvement of valley of Rock Creek.
1. Washington, D. C.—Parks—Rock Creek Park.

New York (*State*) *Commissioners of Fire Island State Park.*
Annual report.
1. Fire Island State Park, N. Y.

New York (*State*) *Allegany State Park Commission.*
Annual report.
1. Allegany State Park, N. Y.

Boston. *Dept. of Parks.*
Notes on the plan of Franklin Park.
1. Boston—Parks—Franklin Park.

Chicago. *Lincoln Park Commissioners.*
Report.
1. Chicago—Parks—Lincoln Park.

148. Cemeteries.

Enter local cemeteries under place. Enter city cemeteries located at a distance from the city under the name of the cemetery, adding the name of the city. Reports issued by cemetery associations are to be entered under the name of the cemetery, with reference from the name of the association.

Boston. South Burying Ground.
Refer from
South Burying Ground, *Boston.*

New York. Calvary Cemetery.
> *Refer from*
> Calvary Cemetery, *New York.*

New York Cemetery of New Jersey, *Hackensack.*
> *Refer from*
> Hackensack, N. J. New York Cemetery of New Jersey.

Gettysburg. National Cemetery.
> *Refer from*
> Soldiers' National Cemetery, *Gettysburg.*

Mt. Auburn Cemetery, *Cambridge, Mass.*
> *Refer from*
> Cambridge, Mass. Mt. Auburn Cemetery.

149. Botanical and zoological gardens.

Enter botanical and zoological gardens under the name of the place where located.

Botanical and zoological gardens whose names are preceded by the titular designations Imperial, Royal, National, etc., are to be entered according to this rule even when supported wholly or in part by public funds.

> **Cincinnati. Zoological Garden.**
> **Brussels. Jardin botanique de l'État.**
> **Kew. Royal Gardens.**

Exceptions.—

A. When distinctly a part of some university or school, enter under the name of the university or school.

> **Cambridge. University.** *Botanic Garden.*
> **Münden, Ger. Forstakademie.** *Botanischer Garten.*

B. When owned or controlled by a society and constantly referred to by its name, enter under the society.

> **Royal Society of Tasmania,** *Hobart. Gardens.*
> **Zoological Society of Philadelphia.** *Garden.*
> **Zoological Society of London.** *Gardens.*

C. When private property, enter under the name of the owner or under the estate to which it belongs.

> **Aken, Hermann von.**
> Verzeichniss sämmtlicher Thiere, welche sich in der Menagerie von Hermann v. Aken befinden . . .

IV. Geographic Headings

150. Language of heading.

A. Give countries, self-governing dominions, colonies and protectorates in the conventional English form.

> **Austria** *not* Oesterreich.
> **Bavaria** *not* Bayern.
> **Morocco** *not* Moghreb-el-Aksa.
> **Sweden** *not* Sverige.

B. Give local geographic names usually in the vernacular form but where a well-established English form differs, prefer the English form.[1]

> **Dauphiné** *not* Dauphiny.
> **Lyon** *not* Lyons.
> **Mainz** *not* Mayence.
> **Marseille** *not* Marseilles.
> **Tucumán** *not* Tucuman.
> *but*
> **Copenhagen** *not* København.
> **Florence** *not* Firenze.
> **Munich** *not* München.
> **Vienna** *not* Wien.

151. States, provinces, etc.

The states of the United States, and the provinces of Canada and the more familiar foreign states, provinces and "départements," do not require the addition of the name of the country.

> **Ohio.**
> **British Columbia.**
> **Liguria.**
> **Seine** (*Dept.*)[2]

---

[1] In deciding between different forms of place names consult U. S. **Geographic Board,** *Sixth report,* 1933, and the *Decisions* of its successor, the U. S. Board on Geographical Names; Canada Geographic Board; Permanent Committee on Geographical Names for British Official Use; *Times gazetteer of the world; Bartholomew's Survey gazetteer; Lippincott's new gazetteer; Longmans' gazetteer; Century Cyclopedia of names; Ritters geographisch-statistisches Lexikon;* Vivien de Saint-Martin, *Nouveau dictionnaire de géographie universelle,* etc., giving preference in all instances to official sources.

[2] Cf. 154.

215

> Bavaria.
> Rajputana.
> Yucatán.

For publications of the colonial and territorial periods of the present states of the United States, see 154C.

152. Counties.

Counties in the United States and Canada when used as entry word are followed by the name of the state or province, elsewhere by the name of the country, in accepted abbreviated form.

> Charlotte Co., *N. B.*
> Durham Co., *Ont.*
> East Feliciana Parish, *La.*
> Washington Co., *Ohio.*
> Washington Co., *Pa.*
> *but*
> Limerick, *Ire.* (*County*)

153. Cities and towns.

A. When used as entry word, cities and towns in the United States and Canada are followed by the name of the state or province, in accepted abbreviated form. (Cf. C, p. 217.)

> Alexandria, *Va.*
> Cumberland, *Md.*
> Victoria, *B. C.*
> Hamilton, *Ont.*

B. Cities and towns other than those in the United States and Canada are followed by the name of the country (not by the name of the province or smaller division) or region. The name of the region is used for cities and towns in areas whose political jurisdiction has been unstable, as, for example, Sardinia.

> Alexandria, *Egypt.*
> Alexandria, *Scot.*
> Eberbach, *Ger.*
> Fulda, *Ger.*
> Saint-Dizier, *France.*
> Smolensk, *Russia.*
> Tananarivo, *Madagascar.*

Designation follows local usage if distinctive.

> Frankfurt am Main.
> Freiburg i. B.

The name of the country is used in direct form even though inverted for its own entry.

> Elisabethville, *Belgian Kongo.*
> *not* Elisabethville, *Kongo, Belgian.*

C. Exception.—Enter largest or best-known city of its name, in America or elsewhere, without further designation.[3]

> **Athens** *but* **Athens,** *Ga.,* **Athens,** *Ohio,* etc.
> **Berlin.**
> **Boston.**
> **Chicago.**
> **Dublin.**
> **Johannesburg.**
> **London.**
> **Montreal.**
> **Paris.**

D. Suburbs. Enter publications of a town or village which later became part of a larger place (thus losing administrative entity) under the name of the original unit, followed by the name of the state, province or country according to rule 153.

> **Germantown,** *Pa.*   [*now a part of Philadelphia*]
> **Roxbury,** *Mass.*   [*now a part of Boston*]
> **Charlottenburg.**   [*now a part of Berlin*]

For entry of institutions located in suburbs later absorbed in a metropolitan area see 103.

Note that in some cases towns which are adjacent to a larger place remain administratively independent.

> **West Springfield,** *Mass.*   [*suburb of Springfield*]
> **Brookline,** *Mass.*   [*suburb of Boston*]
> **Schaerbeek,** *Belgium.*   [*suburb of Brussels*]
> **Frederiksberg,** *Denmark.*   [*suburb of Copenhagen*]

154. Political division in heading.

A. When different political or administrative units have the same name, distinguish them by adding the particular designation in parentheses, preferably in English, though a term without a precise English equivalent is given in the vernacular form.

> **New York** (*City*)
> **New York** (*State*)

---

[3] Library of Congress omits designation of state or province in the heading for the following cities and towns in the United States and Canada.

Albany	Grand Rapids	Quebec
Annapolis	Hartford	Richmond
Atlanta	Indianapolis	St. Augustine
Atlantic City	Jersey City	St. Louis
Baltimore	Los Angeles	St. Paul
Boston	Memphis	Salt Lake City
Brooklyn	Milwaukee	San Antonio
Buffalo	Minneapolis	San Francisco
Chattanooga	Montreal	Savannah
Chicago	Nashville	Scranton
Cincinnati	New Haven	Seattle
Cleveland	New Orleans	Spokane
Colorado Springs	New York	Tacoma
Dallas	Oklahoma City	Tallahassee
Denver	Omaha	Toledo
Des Moines	Ottawa	Toronto
Detroit	Philadelphia	Trenton
Duluth	Pittsburgh	Wheeling
Fort Wayne	Providence	

Mexico *(City)*
Mexico *(Federal District)*
São Paulo *(City)*
São Paulo *(Province)*
Kassel *(City)*
Kassel *(Regierungsbezirk)*

B. Add an explanatory designation whenever the particular kind of political or administrative unit needs to be specified.

Bramhall, *Eng. (Manor)*
Bromfield and Yale, *Wales (Lordship)*
Diepholz *(Grafschaft)*
San Marino *(Republic)*

C. For countries or other political units in which a different government needs to be specified in the heading for official publications, add to the usual name of the unit a word or phrase designating the period covered.

Mexico *(Viceroyalty)*
Mexico *(Empire, 1864-1867)*
but Mexico.
    [*for publications since its independence*]
Netherlands *(before 1581)*
Netherlands *(Southern Provinces, 1581-1793)*
Netherlands *(United Provinces, 1581-1795)*
Netherlands *(Batavian Republic, 1795-1806)*
Netherlands *(Kingdom of Holland, 1806-1813)*
Netherlands *(Kingdom, 1815-)*
Netherlands *(Territory under German occupation, 1940-1945)*

Publications of the colonial and territorial periods of states of the United States are distinguished by the designation COLONY or TER.

Georgia *(Colony)*
Oklahoma *(Ter.)*

155. Places of the same name in one country.
Distinguish two or more places of the same name, the same type of unit, and in the same country by the addition, in parentheses, of the name of the province, "département," county, etc.

Athies, *France (Aisne)*
Athies, *France (Pas-de-Calais)*
Athies, *France (Somme)*
Bradford, *Eng. (Devonshire)*
Bradford, *Eng. (Northumberland: Berwick-upon-Tweed Div.)*
Bradford, *Eng. (Northumberland: Wansbeck Div.)*
Templemore, *Ire. (Co. Mayo)*
Templemore, *Ire. (Co. Tipperary)*
Washington, *Ohio (Fayette Co.)*
Washington, *Ohio (Guernsey Co.)*

156. Special rulings.

A. Place names beginning with an article have the article as entry word. Refer from the part of the name following the article. Exception may be made in the case of place names familiarly referred to in English under the part of the name following the article.

> **La Rochelle,** *France.*
> *Refer from*
> Rochelle, La, *France.*

> **Le Mans,** *France.*
> *Refer from*
> Mans, Le, *France.*

> **La Paz,** *Bolivia.*
> *Refer from*
> Paz, La, *Bolivia.*

> *but*
> **Havre.**
> *Refer from*
> Le Havre.

B. Enter German health resorts beginning with the word Bad under the name of the place, omitting "Bad." Refer from name beginning with Bad.

> **Eilsen,** *Ger.*
> *Refer from*
> Bad-Eilsen, *Ger.*
> Eilsen, Bad-

> **Nauheim,** *Ger.*
> *Refer from*
> Bad-Nauheim, *Ger.*
> Nauheim, Bad-

V. Added Entries. References

157. Added entries.

The chief function of an added entry is to enable the user of the catalog to find a work when incomplete knowledge or imperfect memory of the work, or unfamiliarity with the rules of entry, would prevent ready access to the main entry. Added entries serve also the purpose of assembling closely related matter which has main entry under various headings.

If it is desirable to make an added entry for a name not included in the title of the work, an explanatory note or a contents note should make the reason apparent.

The necessity for added entries varies somewhat with the individual library and the extent to which they are made is a matter for each library to determine according to its particular needs. In general, the more indeterminate or divided the responsibility for authorship, the more need for added entries. In the foregoing rules, added entries have been specified wherever they would be appropriate, as follows:

A. Make added entries for joint authors, collaborators, editors, compilers, translators, illustrators (if the illustrations form an important feature of the work)—in short, for any person or corporate body other than the one chosen for the main entry that has a significant part in or responsibility for the production of the work.[1] Names, personal and corporate, used as added entries are established by the same rules as those used as main entries. The designations ED., COMP., TR., ILLUS., JOINT AUTHOR, JOINT COMP., etc., are included in the heading and if the added entry bears more than one relation to the work, e.g., *ed. and tr.*, it is so designated. These designations are used only with personal, never with corporate names.

B. Make added entries for the purpose of assembling closely related matter, e.g., an added entry under the original author of a work when a free adaptation of it has been entered under the adapter; or an added entry under a uniform heading for the various versions of an anonymous classic whose main entries are under their own titles. (Cf. 33C (3).)

---

[1] Make added entry for a foundation, corporation, or other body that provides funds for publication or carrying on of studies, only when the work is done on the initiative of the body supplying the funds, or as one of its acknowledged interests. An added entry is not ordinarily made for a foundation, corporation, etc., that makes a grant to another corporate body or to an individual who assumes responsibility for the work.

In libraries which make use of printed cards, the use of an added entry on the unit card may serve to list the contents of a series.

C. Make added entries for titles also; in general, whenever an entry under the title will insure the ready finding of the book, in particular:

(1) For all single works of the imagination such as novels, plays, poems, and other literary forms

(2) For all works entered under author which were published anonymously

(3) For composite works and collections where main entry is not under title

(4) For works (except Reports, Transactions, Proceedings, etc.) the author entries for which are corporate names

(5) For all works of any character bearing a distinctive or striking title; make partial title entry in cases where a subtitle, alternative title, or some striking part of the title (catchword title) is likely to be remembered, but prefer a subject heading, or a reference to a subject heading, where the title added entry would be substantially the same.

D. In a library which uses printed cards chiefly, added entries may serve as analytics (e.g., when a work includes a brief work by another author) or added entries may take the place of references. (Cf. 158.) On the other hand, in some cases a reference may take the place of several added entry cards, e.g., from title to author where there are many editions of a given work in which there is little or no change of title; or under similar conditions, from editor to work edited. Added entry and reference may be combined by making a regular added entry for one edition and writing or stamping on the card: "Other editions under author." If the reference to author heading is not clear, or if the entry referred to is not an author entry, instead of "author" give the exact heading to which reference is made.

158. References.

The function of a reference is to direct the user of a catalog from one of several headings under which an entry might be looked for to the one adopted (*see reference*), or to indicate other headings under which related material may be found (*see also reference*). This latter type of reference occurs most often in subject headings. The following rules deal with the most frequently recurring instances in author and title entries where references are required. Other specific cases where references are necessary are noted throughout the rules. A reference may always be made wherever good judgment and experience agree upon its usefulness. In making references, bear in mind the following points: (1) There must always be an entry in the catalog under the heading to which reference is made; (2) There must always be something in the catalog under the heading from which a *see also* reference is made; (3) Every reference must be carefully recorded so that in the event of future changes all references may be brought into line.

Whenever a heading, whether for main or added entry, is chosen from two or more possible forms, make references freely from the alternative forms to the form of heading chosen, e.g.,

A. From full name to shorter form used by author and adopted as heading.

> **Tarkington, Newton Booth**
> *see*
> **Tarkington, Booth,** 1869-1946.

B. From original name to name adopted in civil or religious life.

> **Herzog, Émile Salomon Wilhelm**
> *see*
> **Maurois, André,** 1885-

> **Hess, Lawrence Anthony**
> *see*
> **Cuthbert,** *Father,* 1866-1939.

C. Conversely, refer from name in religion to real name if the latter is chosen as heading.

> **Mary Alphonsa Lathrop,** *Mother*
> *see*
> **Lathrop, Rose (Hawthorne)** 1851-1926.

> **Lathrop, Mary Alphonsa,** *Mother*
> *see*
> **Lathrop, Rose (Hawthorne)** 1851-1926.

D. From parts of a compound name to the part selected as entry word.

> **Salignac de La Mothe-Fénelon, François de**
> *see*
> **Fénelon, François de Salignac de La Mothe-,** *Abp.,* 1651-1715.

> **La Mothe-Fénelon, François de Salignac de**
> *see*
> **Fénelon, François de Salignac de La Mothe-,** *Abp.,* 1651-1715.

E. From the part of a prefix name following the prefix if entry is under prefix, and conversely.

> **Essarts, François des**
> *see*
> **Des Essarts, François.**

> **D'Alembert, Jean Lerond**
> *see*
> **Alembert, Jean Lerond d',** 1717-1783.

F. From family name to title when entry is under title, and conversely.

222

> **St. Leonards, Edward Burtenshaw Sugden,** *baron*
> *see*
> **Sugden, Edward Burtenshaw,** *baron St. Leonards,* 1781–1875.

> **Disraeli, Benjamin,** *1st earl of Beaconsfield*
> *see*
> **Beaconsfield, Benjamin Disraeli,** *1st earl of,* 1804–1881.

G. From maiden name to married name when entry is under the latter, and conversely, if both names have been used by the author.

> **Duncan, Sara Jeannette**
> *see*
> **Cotes, Sara Jeannette (Duncan)** 1862?–1922.

> **Boissevain, Edna St. Vincent (Millay)**
> *see*
> **Millay, Edna St. Vincent,** 1892–

H. From pseudonym to real name when entry is under real name, and conversely.

> **Morgan, De Wolfe,** *pseud.*
> *see*
> **Williamson, Thames Ross,** 1894–

> **Webb, Frances (Vinciguerra)** 1900–
> *see*
> **Winwar, Frances,** *pseud.*

I. When such pseudonyms as Aristides, Spectator, etc., have been used by different writers, include in the reference a brief title.

> **Aristides,** *pseud.*
>   An address to the country.
> *see*
> **Evans, Estwick,** 1787–1866.

> **Aristides,** *pseud.*
>   Essays on the spirit of Jacksonism.
> *see*
> **McKenney, Thomas Loraine,** 1785–1859.

J. When an author's works may appear in the catalog under his personal name and also under an official heading connect the different headings by references.

> **Roosevelt, Franklin Delano,** *Pres. U. S.,* 1882–1945.
> *see also*
> **New York** (*State*) *Governor, 1929–1932* (*Franklin D. Roosevelt*)
> **U. S.** *President, 1933–1945* (*Franklin D. Roosevelt*)

K. General references should be made between variant spellings of the same name.

Smith	**Smyth**	**Smythe**
see also	*see also*	*see also*
Smyth	**Smith**	**Smith**
Smythe	**Smythe**	**Smyth**

A reference similar to the following one should be made under each of the variant spellings if widely enough separated in the catalog to make the reference useful.

Catharine
For sovereigns, princesses of sovereign houses, and saints:

Bohemian	*see*	**Katerina**
Dutch		**Katharina**
English		**Catharine**
French		**Catherine**
German		**Katharine**
Italian		**Caterina**
Portuguese		**Catharina**
Spanish		**Catarina**
Swedish		**Katarina**
Danish and Norwegian		**Katharina**

For Russian, Greek and other languages not using the Roman or Gothic alphabet, the English form, Catharine, has been used.

L. Corporate bodies entered under name require reference from place of headquarters,[2] while those entered under place must have reference from name of body. Change of name or variation in the form used necessitates reference from any name by which a body has been or is known to the one adopted as heading. Reference should also be made from an inverted form of name if the distinctive word is not the first word of the corporate name, unless the use of a subject heading or a subject reference obviates such a necessity.

London. Society of Antiquaries
see
Society of Antiquaries of London.

Metropolitan Museum of Art, *New York*
see
New York. Metropolitan Museum of Art.

Association of Government Officials in Industry of the United States and Canada
see
International Association of Governmental Labor Officials.

Paris. Exposition des arts et des techniques dans la vie moderne, 1937
see
Paris. Exposition internationale, 1937.

Kings Daughters and Sons, International Order of
see
International Order of Kings Daughters and Sons.

M. In national or local official documents where the entry word is a geographical name used as *author* rather than *location*, reference from the office is not ordinarily necessary unless it is popularly re-

[2] In exceptional cases reference from the place of headquarters of a society may not be needed, especially where the society or other body is national in scope, but due to the fact that some catalogs and bibliographies enter all corporate bodies under place, a reference is usually advisable.

ferred to by its name. Individual libraries will naturally be guided by local considerations.

> **Massachusetts.** *Commission on Security Laws*
> *see*
> **Massachusetts.** *Special Commission on Security Laws.*

> **Massachusetts.** *Security Laws, Special Commission on*
> *see*
> **Massachusetts.** *Special Commission on Security Laws.*

> **Massachusetts.** *Special Commission on Study of Laws Regulating Promotion and Sale of Securities*
> *see*
> **Massachusetts.** *Special Commission on Security Laws.*

> **Work Projects Administration**
> *see*
> **U. S.** *Work Projects Administration.*

> **WPA**
> *see*
> **U. S.** *Work Projects Administration.*

> **Works Progress Administration**
> *see*
> **U. S.** *Work Projects Administration.*

> **U. S.** *Works Progress Administration*
> *see*
> **U. S.** *Work Projects Administration.*

> **Illinois.** *Work Projects Administration*
> *see*
> **U. S.** *Work Projects Administration. Illinois.*

N. Refer from a larger body subdivided by a smaller division, bureau, etc., if entry is directly under the smaller body, and, conversely, refer from a subordinate entity to the larger body of which it is a part if entry is under the latter.

> **U. S.** *War Dept. Bureau of Insular Affairs*
> *see*
> **U. S.** *Bureau of Insular Affairs.*

> **U. S.** *Insular Affairs, Bureau of*
> *see*
> **U. S.** *Bureau of Insular Affairs.*

> **Insular Affairs, Bureau of**
> *see*
> **U. S.** *Bureau of Insular Affairs.*

> **Sheffield Scientific School**
> *see*
> **Yale University.** *Sheffield Scientific School.*

O. Refer from any name which a periodical has borne to the name under which it is entered in the catalog. (Cf. 5C.) The reference may be replaced by an added entry when the set is complete.

> **Art** and progress
> *see*
> **Magazine** of art.

> **Art** including "Creative art"
> *see*
> **Magazine** of art.

> The **American** magazine of art.
> *see*
> **Magazine** of art.

P. Refer from variant names by which an anonymous classic is known to the form chosen as uniform heading for it. (Cf. 33.)

> **Roland**
> *see*
> **Chanson de Roland.**

> **Song of Roland.**
> *see*
> **Chanson de Roland.**

Q. Explanatory references are made when a simple reference does not in itself justify its existence, but when a brief explanation will clarify once and for all the method of treatment of a given type of entry. Examples of such references will be found under Bishops (52); Anonymous classics. (33)

For other uses of references see 157D.

Appendixes

I. *Glossary*[1]

Added entry.[2] 1. A secondary entry, i.e., any other than the main entry. There may be added entries for editor, translator, title, subjects, series, etc. 2. The heading chosen for an added entry.

See also Main entry.

The term "General secondary" is sometimes applied to an added entry for a person or a corporate body whose relation to the work in hand cannot be indicated in the heading by the use of some specific designation such as editor, translator, illustrator, etc.

When the unit card system is used an added entry card is a duplicate of the main entry, with the addition of a special heading. If the catalog cards are written or typewritten, added entry cards may be made in an abbreviated form.

Added title page. A title page complementary to the one chosen for the main entry of a work. The added title page may precede or follow the main title page with which it is issued and may be more general, as a series title page, or equally general, as a title page in another language.

See also Title page.

Alternative title. A subtitle introduced by "or" or its equivalent, e.g., The tempest; or, The enchanted island.

See also Subtitle, Catchword title.

Analytical entry. The entry of some part of a work or of some article contained in a collection (volume of essays, serial, etc.).

Anonymous. *See* rules for the entry of anonymous works.

Anonymous classic. For definition and specifications *see* rules for entry.

Arranger. One who translates a whole work, or an integral portion of a work to a medium of performance other than that intended by the original com-

---

[1] For definitions of additional terms see the *A. L. A. Glossary of library terms.* (Chicago, American Library Association, 1943).

[2] Since subject entries are only an incidental concern of this code, the term added entry as used in the rules is restricted to added entries other than subjects. Where reference to a subject has been necessary, the term subject entry has been used and the Library of Congress practice of using arabic notation for subjects and roman notation for all other added entries has been followed.

Note: This logical distinction in tracing may explain in part the desire for a definitive group term limited to additional entries other than subject. To serve this purpose, some would restrict the term added entry to those which the Library of Congress traces in roman notation, and reserve secondary entry as a group term to include (1) such an added entry and (2) subject entry. Others would make the opposite choice, using added entry as the group term to include secondary entry and subject entry.

poser. The arrangement may also be a simplification or amplification, the medium of performance and the musical structure remaining the same.

Atlas. A volume of maps, plates, engravings, tables, etc., with or without descriptive letterpress. It may be an independent publication or it may have been issued to accompany one or more volumes of text.

Author. 1. The writer of a work, as distinguished from the translator, editor, etc. By extension, an artist, composer, photographer, cartographer, etc.

2. In the broader sense, the maker of the work or the person or body immediately responsible for its existence. Thus, a person who collects and puts together the writings of several authors (compiler or editor) may be said to be the author of a collection. A corporate body may be considered the author of publications issued in its name or by its authority. (Cf. rules for entry of publications of corporate bodies.)

Author entry. 1. An entry of a work in a catalog under its author's name as heading, whether this be a main or an added heading. The author heading will consist of a personal or a corporate name or some substitute for it, e.g., initials, pseudonym, etc.

2. The author heading chosen for this entry.

Cadenza. A technically brilliant solo passage toward the close of the first or last movement of a concerto, in which the main themes are given further development.

Catalog. A list of books, maps, etc., arranged according to some definite plan. As distinguished from a bibliography it is a list which records, describes, and indexes the resources of a collection, a library, or a group of libraries.

See also Dictionary catalog.

Catchword title. A partial title consisting of some striking or easily remembered word or phrase. It may coincide with the subtitle or the alternative title. Called also Catch title.

Collection. Three or more separate works or parts of works, not forming a treatise or monograph on a single subject, combined and issued together as a whole.

See also Composite work, Festschrift.

Compiler. One who produces a work by collecting and putting together written or printed matter from the works of various authors. Also, one who chooses and combines into one work selections or quotations from one author. (Cf. Editor.)

Composer. An author of music.

Composite work. An original work produced by the collaboration of two or more authors in which the contribution of each forms a separate and distinct part, although included within a planned whole.

See also Collection, Festschrift, Joint author, Monograph.

Compound name. A name formed from two or more proper names, often connected by a hyphen, a conjunction, or a preposition.

Continuation. 1. A work issued as a supplement to one previously issued.

2. A part issued in continuance of a book, a serial, or a series.

See also Periodical, Serial.

Conventional title. *See* Uniform title.

Corporate entry. 1. An entry under the name of a society, institution, government department, bureau, or other organized body, for works issued in its name or by its authority, whether this be a main or an added **heading.**
2. The heading chosen for this entry.
See also Author entry, Main entry, Added entry.

Cross reference. *See* Reference.

Dictionary catalog. A catalog, usually on cards, in which all the entries (author, title, subject, series, etc.) and their related references are arranged together in one general alphabet. The subarrangement frequently varies from the strictly alphabetical.

Dissertation, Academic. An essay or treatise presented by a candidate in partial fulfillment of the requirements for a degree. (Cf. Program dissertation.)

Edition. One of the successive forms in which a literary text is issued either by the author or by a subsequent editor.

Editor. One who prepares for publication a work or collection of works or articles not his own. The editorial labor may be limited to the preparation of the matter for the printer, or it may include supervision of the printing, revision (restitution) or elucidation of the text, and the addition of introduction, notes, and other critical matter. (Cf. Compiler.)

Entry. 1. A record of a book in a catalog or list.
2. The heading chosen for this record.
See also Heading, and the various types of entry, e.g., Main entry, Author entry, Added entry, Title entry, Analytical entry, Series entry.

Entry word. The word by which the entry is arranged in the catalog, usually the first word (other than an article) of the heading. Called also Filing word. (Cf. Heading.)

Excerpt. A passage reproduced verbatim from a printed work or a manuscript; an extract or selection.

Extract (selection). *See* Excerpt.

Extract (summary or abstract). *See* rules for abridgments.

Facsimile reproduction. A reproduction of a manuscript or printed work by means of a mechanical or a photomechanical process.

Festschrift. A complimentary or memorial publication usually in the form of a collection of essays, addresses, or biographical, bibliographical, scientific, or other contributions, often embodying the results of research, issued in honor of a person, an institution, or a society, as a rule on the occasion of an anniversary celebration.
For festschriften which are not collections see footnote 3, p. 9.

Filing word. *See* Entry word.

General secondary entry. *See* Added entry.

Heading. The name, word, or phrase used at the head of an entry to indicate some special aspect of the book (authorship, subject content, series, title, etc.) and thereby to bring together in the catalog associated and allied material.

See also Entry word.

Issue (verb). Specifically, to produce, or cause to be produced, books or other printed matter and to make them available for purchase by the public or for private distribution.

Joint author. A person who collaborates with one or more associates to produce a work in which the contribution of each is usually not separable from that of the others.

See also Composite work.

Librettist. The author of the text of an opera or other extended choral composition.

Main entry. 1. The basic catalog card, usually the author entry, giving all the information necessary to the complete identification of a work. This entry bears also the tracing of all the other headings under which the work in question is entered in the catalog. It may bear in addition the tracing of related references and a record of other pertinent official data concerning the work.

2. The entry chosen for this main card, whether it be a personal or corporate name, the title of an anonymous work, a collection, composite work, periodical or serial, or a uniform title.

See also Author entry, Corporate entry, Heading, Tracing, Unit card.

Monograph. A systematic and complete treatise on a particular subject, usually detailed in treatment but not extensive in scope. It need not be bibliographically independent.

Monograph series. A series of monographs with a collective title, usually issued serially by a university or a society. There may be more than one monograph in a volume.

See also Serial, Series.

Partial title. One which consists of a secondary part of the title as given on the title page. It may be a catchword title, subtitle, or alternative title. (Cf. rules for added entry.)

See also Alternative title, Catchword title, Subtitle.

Pasticcio. A musical medley made up of parts of, or selections from, different works.

Periodical. A serial in parts which are not monographs and usually contain articles by several contributors. It generally has a distinctive title and the successive numbers or parts are intended to appear at stated or regular intervals, and, as a rule, for an indefinite period.

Newspapers, whose chief function it is to disseminate news, and the *Memoirs, Proceedings, Journals,* etc., of societies are not considered periodicals under the rules.

See also Continuation, Serial.

Praeses. The person or persons who open an academical disputation by propounding objections to some tenet or proposition, usually moral or philosophical, as distinguished from the respondent who defends it. The praeses is called also the opponent.
See also Respondent.

Program dissertation. A dissertation accompanying one of the "programs" (i.e., announcements of memorial exercises, lectures, etc.) published by universities and schools, especially those of Germany, Austria, Switzerland, and the Scandinavian countries.

Pseudonym. A false name assumed by an author to conceal his identity.
See also Sobriquet.

Publisher. The person, firm, or corporate body undertaking the responsibility for the issue of a book or other printed matter to the public.
See also Issue (verb)
The same person or firm may be printer, publisher, and bookseller, or printer and publisher, or publisher and bookseller, but since the opening years of the nineteenth century publishing has been, for the most part, a separate business.

Publisher's series. A series of publications whose only link may be the collective title assigned by the publisher.
See also Series, definition 1.

Reference. A direction from one heading to another.

Respondent. The candidate for a degree who, in an academical disputation, defends a tenet or thesis against the objections proposed by the praeses. The respondent is called also the defendant.
See also Praeses.

Secondary entry. *See* Added entry.

Serial. A publication issued in successive parts, usually at regular intervals, and, as a rule, intended to be continued indefinitely. Serials include periodicals, newspapers, annuals (reports, yearbooks, etc.) and memoirs, proceedings, and transactions of societies, and may include monographic series and publishers' series.
See also Continuation, Periodical, Monograph series, Publisher's series.

Series. 1. A number of separate works, usually related to one another in subject or otherwise, issued in succession, normally by the same publisher and in uniform style, with a collective title which generally appears at the head of the title page, on the half title, or on the cover.
2. Each of two or more volumes of essays, lectures, articles, or other writings, similar in character and issued in sequence, e.g., Lowell's Among my books, second series.
3. A separately numbered sequence of volumes within a series or serial, e.g., Notes and queries, 1st series, 2d series, etc.
See also Continuation, Monograph series, Publisher's series.

Series entry. An entry, usually brief, of the several works in the library which belong to a series under the name of that series as a heading.

Sobriquet. A fanciful or humorous appellation given by others; a nickname. *See also* Pseudonym.

Society. For definition and specifications *see* rules for the entry of societies and institutions.

Subtitle. The explanatory part of the title following the main title; e.g., The creative adult; self-education in the art of living.
See also Alternative title, Catchword title.

Thematic catalog. A list of a composer's works, with the theme given for each composition or for each section of large compositions, usually arranged in chronological order or by categories.

Thesis. *See* Dissertation, Academic.

Title. 1. In the broad sense, the distinguishing name of any written production as given on the title page, including the name of the author, editor, translator, the edition, etc., but excluding the imprint.
2. In the narrow sense the title does not include the name of the author, editor, etc.
See also Alternative title, Partial title, Subtitle, Title page.

Title entry. 1. The record of a work in the catalog under the title, generally beginning with the first word not an article. A title entry may be a main entry or an added entry.
2. The title chosen for this entry.

Title page. A page at the beginning[3] of a book or work, bearing its full title and usually, though not necessarily, the author's (editor's, etc.) name and the imprint.[4] The leaf bearing the title page is commonly called the "title page" although properly called also the "title leaf."
See also Added title page.

Tracing. The record on the main entry card of all the additional headings under which the work is represented in the catalog. Also, the record on a main entry card or on an authority card of all the related references made.
The tracing may be on the face or on the back of the card, or on an accompanying card.
See also Main entry.

Translator. One who renders from one language into another, or from an older form of a language into the modern form, more or less closely following the original.

Transliteration. A representation of the characters of one alphabet by those of another.

---

[3] In the case of works in Oriental languages, the title page and the beginning of the text are normally at the back of the volume.
[4] For the evolution of the title page from the colophon and the label title, cf. R. B. McKerrow, *An introduction to bibliography for literary students* (Oxford, Clarendon Press, 1927), p. 88-95; A. J. K. Esdaile, *A student's manual of bibliography* (London, Allen & Unwin, 1931), p. 85-86; A. W. Pollard, *Last words on the history of the title-page* (London, Nimmo, 1891).

Uniform title. The distinctive title by which a work which has appeared under varying titles and in various versions is most generally known. *See also* rules for anonymous classics.

Unit card. A basic catalog card, in the form of a main entry, which when duplicated may be used as a unit for all other entries for that work in the catalog by the addition of the appropriate heading. Library of Congress printed cards are the most commonly used unit cards.
See also Added entry, Main entry.

Volume. In the bibliographical sense, a book distinguished from other books or from other major divisions of the same work by having its own inclusive[5] title page, half title, cover title, or portfolio title, and usually independent pagination, foliation, or register.

This major bibliographical unit may have been designated "part" by the publisher, or it may include various title pages or paginations. Occasionally other bibliographical characteristics must be taken into consideration.

---

[5] The most general title page, or half title, or the cover title, will be the determining factor in deciding what constitutes the volume; e.g., a reissue in one binding, of a work previously issued in two or more volumes, should be considered one bibliographical volume.

II. *Abbreviations Used in Headings*

Term	Abbreviation	Term	Abbreviation
anno Domini	A.D.	Honorable	Hon.
Archbishop	Abp.	illustrator	illus.
arranger	arr.	incorporated	inc.
baronet	bart.	Junior	Jr.
Before Christ	B.C.	limited	ltd.
Bishop	Bp.	Madame	Mme.
born	b.	manuscript, — s	ms., mss.
century	cent.	Mistress	Mrs.
circa	ca.	New Testament	N. T.
Company	Co.	Old Testament	O. T.
compiler	comp.	President	Pres.[1]
Congress	Cong.	pseudonym	pseud.
County	Co.	publisher	pub.
Department	Dept.	Regiment	Regt.
died	d.	Reverend	Rev.
editor	ed.	Saint	St.[2]
engraver	engr.	Senior	Sr.
et alii	et al.	session	sess.
et cetera	etc.	Territory	Ter.
flourished	fl.	translator	tr.

Abbreviations are not to be used for geographical names that form an integral part of a corporate name, nor, with the exception of U. S. and Gt. Brit., for geographical names occurring as the first word of an official heading.

The following abbreviations for names of states and territories of the United States are permissible in headings after the name of a city, county, etc. Names not in this list are written in full.

Ala.	Ill.	Minn.	N. Y.	Tenn.
Ariz.	Ind.	Miss.	N. C.	Tex.
Ark.	Kan.	Mo.	N. D.	Vt.
Calif.	Ky.	Mont.	Okla.	Va.
Colo.	La.	Neb.	Or.	Wash.
Conn.	Me.	Nev.	Pa.	W. Va.
Del.	Md.	N. H.	R. I.	Wis.
Fla.	Mass.	N. J.	S. C.	Wyo.
Ga.	Mich.	N. M.	S. D.	

D. C. District of Columbia   P. R. Puerto Rico   T. H. Territory of Hawaii

[1] Only when used in the personal name heading.
[2] Only when preceding the name, as St. Paul's Cathedral.

Other abbreviations commonly used:

Alta.	Alberta	Ont.	Ontario
B. C.	British Columbia	P. E. I.	Prince Edward Island
Can.	Canada	Que.	Quebec
C. P.	Cape Province	R. S. F. S. R.	Russian Soviet
D. F.	Distrito Federal		Federated Socialist
Eng.	England		Republic
Ger.	Germany	Sask.	Saskatchewan
Gt. Brit.	Great Britain	Scot.	Scotland
Ire.	Ireland	U. S. S. R.	Union of Soviet
N. B.	New Brunswick		Socialist Republics
N. Z.	New Zealand	U. S.	United States
N. S.	Nova Scotia	V. I.	Virgin Islands

III. *Rules of Style for Headings*

A. Punctuation.

  1. Brackets.

  (a) Inclose in brackets the name of a personal author if it does not appear openly in the book. Include within the brackets titles of nobility and office, but not dates of birth and death, nor approximate dates substituted for them, nor terms added for identification. Do not bracket parts of names, e.g., forenames, or forenames of which initials only appear on the title page.

  (b) Inclose in brackets the name of a corporate body, when entry is under the name of the body, if no part of the name appears in the book. When entry is under country, city, or other jurisdiction, however, do not use brackets in any case.

When the name of a corporate body contains initials which need to be explained, insert the explanation in the heading within brackets.

  (c) Do not inclose in brackets the uniform heading of an anonymous classic entry.

  2. Parentheses. Use parentheses

  (a) In personal headings to indicate the maiden names of married women.

    Andrews, Mary (Beckwith)

  (b) In corporate headings and uniform headings to inclose a word or phrase used for the purpose of definition or identification.

    Hereford, *Eng.* (*Diocese*) *Bishop, 1516–1535* (*Charles Bothe*)
    New York (*State*) *Governor.*
    Paris. Notre Dame (*Cathedral*)
    Baltimore. St. James Church (*Catholic*)
    Bible. *French* (*Old French*)
    Antioche (*Chanson de geste*)
    Sirius (*Ship*)

  (c) To inclose *ca.* when used after a date of birth, e.g., Smith, John, 1837 (*ca.*)-1896.

  3. Dash. The dash is used to connect numbers, signifying "to and including," e.g., 1940–1941. Following a number, it signifies continuation.

4. Interrogation point. The interrogation point following a date signifies uncertainty.

5. Period. Use the period

(a) For abbreviations.

(b) To separate the main heading from the subheading.

(c) At the end of a completed heading, if there is no other mark of punctuation.

B. Modified vowels.

In the heading write modified vowels in whatever language they may occur (German, Swedish, Hungarian, etc.) according to the usage of the author.

C. Accents.

In the heading supply accents in French on lower-case letters and on capital E, and in Spanish on lower-case letters. In title entries, however, supply accents in French only for books published after 1800; and in Spanish after 1890. Do not use accents in headings in Portuguese, except on the names José and Sá, nor supply accents in title entries in Portuguese.

D. Figures.

1. Use roman numerals in headings after the names of sovereigns, princes, and popes.

Richard III, Leo XIII.

2. Use arabic numerals in headings for numbered congresses and conferences.

International Geographical Congress. *4th, Paris,* 1889.
Baptist Training Union. *Southwide conference. 4th, Birmingham, Ala.,* 1925.

3. For numerals in headings for the Army of the United States and of Great Britain, see 76B (1).

E. Capitalization.[1]

In **English**, capitalize:

1. Proper names
2. Derivatives of proper names
3. Common nouns and adjectives forming an essential part of a proper name
4. Names of organized bodies (first word and all important words)
5. Names of countries and administrative divisions
6. Names of regions, localities and geographic features
7. Names of calendar divisions

---

[1] These rules summarize those approved for use by the Library of Congress, beginning July 1, 1947. This capitalization has been applied to the examples in the *A. L. A. Cataloging rules* because it affects the headings. No other rulings from the Library of Congress *Rules for descriptive cataloging,* issued in a provisional edition, June 1947, have been applied to the examples.

8. Names of historic events

9. Religious terms: words denoting the Deity; names for the Bible and other sacred writings; names of confessions of faith and of religious bodies and their adherents.

10. Titles of persons

(a) when immediately preceding a name

(b) when immediately following a name or used alone as a substitute for the name in the following cases:

Title of a head or assistant head of state

Title of a head or assistant head of an existing or proposed National or District governmental unit

Titles of members of diplomatic corps

Title of a ruler or prince

11. The first word of the title of a book, periodical or series; all principal words in the title of a newspaper. If the first word of a title used as main entry is an article, capitalize the following word, except in the entry of anonymous works, which, theoretically, are only temporarily main entries. If the first word of a title is preceded by symbols indicating that the beginning of the phrase has been omitted, do not capitalize it.

12. The first word of a sentence

In **foreign languages,** the capitalization is to conform to national practice in each language, including the capitalization of common nouns in German.

F. Library of Congress Typography[2].

General. The use of various types on the catalog card adds to intelligibility of the entry, gives relative emphasis to its different parts, and may be a clue to arrangement in the catalog.

Bold-faced type and italics are used in the heading to give prominence to certain elements. The body of the title is printed in light-faced roman type.

The typography of **main entries** is treated in the following rules.

1. Boldface.

(a) Author heading. Print the author heading in bold-faced type.

> **Franklin, Benjamin.**
> **American Library Association.**
> **National Society of United States Daughters of 1812.**
> **France.**
> **Havana. Universidad.**

(b) Title entries. Print in bold-faced type the first word or group of closely related words, exclusive of an initial article, in a title entry.

> The **Spectator.**

---

[2] These rules are for Library of Congress usage in force at the time the examples were selected and prepared. They are included here to explain the examples and to assist catalogers who prepare copy for the Library of Congress.

The **George Washington** law review.
The **two hundred and fiftieth** anniversary of the settlement.

Anonymous classic headings are printed in boldface.

Bible.
Chanson de Roland.

2. Italics. Print in italics:
(a) Connective words and abbreviations in the author heading.

Tintoretto, *i.e.* **Jacopo Robusti,** *known as.*
Eliot, George, *pseud., i.e.* **Marian Evans,** *afterwards* **Cross.**
Molitoris, Johannes, *fl.* 1480.
Smith, John, 1836 *or* 7-1896.

(b) Defining and qualifying words and phrases[3] added in the author heading, including geographic names, titles, and epithets.[4]

New York (*Archdiocese*)
Charlemagne (*Play*)
Cohen, Gustave, *ed.*
Schuebler, Gustav, *praeses.*
Eastman Kodak Company of New Jersey, *defendant-appellant.*
Rockwood, Roy, *pseud.*
Brown, John, *genealogist.*
Brown, George, *F.R.A.S.* [initials in small capitals]
Wilson, William, *first mate of the ship Duff.*
Cook, T., *firm, publishers, London.*
   (*1913. Thomas Cook and Son*)
International Association for Testing Materials. (*Founded 1927*)
Akademie der Wissenschaften, *Vienna.*
The Times, *London.*
Karl, *Archduke of Austria.*
Jan III *Sobieski, King of Poland.*
Bacon, Francis, *viscount St. Albans.*
Washington, George, *Pres. U. S.*
Jones, *Mrs.* **Paul.**
Frederick *the Great.*

(c) Subdivisions
(1) Of governments.[5]

---

[3] Exceptions: When the defining word precedes the name of an institution, printed in boldface, the defining word or phrase is also printed in boldface.
    Mexico (City)   Museo Nacional de Arqueología, Historia y Etnografía.
When the defining word follows a subdivision which is printed in italics, the defining word or phrase is printed in roman.
    Kansas. *Office of State Fire Marshal* (1939-   )
[4] Exception: Anonymous classic headings consisting of a personal name with a byname or epithet affixed are printed in boldface.
    Arthur, King (*Romances, etc.*)
    Berthe aux grands pieds (*Romance*)
[5] Note that the names of institutions entered under place are not given in italics, since they are not subdivisions of governments. (Cf. (1a) above **Havana. Universidad.**)

   Gt. Brit. *Public Record Office.*
   U. S. *President, 1789–1797 (Washington)*
   U. S. *Army. 101st Cavalry Group.*

(2) Of institutions and societies.

   Yale University. *Sheffield Scientific School.*
   Columbia University. *School of Law. Alumni Association.*
   American Library Association. *Books for Latin America Project.*

(3) As form headings.

   Aristoteles. *Spurious and doubtful works.*
   The Classical journal *(Indexes)*
   South Africa. *Treaties, etc.*
   Bible. *O. T. Psalms. English. 1873.*

3. Lightface. Print in light-faced roman type:
 (a) Dates of birth and death of personal authors,[6] and the abbreviations B.C. and A.D. when used with them.

   Washington, George, *Pres. U. S.,* 1752–1799.
   Tiberius, *Emperor of Rome,* B.C. 42–A.D. 37.

 (b) Dates showing when a body convened, or how long it existed.
   Dordrecht, Synod of, 1618–1619.
   World Conference on Faith and Order, *Lausanne,* 1927.

---

[6] Designation of the century is printed in italics.
  Malory, *Sir* **Thomas,** *15th cent.*

IV. *Transliteration*

New Russian Orthography

The introduction of a new Russian orthography was one of the early acts of the Soviet government. The changes made were not, however, unpremeditated, for the question had been under consideration by scholars before the revolution, and had been the subject of investigation by official commissions. The new law was based on this previous work, and as a result the new system is thoroughly scientific, and there is no question as to its simplicity as compared with the old spelling.

Books printed in the U. S. S. R. must conform to this spelling, and it is necessary, therefore, for libraries acquiring modern Russian books to consider the effect of the new rules on the alphabeting of names and titles in their card catalogs, and to provide rules which will guard against future confusion. It is not a practicable solution to spell the names of contemporary writers the new way and to leave the pre-revolution writers under the old forms, for new editions of the older authors are being printed in which the new spelling is adopted, and bookdealers in Russia are sending out book lists in which they regularly use the new spelling in listing the older books, to the confusion of the library assistant who is not prepared for this change.

Fortunately, while there are about a dozen changes in the new rules for spelling, only two seriously affect the alphabetization of names and titles in the catalog. Formerly there were two characters in Russian pronounced alike: one, the *yat*, was transliterated by ie; the other, exactly like our letter e in form, was transliterated by e. Under the new spelling, the letter *yat* drops out, and in every case where it was used, the letter e is substituted. Thus: in the word Soviet, the letter before t was a *yat*, transliterated ie. It now becomes an e, changing the spelling of the word to "Sovet;" the author whose name was formerly transliterated Bieliaev, now becomes Beliaev.

Another Russian character is transliterated by the letter z. Under the new rules, this z becomes an s in the prefixes voz, vz, iz, niz, raz, bez, chrez, and cherez when standing before k, p, t, kh, ch, sh,

---

[1] Report of the A. L. A. Cataloging Committee's subcommittee on Russian orthography, 1927.

shch, s, and f. This change will create confusion in the catalog, especially if it comes near the beginning of a word; thus, Razskaz is now spelled Rasskaz.

It is hereby recommended that in the headings of catalog cards the new Russian orthography be adopted not only for contemporary publications, but for pre-revolution books.

When transcribing titles for the catalog card, no change should be made in the established principle of exact transcription of the title page in hand, whatever may be its system of spelling. This ruling will apply even in the case of title entries beginning with a word the orthography of which would differ under the old and new systems (Lietopis). The catalog treatment should in such cases correspond to the treatment now accorded such words as Almanac (Almanack), Centralblatt (Zentralblatt), which is to copy exactly the spelling of the title page and to gather together under one of the spellings (the current form or the form most used) all titles beginning with the word in question, whatever the spelling may be on the title page in hand.

A summary of the new Russian rules is appended (see p. 245).

The Committee comprised: Archibald Cary Coolidge, Harvard University, chairman; Samuel A. Chevalier, Boston Public Library; George Rapall Noyes, University of California.

RULES OF THE NEW RUSSIAN ORTHOGRAPHY

1. In place of Ѣ write Е.

   Люди за дело, а мы за еду.   На языке мед, а на душе лед.

2. In place of I write И.

   Язык до Киева доведет.   Нищий—человек Божий.

3. In place of Ѳ write Ф.

   Напала зевота на Федота.   Ты про Фому, а он тебе про Ерему.

4. Omit Ъ at end of a word.

   Орел мух не ловит.   Не пером пишут, а умом.

5. In the middle of words Ъ is retained to separate consonant and vowel sounds.

   До того дожили, что ножки съежили.   Горе безъязыкому.

6. The prefixes, ВОЗ, ВЗ, ИЗ, НИЗ, РАЗ, БЕЗ, ЧРЕЗ and ЧЕРЕЗ before К, П, Т, Х, Ч, Ш, Щ, Ф, С are to be written with a final С in place of З.

   Воспитание. Расценка. Бесконечный. Всходы. Беспечный. Источник. Иссушить. Чересседельник. Рассказ. Бесценный.

7. In place of the ending АГО and ЯГО in the genitive and accusative singular of adjectives, participles, numerals and pronouns write ОГО and ЕГО.

   Вкусивший сладкого не захочет горького.   С третьего на пятое, с пятого на десятое.   У всякого Филатки свои ухватки.   Обещанного три года ждут.   Лежачего не бьют.

8. In place of final ЫЯ and IЯ in the nominative and accusative plural of adjectives, numerals and pronouns write ЫЕ and ИЕ.

   Певчие птицы. Какие жирные утки! Хорошие дети. Срубленные деревья. Первые строки. Добрые дела.

9. Instead of the form ОНѢ, ОДНѢ, ОДНѢХ, ОДНѢМ, ОДНѢМИ write ОНИ, ОДНИ, ОДНИХ, ОДНИМ, ОДНИМИ.

   Рукавиц ищет, а они за поясом.   Только и родни, что бабушки одни.   Барыши с убытком на одних санях ездят.   Где мои книги? Где они?

10. Instead of the pronoun form ЕЯ write ЕЕ.

    Не змея страшна, а ее жало.

11. Adverbs formed by the combination of substantives, adjectives and numerals with prepositions may be written with the two parts either joined or separated.

    В течение. С верху. В стороне. В трое. Втечение. Сверху. Всто-роне. Втрое.

SLAVIC TRANSLITERATION

Russian [1]			Ukrainian [5]			White Russian			Bulgarian			Serbian [8]		
А	а	*a*	А	а	*a*	А	а	*a*	А	а	*a*	А	а	*a*
Б	б	*b*	Б	б	*b*	Б	б	*b*	Б	б	*b*	Б	б	*b*
В	в	*v*	В	в	*v*	В	в	*v*	В	в	*v*	В	в	*v*
Г	г	*g*	Г	г	*h*	Г	г	*h*	Г	г	*g*	Г	г	*g*
			Ґ	ґ	*g*	Ґ	ґ	*g*						
Д	д	*d*	Д	д	*d*	Д	д	*d*	Д	д	*d*	Д	д	*d*
												Ђ	ђ	*đ*
Е	е	*e*	Е	е	*e*	Е	е	*e*	Е	е	*e*	Е	е	*e*
			Є	є	*ĩe*									
Ё	ё	*ë*				Ё	ё	*ĩo*						
Ж	ж	*zh*	Ж	ж [6]	*ẑh*	Ж	ж	*zh*	Ж	ж	*zh*	Ж	ж	*ž*
З	з	*z*	З	з	*z*	З	з	*z*	З	з	*z*	З	з	*z*
И	и	*i*	И	и	*y*				И	и	*i*	И	и	*i*
І	і [2]	*ī*	І	і	*i*	І	і	*i*						
			Ї	ї	*ï*									
Й	й	*ĭ*	Й	й	*ĭ*	Й	й	*ĭ*	Й	й	*ĭ*			
												Ј	ј	*j*
К	к	*k*	К	к	*k*	К	к	*k*	К	к	*k*	К	к	*k*
Л	л	*l*	Л	л	*l*	Л	л	*l*	Л	л	*l*	Л	л	*l*
												Љ	љ	*lj*
М	м	*m*	М	м	*m*	М	м	*m*	М	м	*m*	М	м	*m*
Н	н	*n*	Н	н	*n*	Н	н	*n*	Н	н	*n*	Н	н	*n*
												Њ	њ	*nj*
О	о	*o*	О	о	*o*	О	о	*o*	О	о	*o*	О	о	*o*
П	п	*p*	П	п	*p*	П	п	*p*	П	п	*p*	П	п	*p*
Р	р	*r*	Р	р	*r*	Р	р	*r*	Р	р	*r*	Р	р	*r*
С	с	*s*	С	с	*s*	С	с	*s*	С	с	*s*	С	с	*s*
Т	т	*t*	Т	т	*t*	Т	т	*t*	Т	т	*t*	Т	т	*t*
												Ћ	ћ	*ć*
У	у	*u*	У	у	*u*	У	у	*u*	У	у	*u*	У	у	*u*
						Ў	ў	*ŭ*						
Ф	ф	*f*	Ф	ф	*f*	Ф	ф	*f*	Ф	ф	*f*	Ф	ф	*f*
Х	х	*kh*	Х	х	*kh*	Х	х	*kh*	Х	х	*kh*	Х	х	*h*
Ц	ц	*t͡s*	Ц	ц	*ts*	Ц	ц	*ts*	Ц	ц	*ts*	Ц	ц	*c*
Ч	ч	*ch*	Ч	ч	*ch*	Ч	ч	*ch*	Ч	ч	*ch*	Ч	ч	*č*
												Џ	џ	*dž*
Ш	ш	*sh*	Ш	ш	*sh*	Ш	ш	*sh*	Ш	ш	*sh*	Ш	ш	*š*
Щ	щ	*shch*	Щ	щ	*shch*				Щ	щ	*sht*			
Ъ	ъ [3]	*''*							Ъ	ъ [7]	*ŭ or ''*			
Ы	ы	*y*				Ы	ы	*y*						
Ь	ь [4]	*'*	Ь	ь	*'*	Ь	ь	*'*	Ь	ь	*'*			
Ѣ	ѣ	*ĩe*							Ѣ	ѣ	*ĩe*			
Э	э	*é*				Э	э	*é*						
Ю	ю	*ĩu*	Ю	ю	*ĩu*	Ю	ю	*ĩu*	Ю	ю	*ĩu*			
Я	я	*ĩa*	Я	я	*ĩa*	Я	я	*ĩa*	Я	я	*ĩa*			
Ѳ	ѳ	*f*												
Ѵ	ѵ	*ẏ*												
									х		*ŭ*			

[1] The present practice of the Library of Congress is in agreement with this table.

[2] Do not confuse with similar part of the letter Ы (*y*).

[3] Final disregarded.

[4] Do not confuse with similar part of the letter Ы (*y*).

[5] This transliteration takes account of only the accepted Ukrainian alphabet and orthography, disregarding the older ones, like the "Ĩàryzhka," the "Drahomanivka," and the so-called etymological orthography of Maksymovych.

[6] The ligature is necessary here in order to distinguish Ж from the combination ЗГ.

[7] Transliterate as *ŭ* in the middle of a word, disregard at the end.

[8] This transliteration insures correspondence between the Serbian and present day Croatian alphabets.

Ligatures may be used in the cases indicated. They are an aid in determining the exact form of the name in the original, but may be omitted by libraries where less exact transcription is permitted.

Russian names of non-Russian origin (more particularly Western European) are not transliterated from the Russian, but are given in the original form, if the original form used by the bearer of the name can be determined.

> Hertzen *not* Gertsen.
> Rubinstein *not* Rubinshtein.
> Witte *not* Vitte.
> Benois *not* Benua.

MODERN GREEK TRANSLITERATION [1]

A	*a*	*a*	I	*ι*	*i*	'P	*ρ*	*rh**
B	*β*	*b**	K	*κ*	*k*	Σ	*σ*	*s*
Γ	*γ*	*g* (*γ* before *γ*,	Λ	*λ*	*l*	T	*τ*	*t*
		κ, *χ*=*n*)	M	*μ*	*m*	Υ	*υ*	*y*
Δ	*δ*	*d*	N	*ν*	*n*	Φ	*φ*	*ph*
E	*ε*	*e*	Ξ	*ξ*	*x*	X	*χ*	*ch**
Z	*ζ*	*z*	O	*o*	*o*	Ψ	*ψ*	*ps*
H	*η*	*ē**	Π	*π*	*p**	Ω	*ω*	*ō*
Θ	*θ*	*th*	P	*ρ*	*r*			

Αι	αι	*ai*	Ευ	ευ	*eu*
Αυ	αυ	*au*	Ηυ	ηυ	*ēu*
Αϋ	αϋ	*ay*	Ου	ου	*ou*

Spiritus asper (')=*h*, *e. g.* ῾Εταιρία=Hetairia.

*Certain exceptions are reserved. Names of Greek writers who have published books in any of the western European languages and are better known under a form of name transliterated differently may be given in that form. The exceptions involve chiefly the transliteration of the following letters:

B, *β* transliterated by *v*.   H, *η* transliterated by *i*.
'P, *ρ* transliterated by *r* only.   *π* (after *μ*) transliterated by *b*.
X, *χ* transliterated by *h*.
> *e. g.* Βλάχος=Vlachos; ῾Ραγκαβῆς=Rankabēs (Rangabé);
> Χαραλάμπης=Haralambis.

[1] Library of Congress Cat. rules (Suppl.) Rule 11, printed Jan. 26, 1905.

SEMITIC TRANSLITERATION[1]

ARABIC		HEBREW	
١	'	א	'
(m.' , f.') ﺑ	b	ב	v
(m. ﺘ, f. ﺗ) ﺗ	t	בּ	b
(m. ﺜ, f. ﺛ) ﺛ	th	ג	gh
(m. ﺠ, f. ﺟ) ﺟ	j	גּ	g
(m. ﺤ, f. ﺣ) ﺣ	ḥ	ד	dh
(m. ﺨ, f. ﺧ) ﺧ	kh	דּ	d
د	d	ה	h
ذ	dh	ו	w
ر	r	ז	z
ز	z	ח	ḥ
(f. س) ﺳ	s	ט	ṭ
(f. ش) ﺷ	sh	י	y
(f. ص) ﺻ	ṣ	(f. ך) כ	kh
(f. ض) ﺿ	ḍ	כּ	k
ط	ṭ	ל	l
ظ	ẓ	(f. ם) מ	m
(m. ﻋ, f. ع) ﻋ	'	(f. ן) נ	n
(m. ﻏ, f. غ) ﻏ	gh	ס	s
(m. ﻓ, f. ف) ﻓ	f	ע	'
(m. ﻗ, f. ق) ﻗ	ḳ	(f. ף) פ	f
(m. ﻛ, f. ك) ﻛ	k	פּ	p
(m. ﻟ, f. ل) ﻟ	l	(f. ץ) צ	ẓ
(f. م) ﻣ	m	ק	ḳ
(m. ﻧ, f. ن) ﻧ	n	ר	r
(m. ﻬ, ﻫ, f. ﻪ, ﺔ) ﻫ	h	שׁ	sh
و	w	שׂ	ś
(m. ﻳ, f. ى) ﻳ	y	ת	th
		תּ	t

[1] This table is based on the system indicated in the Jewish Encyclopedia and recommended in A. L. A. Catalog rules, 1908.
[2] m. = medial; f. = final.

Index

Bertha M. Frick

References in bold-face type are to rule numbers.

251

TRANSLITERATION OF HEBREW AND YIDDISH

As a result of the increased amount of cataloging of Hebraica at the Library of Congress during the last five years, rules for the transliteration of Hebrew and Yiddish have been subjected to scrutiny, and certain changes have been adopted. The purpose of the changes is to establish a consistent and logical system of transliteration requiring a minimum use of diacritical marks. The transliteration attempts to represent the sound of the Hebrew or Yiddish word; for this the Hebrew follows the modern Palestinian (Sephardic) pronunciation and the Yiddish follows the Lithuanian Yiddish pronunciation. In transliterating Yiddish the etymology of the words is ignored.

The Yiddish transliteration system now in use is identical with that used by the Yiddish Scientific Institute (YIVO) in New York.

Hebrew			Hebrew	
א	initial and final disregarded; otherwise ' (prime)		ל	l
			מ (final, ם)	m
ב	b		נ (final, ן)	n
ב	v (in Yiddish, b)		ס	s
ג	g		ע	' (inverted comma)
ד	d		פ	p
ה	h		פ (final, ף)	f
ו	v		צ (final, ץ)	ts
וו	v		ק	k
ז	z		ר	r
ח	ḥ		שׁ	sh
ט	t		שׂ	s
י	y (at beginning of word or syllable; otherwise, i)		ת	t
			ת	t (in Hebrew words; in Yiddish, s)
כ	k			
כ (final, ך)	kh			

Vowels used in Hebrew		Vowels used in Yiddish	
ִ	a	א	a or o
ַ	a		
ֶ	e	ו, או	u
ֵ	e		
וֹ	o	וי, אוי	oy
וּ	u		
ִ	u	י, אי	i
ׅ	i		
ִ	i	ע	e
ְ	e	יי, איי	ay (as ai in aisle) or ey (as ei in weigh)

Adopted March, 1948. The examples in rules 35A, 65 and 121 are from entries prepared before the adoption of this system.

THE AMERICAN LIBRARY ASSOCIATION

The American Library Association, established in 1876, is an organization of libraries, librarians, library trustees and others interested in the responsibilities of libraries in the educational, social and cultural needs of society. It is affiliated with more than fifty other library associations in this country and abroad. It works closely with many organizations concerned with education, recreation, research, and public service. Its activities are carried on by a headquarters staff, voluntary boards and committees, and by divisions, sections, and round tables, all interested in various aspects or types of library service. Its program includes information and advisory services, personnel service, field work, annual and midwinter conferences, and the publication—not for profit—of numerous professional books, pamphlets and periodicals.